THE PRO-CHOICE MOVEMENT

THE PRO-CHOICE MOVEMENT

Organization and Activism in the Abortion Conflict

SUZANNE STAGGENBORG

OXFORD UNIVERSITY PRESS
New York Oxford

Oxford University Press

Oxford   New York   Toronto
Delhi   Bombay   Calcutta   Madras   Karachi
Kuala Lumpur   Singapore   Hong Kong   Tokyo
Nairobi   Dar es Salaam   Cape Town
Melbourne   Auckland   Madrid

and associated companies in
Berlin   Ibadan

Library of Congress Cataloging-in-Publication Data
Staggenborg, Suzanne.
The Pro-choice movement : organization and activism
in the abortion conflict / Suzanne Staggenborg.
p. cm.   Includes bibliographical references and index.
ISBN 0-19-506596-4
ISBN 0-19-508925-1 (pbk)
1. Pro-choice movement—United States.
2. Abortion—United States.   I. Title.
HQ767.5.U5S73   1991   363.4′6′0973—dc20
90-23877

9 8 7 6 5 4 3 2 1

Printed in the United States of America
on acid-free paper

To Rod

ACKNOWLEDGMENTS

Many past and present pro-choice movement activists gave me hours of their time and the benefit of their memories and insights; this book could not have been written without their help. In addition to talking to me, many persons also dug into their closets and basements for memos, newsletters, and notes. I am particularly grateful to Jean Robinson and Jenny Knauss, who each lent me several boxes of invaluable private papers. The staffs at the special collections departments of Northwestern University library and the University of Illinois at Chicago library, the Chicago Historical Society, the manuscripts department of the New York Public Library, and the Schlesinger Library at Radcliffe College were also all very helpful in routing out documents.

This work began as my doctoral dissertation at Northwestern University. I am grateful for the support I received there, and particularly for the freedom I had to pursue my own project in my own way. My dissertation advisor Allan Schnaiberg and committee members Albert Hunter and Charles Ragin were very much a part of the support and freedom I enjoyed at Northwestern.

Comments from a number of colleagues and reviewers greatly improved the manuscript. I am particularly grateful to John McCarthy, Carol Mueller, Rod Nelson, Ronnie Steinberg, Verta Taylor, and an anonymous reviewer for their suggestions. At Oxford University Press, Valerie Aubry, my editor, and Niko Pfund were extremely supportive and helpful.

The research was supported by a dissertation grant from the National Science Foundation (#SES-8315574) and a small grant from the Institute of Social Research at Indiana University. A leave from teaching in the spring of 1990 at Indiana University enabled me to complete work on the manuscript.

Contents

ABBREVIATIONS

ACS	Abortion Counseling Service (Jane)
ARA	Abortion Rights Association of Illinois
ATF	Abortion Task Force
AGI	Alan Guttmacher Institute
AAUW	American Association of University Women
ABA	American Bar Association
ACLU	American Civil Liberties Union
AFSC	American Friends Service Committee
ALI	American Law Institute
AMA	American Medical Association
ASA	Association for the Study of Abortion
AVS	Association for Voluntary Sterilization
CFFC	Catholics for a Free Choice
CWHTF	Chicago Women's Health Task Force
CWLU	Chicago Women's Liberation Union
CCS	Clergy Consultation Service
CARASA	Committee for Abortion Rights and Against Sterilization Abuse
CESA	Committee to End Sterilization Abuse
ECDC	Emergency Clinic Defense Coalition
FFP	Friends of Family Planning
HEW	Health, Education, and Welfare (Department of)
HERS	Health Evaluation and Referral Service
ICMCA	Illinois Citizens for the Medical Control of Abortion
IRCAR	Illinois Religious Coalition for Abortion Rights
IWAC	Illinois Women's Abortion Coalition
NARAL	National Abortion Rights Action League
NARAL	National Association for Repeal of Abortion Laws
NOW	National Organization for Women
NWHN	National Women's Health Network
NAM	New American Movement

PAC	Political Action Committee
RCAR	Religious Coalition for Abortion Rights
R2N2	Reproductive Rights National Network
SWP	Socialist Workers Party
SOS	Students Organizing Students
TRIAL	Total Repeal of Illinois Abortion Laws
VC	Voters for Choice
WISC	Washington Inter-religious Staff Council
WORC	Women Organized for Reproductive Choice
WONAAC	Women's National Abortion Action Coalition
ZPG	Zero Population Growth

THE PRO-CHOICE MOVEMENT

1

Introduction

The conflict over abortion has a long history in American political life.[1] The states were originally guided on the matter of abortion by British common law, which permitted abortion until "quickening," the point about midway through pregnancy when the woman first perceives fetal movement. Although abortion before quickening was socially acceptable and there was no grass-roots anti-abortion movement before the twentieth century, there was a successful campaign to outlaw abortion in the nineteenth century that was initiated not by religious leaders—as might be expected—but by physicians. The physicians who led this campaign were "regular" doctors motivated in large part by their desire to regulate medicine and to drive out the "irregular" doctors who were most likely to perform abortions. The power of these regular physicians grew with the formation of the American Medical Association (AMA) in 1847 and later from a political alliance with the anti-obscenity movement led by Anthony Comstock in the 1870s. But because there was no popular movement to resist the pressure exerted by the AMA and its members, by 1900 abortion had been outlawed by every state in the nation (see Mohr, 1978).

On January 22, 1973, the abortion conflict came full circle when the U.S. Supreme Court, with its landmark *Roe* v. *Wade* ruling, legalized abortion throughout the United States. The Court ruling was the result of another organized effort to alter the legal status of abortion, but this time the goal was legalization, and the cast of characters had changed. Although many physicians became involved in efforts to reform the anti-abortion laws for which their predecessors had lobbied, they were not the main leaders of the campaign for legalization. Rather, it was feminists and family-planning activists who led the twentieth-century movement to legalize abortion.

The social movement that became known as the "pro-choice" movement originated in the 1960s as a loose coalition of women's movement, single-issue "abortion" movement, and population movement activists and organizations.[2] Paradoxically, the movement achieved its most spectacular victory—the legalization of abortion in 1973—before pro-choice forces became very well organized or powerful.

This book recounts the sociological history of the movement's transformation from a small band of entrepreneurs to a strong social movement consisting of

3

professional leaders and formal organizations as well as grass-roots activists. Before 1973, the story is one of a movement that patched together different types of resources from different sources: the enthusiasm of young constituents, particularly feminists, willing to demonstrate for abortion rights in the streets; the skills of seasoned family-planning activists and volunteers who knew how to raise money and lobby their legislators; the moral concern and counseling skills of clergy members who organized abortion referral services; and the ingenuity of civil liberties and women's movement lawyers anxious to test the abortion laws. With these resources, the movement engaged in a successful combination of direct-action and institutionalized tactics.[3] Although loosely organized, the movement coalition proved stronger than the emerging anti-abortion countermovement.

After the legalization of abortion, the balance of power shifted. One of the unfortunate side-effects of victory is that it often provokes opponents into action while the victors may be lulled into complacency. *Roe* v. *Wade* was indeed a powerful stimulus for the anti-abortion countermovement, which grew enormously after 1973. Contrary to popular belief, however, the pro-choice movement did not simply fold up shop after 1973, only to revive again in the late 1970s. The pro-choice coalition was too diverse, and the reaction of the countermovement too swift, for that to have happened. The movement was, however, forced into a reactive stance as the countermovement began to shape the pro-choice agenda. Countermovement activities precluded the adoption of broader goals and tactics, which might have been pursued following the victory of 1973, but they also prevented the decline of the pro-choice movement, which might also have occurred after the victory. Instead, the pro-choice movement began to lay the organizational groundwork that would enable it to become a long-term single-issue defender of legal abortion.

It was after the countermovement achieved its first major victories, beginning with Congressional passage of the Hyde Amendment banning Medicaid funding of abortions in 1976, that the pro-choice movement received the spur it needed in order to expand. At the same time, the countermovement was also encouraged, rather than lulled, by its partial victories, and the movement continued to be limited in its strategic and tactical options by the need to respond to countermovement initiatives. Despite the growth in the late 1970s of a "reproductive rights" component of the pro-choice movement that favored direct-action tactics and attempted to promote a broad definition of reproductive "choice," the movement as a whole did not broaden its objectives and repertoire of collective action. Rather, the goals of the movement became increasingly narrow in response to the single-issue countermovement. Major movement organizations became increasingly formalized, employing tactics that were largely institutionalized. At the same time, however, the movement was also able to mobilize an impressive number of grass-roots activists around the single issue of abortion rights. By 1989, when the Supreme Court struck an important blow at *Roe* v. *Wade* in *Webster* v. *Reproductive Health Services,* a ruling that allowed the states to place important restrictions on abortion rights, the pro-choice movement was prepared to continue the abortion battle on a number of fronts.

Despite its ups and downs, the pro-choice movement has remained continually mobilized since its 1973 victory. A major argument of this book is that the movement has been able to maintain itself and grow in strength since the legalization of abortion by acquiring professional leadership and formalized organizational structures. In part, this transformation was necessary because the protest movements of the 1960s that had nourished the abortion movement prior to legalization were declining. Whereas the strength of the "social movement sector"[4] helped compensate for organizational deficits in the movement before legalization, by the late 1970s the pro-choice movement had to develop stronger organizational structures to compensate for the demise of other social movements, notably the women's liberation and population movements, which had previously provided grass-roots support for the abortion movement. This strengthening of pro-choice organizations was made possible in part by the legitimacy created for the movement by the *Roe* v. *Wade* victory and in part by the threats created by the anti-abortion countermovement. Contrary to some theories of what happens to movements when they become "institutionalized," however, these developments actually facilitated, rather than hindered, the growth of grass-roots movement activities.

Beyond explaining the course of the pro-choice movement, this book develops arguments that are relevant to more general theories of social movements. In particular, I address two broad sets of issues: (1) the role of social movements in the political system and (2) their growth, maintenance, and decline.

Social Movements and the Political Process

The role of social movements in the larger political process is a long-standing concern of social movement theorists. At one time, social movements were commonly treated as deviant or extraordinary behavior rather than as "normal" political phenomena. This perspective changed, in part, because many students of social movements either became active themselves or observed at close range the activities of social movements emerging in the 1960s (cf. Zald, 1980:61). As theorists began to focus on the processes of "resource mobilization" and the strategies of collective action, they came to see movements as legitimate political means of bringing about social change.[5] Despite this emerging consensus, however, important questions remain regarding the status of movement actors vis-à-vis the established political system.

One key issue is the extent to which movements originate and operate independently of elites and established organizations. In one view, movements originate from *within* the established power structure with the aid of institutionalized actors such as government authorities or interest groups (cf. Zald, 1988:39, n. 1). In another view, protest is created by "challenging groups" *outside* the established political system or "polity" (see Gamson, 1975; Tilly, 1978).[6] These contrasting theoretical models produce different expectations as to the kinds of resources needed to launch social movements, and they place somewhat different emphases on the grievances of grass-roots constituents as a source of collective action. In the case of the pro-choice movement, we shall see that from the start it relied on a mix of different types of resources and immediately felt grievances and was never a complete "insider" or "outsider" to the political system.

The growing trend toward "professionalization" in social movements provides some evidence for the view that movements emerge from within the system. Many movement organizations—including environmental, feminist, and pro-choice groups—are increasingly led by paid professionals, whereas their "members" are recruited by direct mail to provide largely financial support.[7] Observers of this phenomenon have argued that groups and individuals with grievances—who are the potential recipients of the benefits won by a movement (the "beneficiary" constituents)—are no longer essential because professional movements typically mobilize "conscience" constituents who do not stand to gain directly from the achievement of the movement's goals (McCarthy and Zald, 1973, 1977). In this "professional" model of movement mobilization, support from groups with resources to spare, rather than the participation of the dispossessed, becomes the key to movement success and movement organizations look much like other kinds of organizations.

In contrast with "hearts and minds of the people" theories,[8] the professional model deemphasizes the role of grievances as a motor of collective action. Grievances may exist, but resources and organizational structures are necessary for the emergence of a social movement. Moreover, as McCarthy and Zald (1973, 1977) contend, professional movement "entrepreneurs" can draw on an ever-present supply of grievances to create interest in a movement. Work compatible with this model also downplays grievances and stresses the importance of support from established organizations or other elites with access to political power in the mobilization of social movements. Research on the farm worker movement of the 1960s (Jenkins, 1985; Jenkins and Perrow, 1977), for example, reveals the critical role of liberal support organizations in the success of the movement. Both grassroots participation and grievances may be important, but they are not always sufficient to generate successful collective action, and they may not always be necessary.

In contrast, other research demonstrates the significance of grass-roots protest by groups excluded from the institutionalized power structure in pressuring elites to support movements (e.g., Jenkins, 1987; Jenkins and Eckert, 1986; Morris, 1981, 1984; Piven and Cloward, 1977). For example, in a study of the civil rights movement, Morris (1984) shows that resources derived from the black community itself were critical. Although, in his "indigenous approach," Morris places more emphasis on grass-roots resources than on grievances, other theorists stressing the importance of grass-roots participation in social movements have pointed to the role of grievances in mobilizing movement support: If protest originates with grass-roots activists rather than professional political organizers, the discontent that people feel is much more relevant. In this regard, Walsh (1988) demonstrates the importance of "suddenly imposed grievances" in persuading citizens to participate in the anti-nuclear protest movement that formed after the nuclear accident at Three Mile Island, Pennsylvania. Although the lack of access to legal abortion has not (as of yet) been so suddenly imposed, women's very immediate concerns about abortion have, as we shall see, been essential to promoting grass-roots participation in the pro-choice movement.

Thus, one set of theoretical issues concerns the nature of the social movement as a political phenomenon. How necessary are grass-roots activists and their grievances compared with professional movement organizers? In what sense are movement organizations "challenging groups," and how do they differ from established interest groups? If movements originate from outside the political establishment, do successful or surviving movements inevitably become "established" in the sense that leadership becomes professionalized, movement organizations become bureaucratic, and tactics become institutionalized? If movements do become professionalized, will this lead to the decline of insurgency? Is the real work of social movements increasingly carried out behind the scenes rather than in the streets?

Growth, Maintenance, and Decline of Social Movements

Related to the role of social movements in the political process is the problem of how to account for the growth, maintenance, and decline of social movements. Not only do individual movements rise and fall, but in some periods, such as the 1960s, many different social movements thrive; at other times, there is little collective action in evidence. To describe this phenomenon of the rise and decline of periods of widespread movement mobilization, social movement theorists have developed the concept of "cycles of protest" (see Tarrow, 1983, 1988, 1989). As Tarrow (1989) emphasizes, cycles of protest are related to the "structure of political opportunity." Widespread protest is likely to occur when political conditions reduce the costs of collective action and increase the likelihood of success. For example, political opportunities exist when elites are divided among themselves or are open to the demands of protestors, allies are available, and resources are plentiful.[9]

Beyond explaining periods of widespread protest, the concept of cycles of protest is useful in pointing to changes that occur over the course of a period of widespread movement activity. During a cycle of protest, the social movement sector expands in size, with important consequences for the movements and organizations that compose it, including the potential for both cooperation and competition among movement organizations and other actors drawn into movement activity. As Tarrow (1989:23) notes, the political opportunity structure changes once a cycle of protest is under way, because "early riser" movements provide models of action and evidence of elite vulnerability for movements that emerge later in the cycle. Existing movements may also supply resources and activists for later movements. The civil rights movement, for example, directly or indirectly aided the growth of numerous other movements of the 1960s, including the abortion movement.

The collective action of social movement actors also produces victories and defeats that affect opportunities for subsequent mobilization and collective action. Social movement theorists need to take into account how the outcomes of one "round" of collective action affect the resources, organization, and tactics of the next (cf. Snyder and Kelly, 1979). One of the outcomes that may result from a movement's victories is the growth of a countermovement. Depending on its strength, a countermovement may severely limit the strategic and tactical options of the original movement, while at the same time increasing the movement's resources as supporters become alerted to threats from the opposition. In this regard, the pro-choice movement is somewhat unusual in that it has provoked one of the most vigorous and lasting countermovements in the history of American reform movements.

When a cycle of protest wanes, we can expect movements to have a more difficult time surviving. Piven and Cloward (1977) predict an inevitable decline in "poor people's movements" when conditions of political opportunity dissipate, but studies of other kinds of movements reveal that certain types of movement organizations do survive. Rupp and Taylor's (1987) study of the women's movement in the years between the passage of women's suffrage and the 1960s shows that the movement was kept alive "in the doldrums" by its "elite-sustained" structure consisting of a small, exclusive, and affluent core of women activists. This finding points to the more general proposition that movements with different organizational structures have different capacities to survive "dry" periods for mobilization. As we shall see in the case of the pro-choice movement, the formalization of movement organizations also can facilitate ongoing mobilization.

In sum, a number of questions are involved in the problem of explaining the growth, maintenance, and decline of social movements. What kinds of political opportunities are important to the growth of social movements? How does the position of a social movement in a cycle of protest affect opportunities for mobilization and collective action? Under what circumstances do movement organizations cooperate and compete with one another? How do victories and defeats affect subsequent mobilization? What impact does countermovement activity have on a social movement? And how do the characteristics of movement organizations affect mobilization and collective action?

The Study

This study addresses these questions through a sociological examination of the development of the pro-choice movement. Based on a theoretical assumption of the importance of social movement organizations to modern social movements (cf. McCarthy and Zald, 1977; Zald and Ash, 1966), I have focused on the experiences of thirteen major movement organizations, including six national organizations and seven local organizations active in Chicago and Illinois. Newsletters and other organizational documents (see Appendix B) were used to trace the activities of these movement organizations from their origins to the 1980s. Interviews with past and present activists supplement the documentary data (see Appendix C).

The movement organizations that I studied intensively are the most important of three major types of pro-choice movement organizations identified through a preliminary study of historical documents and secondary sources: single-issue, population, and women's movement organizations. The six national organizations include two single-issue organizations (one secular and one religious), the National Abortion Rights Action League (formerly called the National Association for Repeal of Abortion Laws), and the Religious Coalition for Abortion Rights; one population organization, Zero Population Growth; and three types of women's movement organizations, the National Organization for Women (a women's rights organization), the National Women's Health Network (a women's health movement organization), and the Reproductive Rights National Network (a reproductive rights organization). The local organizations include two single-issue organizations, the National Abortion Rights Action League of Illinois (formerly called Illinois Citizens for the Medical Control of Abortion and the Abortion Rights Association of Illinois) and the Illinois Religious Coalition for Abortion Rights; one population group, Chicago-area Zero Population Growth; and four different types of women's movement organizations, Chicago National Organization for Women (a women's rights group), the Chicago Women's Liberation Union (a women's liberation group), the Chicago Women's Health Task Force (a women's health movement organization), and Women Organized for Reproductive Choice (a reproductive rights organization). Appendix A provides detailed descriptions of these organizations.

Study of the movement on both national and state and local levels allows for a close-up view of local grass-roots activism as well as nationwide movement activity. The site of Chicago was chosen for practical reasons, including the excellent documentary sources available for the local movement, but it is also important as the center of a well-developed and long-standing movement in Illinois. Moreover, this state and local movement has received less attention than have the abortion movements in several other states (see Faux, 1988, on Texas; Lader, 1973, on New York; Luker, 1984, on California; Mohr, 1989, on Iowa; and Steinhoff and Diamond, 1977, on Hawaii).

The focus on a single state and local movement does raise the question of how typical the movement's activity in Illinois is, a problem shared by other case studies. In this book, however, the problem is mitigated in several ways: First, the national-level analysis reveals many processes parallel to those found locally, which suggests that the local findings are likely to be generalizable. Moreover, in studying the national movement as well as the state and local movements, some information pertaining to other states beside Illinois was obtained from knowledgeable national leaders. For example, I learned that certain programs being implemented by national organizations in their Illinois chapters were also being implemented in other states. Finally, in the case of the pro-choice movement, there are published accounts of movement activity in several other states. Although these accounts do not all provide the same detail or focus on the same concerns as does my study of the Illinois movement, and most cover only the period before the legalization of abortion, I draw on them wherever possible to compare the Illinois movement with those in other states.

Chapter Plan

In the first part of this book, I examine the origins and development of the movement before legalization. Chapter 2 takes up the question of how the movement to legalize abortion came into being, arguing that it relied on both individuals with ties to established organizations and "outsider" beneficiary constituents. Movement organizations did not enjoy strong support from established organizations or elites, but the cycle of protest under way in the 1960s was a source of political opportunity for the movement. In Chapters 3 and 4, I examine the forms of collective action that led to legalization, showing how the movement's internal organization and the external political environment produced a combination of institutionalized and direct-action strategies and tactics.

Part II considers the impact on the movement of the 1973 victory—the legalization of abortion. Chapter 5 demonstrates that there was no demobilization of the movement following victory; rather, the leadership of the movement began to "professionalize," and movement organizations began to formalize. Developments in the movement are explained not only in terms of internal organizational dynamics but also as responses to changes in the movement's political environment, including the growth of the anti-abortion countermovement and increased support for the movement from established organizations. In Chapter 6, I look at the effects of these developments on the strategies and tactics employed by movement organizations following the critical victory.

Part III describes the period of tremendous growth for the movement that followed the first major countermovement victory, Congressional passage of the Hyde Amendment banning Medicaid funding of abortions in late 1976. Chapter 7 shows how a hostile political environment was, paradoxically, beneficial to the organization of the movement. The analysis contributes to theoretical debates about the consequences of different types of organizational arrangements by showing how formalized organizational structures and professional leadership enabled the movement to take advantage of political opportunities. Chapter 8 extends this analysis by demonstrating how organizational structures, together with countermovement actions, caused the strategies and tactics of the major movement organizations to become increasingly narrow and institutionalized. Chapter 9 focuses on the rise of the reproductive rights component of the movement and the dilemmas it faced in attempting to broaden the movement's goals and tactics.

In Part IV, Chapter 10 explains how the movement remained alive in the 1983–89 period of stalemate between movement and countermovement forces. Chapter 11 looks at the movement's responses to the 1989 U.S. Supreme Court ruling challenging *Roe* v. *Wade,* which marked an important turning point in the abortion conflict. In Chapter 12, I conclude by assessing the implications of the history of the pro-choice movement for theories of social movements.

I

ORIGINS OF THE MOVEMENT
TO LEGALIZE ABORTION

2

The Emergence of the Movement

When it began in the 1960s, the movement to legalize abortion "was just a brave tiny army."[1] There were no large national organizations with professional staffs advocating legal abortion. Nevertheless, a movement did take shape and in 1973 abortion became legal throughout the United States. How did this social movement emerge, and what did it look like before *Roe* v. *Wade*?

An "insider" model of social movements would predict that the movement arose from within established institutions, with support from elites, or that professional movement organizers engineered the movement. After legalization of abortion, as we shall see, the movement did indeed develop professional leadership and formalized organizational structures, which played a major role in maintaining the pro-choice movement. But before *Roe* v. *Wade,* the movement relied much more on the challenging groups of the 1960s, including the women's movement, than on the world of established interest groups. Nevertheless, the movement was not a complete "outsider" to the established political process. The abortion movement mobilized both grass-roots constituents activated by other movements of the 1960s and individuals with many years of experience in established political and voluntary organizations.

Professionals and Established Organizations
in the Abortion Reform Movement

One possible "insider" explanation of why the movement formed when it did centers on the role of doctors and other professionals and their organizations. Some movements do originate within established institutions (cf. Zald, 1988:37; Zald and Berger, 1978), which can provide resources and organizational bases for movements. Medical and legal interest groups and family-planning organizations such as Planned Parenthood might have performed this function in the abortion movement. They certainly helped bring about change in the abortion laws; the issue is whether such groups were the entrepreneurs of the movement.

If physicians, along with other professionals, did lead the crusade to legalize abortion in the 1960s, this would indeed be ironic, given their role in making abortion illegal in the United States in the nineteenth century (see Mohr, 1978).

Physicians did change their stance toward abortion in the twentieth century, as they were no longer threatened by "irregular" competitors and now had an interest in reforming abortion laws that interfered with their ability to make medical decisions about abortion. As early as the 1930s, there were doctors and family-planning advocates interested in changing the abortion laws, but few called for radical changes in the laws, and no movement for legalization emerged at that time (see Francome, 1984:74–76). Discussions of abortion in the 1940s and 1950s were quite cautious, and deliberately conservative appeals were made to doctors and lawyers by abortion law reform advocates such as Harold Rosen, who in 1954 published *Therapeutic Abortion,* a collection of essays calling for greater freedom for doctors to make decisions about abortion, and Glanville Williams, who in 1957 similarly appealed to the interests of lawyers in *The Sanctity of Life and the Criminal Law* (Olasky, 1988–89:17–18). Some articles suggesting needed reforms were also published in professional journals in the 1950s, and several conferences on abortion were held, including one sponsored by Planned Parenthood that called on the American Law Institute to study the abortion laws (Francome, 1984; Rubin, 1987). The American Law Institute (ALI) subsequently drafted a model abortion law allowing for therapeutic abortions under limited conditions[2] as part of a Model Penal Code intended to standardize state criminal laws. A draft of the recommendations was released in 1959, and a final version of the Model Penal Code was adopted by the ALI in 1962. The ALI recommendations became the basis for a number of limited reforms of abortion laws enacted by state legislatures in the 1960s.

This sequence of events seems to support the view that the movement to legalize abortion originated within professional associations and other established organizations. The difficulty with this explanation, however, is that it fails to take into account the role of external events in pulling doctors and other professionals into the abortion controversy. Moreover, the support that established interest groups and organizations did provide, particularly in the early years of the movement, was quite limited. Dissatisfaction with the limited actions and policies of these groups forced those who wanted significant change in the abortion laws to build a movement outside the established power structure.

Support for abortion law reform among professionals and professional associations was very quiet in the 1950s and early 1960s, receiving little media attention (cf. Tatalovich and Daynes, 1981:34). Reform efforts might have remained practically invisible were it not for two events that created unexpected opportunities by generating media attention and public support for abortion law reform. The first, in 1962, was the highly publicized case of Sherri Finkbine, a woman who attempted to get a legal abortion in the United States after learning that she had taken thalidomide, a drug that causes fetal deformity, and who ended up having an abortion in Sweden. The incident touched off nationwide concern about thalidomide as well as a debate over abortion (see Faux, 1988:42–51; and Tatalovich and Daynes, 1981:44–46, for detailed accounts). The second "event" was an epidemic of rubella measles in the United States in the early 1960s, a disease that can cause fetal deformity when contracted by a pregnant woman. Both events influenced public opinion toward reform of the abortion laws and gave impetus to the movement (cf. Lader, 1973; Rubin, 1987; Steinhoff and Diamond, 1977; Tatalovich and Daynes, 1981). As Luker (1984:80–81) argues, these events forced doctors to confront differences within their profession over abortion, causing some of the more liberal doctors to support reform of the abortion laws.

The medical community did become involved in lobbying for abortion reform laws in a number of states (Mohr, 1989). However, most professional associations endorsed limited reform rather than total repeal of the abortion laws,[3] and support for the movement from established organizations like Planned Parenthood was slow in coming. In 1967 the American Medical Association (AMA) endorsed the ALI model of reform, and in 1968 the American College of Obstetricians and Gynecologists endorsed the same model of limited reform (Tatalovich and Daynes, 1981:53–58). The AMA debated the repeal position in 1970, the year in which four states passed very liberal abortion bills,[4] but, because of divisions among its members on the issue, ended up adopting a position short of repeal, although more liberal than the ALI model (Tatalovich and Daynes, 1981:56). In 1968 the American Public Health Association became the first professional organization to take a repeal rather than a reform position. Other professional associations, including the American Bar Association and the American College of Obstetricians and Gynecologists, also eventually endorsed repeal in the early 1970s, after the repeal movement had been active for a number of years. Planned Parenthood, the leading family-planning organization, did not vote to endorse abortion law repeal until 1969 and gave little organizational support to the movement before the legalization of abortion (Lader, 1973:84).[5] The board of the American Civil Liberties Union (ACLU) endorsed abortion law repeal in 1967 (Walker, 1990), but the New York Civil Liberties Union was much more active than was the national organization in the years before legalization.[6]

An organization devoted to the single issue of abortion, the Association for the Study of Abortion (ASA), was formed as a result of the professional interest in abortion but, again, was notable for its limited approach. ASA was found in 1964 by Dr. Alan Guttmacher of Planned Parenthood as an educational association consisting largely of doctors, lawyers, and other professionals. Although "national" in its outlook, ASA was based in New York and consisted of only about twenty active members (interview with Lawrence Lader, 1984). The organization initially advocated reform, rather than repeal, of the abortion laws, and its activities consisted largely of publishing and distributing educational materials and supporting research projects on abortion.

ASA was important in lending "prestige and authority" to the abortion reform cause in the early years when this was badly needed (Lader, 1973:58). The organization did eventually come around to the repeal position and played an essential role in the effort to legalize abortion. After the U.S. Supreme Court agreed to hear the *Roe* v. *Wade* case, ASA provided Sarah Weddington and Linda Coffee, the lawyers who filed the case, with access to legal counsel from abortion experts, including Harriet Pilpel, who had worked on several major birth cases before *Roe* v. *Wade,* and law professor Cyril Means. ASA also funded research by Means that resulted in an article on the history of abortion that was cited in the 1973 decision and widely regarded as an important influence on the Court. And ASA's executive director, Jimmye Kimmey, coordinated the *amicus curiae* briefs for *Roe* v. *Wade,* mobilizing professional groups and others to submit a total of forty-two briefs in favor of legal abortion (see Faux, 1988:217–18, 224–28).

ASA was not, however, in the forefront of the movement. In the early years, the group refused to support more aggressive efforts to change the abortion laws (Lader, 1973) and in general moved quite slowly on the issue. Significantly, ASA had itself been interested in developing a test case in the courts but was so cautious that an "ideal plaintiff" was never located (Faux, 1988:217–18).

The Creation of a Repeal Movement

Although established interest groups and organizations of professionals were not the entrepreneurs of the abortion movement, they did play an important role in bringing together activists who were interested in abortion and frustrated by the limited activity of existing organizations. A number of early repeal activists were volunteers or staff in family-planning organizations like Planned Parenthood who, in dealing with women seeking abortions, became concerned about the issue. Through their firsthand experience, these activists were acutely aware that limited reform of the abortion laws, as opposed to repeal, would not meet women's needs for access to abortion.

In addition to family-planning organizations, the Association for the Study of Abortion was crucial in bringing together key activists who disagreed with ASA's cautious approach and who later worked together to found the National Association for Repeal of Abortion Laws (NARAL). Lawrence Lader, a NARAL founder, had become an ASA board member as a result of his research on abortion (Lader, 1966). Ruth Proskauer Smith, another NARAL founder, had served as executive director of ASA. Lader came into contact with a third person instrumental in founding NARAL, Dr. Lonny Myers of Illinois, through her contacts with the Association for the Study of Abortion. As Lader, who was making public appearances as the author of a controversial book on abortion, reported:

> In October 1966, I flew to Chicago to make an abortion speech, and decided to use this chance to have a breakfast conference with one of the stormy petrels of the movement, Dr. Lonny Myers. Annoyed with the approach of the Association for the Study of Abortion, Dr. Myers had constantly peppered ASA with pungent notes to pierce its sleepy dignity. Although I had been a founding, board member of ASA, and chaired two of its committees, I was delighted to find after two hours of talk that Myers' platform was a rational and constructive force for repeal. (Lader, 1973:61)

In Illinois, Lonny Myers and other activists previously involved in population and family-planning work founded in 1966 the repeal organization called Illinois Citizens for the Medical Control of Abortion (ICMCA). One of the ICMCA founders, Don Shaw, was then an Episcopal priest employed by Planned Parenthood as an educational director. In the early 1960s, Shaw had become concerned that social workers were not permitted by law to give information on family-planning services to their public aid clients. As he recalled in an interview:

> We were concerned to make birth control information available to the poor, and someone told me, "you ought to get hold of Lonny Myers," who was working as an anesthesiologist and who had become interested in the population issue—was just starting to get involved in causes and had a lot of energy. So I did and we also hooked up with Ralph Brown, a lawyer who was concerned about the issue. The three of us founded Citizens for the Extension of Birth Control Services in 1961. We were a great triumvirate—I was an Episcopal priest at the time and had connections to ministers, Lonny had connections in the medical profession, and Ralph in the legal profession, so together we were really effective. Well, we won that battle in 1965 [changing the law to allow distribution of family-planning information]. I was ready to relax at that point, but Lonny said, "Now we're going to tackle abortion—make it legal." I said, "You've got to be kidding," but she wasn't.

The three organizers again used their connections to recruit activists such as Rev. Spencer Parsons and law professor Norval Morris, both of the University of Chicago (Lader, 1973:61). There was definitely an emphasis on recruiting professionals who could lend prestige and influence to the movement. The first meeting of ICMCA was held at the University of Chicago's Center for Continuing Education and was attended by "about a dozen physicians, businessmen, sociologists, ministers and others interested in reforming Illinois' archaic abortion law" (ICMCA newsletter, May 1, 1967). Among the early activists, family-planning supporters (including Planned Parenthood volunteers and staff) and church activists were particularly prominent as the organization built on the networks of its founders.

In other states, the pattern appears similar: In Hawaii, a woman with previous experience as a lobbyist in Washington, D.C., who was involved at the time in the local American Association of University Women (AAUW) chapter spearheaded the state repeal campaign, organizing it through the AAUW, labor unions, the YWCA, churches, and many other established organizations (Steinhoff and Diamond, 1977). In Texas, a Planned Parenthood board member was an important entrepreneur of the local Dallas movement, which drew support from volunteers in Planned Parenthood, the Unitarian Church, the Council of Jewish Women, and other local organizations (Faux, 1988). In New York, Lawrence Lader was previously involved in the New York Democratic Club, where he met people like city councilwoman Carol Greitzer, who became NARAL's president (interview with Lawrence Lader, 1984), and the movement was organized through local political organizations, churches, unions, and other established organizations.

In Illinois and elsewhere, the abortion movement was initiated by a small number of activists who were in no way "outsiders" to their communities and their organizations. Rather, they were persons with extensive experience in professional, political, and voluntary organizations who recruited other "solid citizens" to join them. But the new movement did not speak for powerful established interest groups such as the AMA or even Planned Parenthood. The entrepreneurs of the movement were volunteers, albeit experienced ones, who formed new organizations and who needed grass-roots constituents from outside established interest groups.

Grass-Roots Participation:
The Cycle of Protest

Although a few politically experienced individuals helped start the abortion movement, its success was very much dependent on the cycle of protest under way in the 1960s. Other social movements in the expanded social movement sector of the period aided the mobilization of the abortion rights movement in several ways. The civil rights movement was an important precursor that generated social activism among liberal churches and clergy and offered tactical models to numerous other movements, including the abortion movement. Women, college students and other young people who were activated by earlier movements of the 1960s became the grass-roots constituents of the movement to legalize abortion. The family-planning, population, and women's movements directly aided mobilization by providing organizational bases and constituents for the abortion movement.

Not only were these previously organized constituents available, but they were people who felt intensely about the abortion issue. Some early constituents were women who had themselves undergone illegal abortions or who had helped friends arrange abortions. College students in an era of "sexual revolution" and expanded university enrollments were particularly likely to have had such experiences, and many participants in the population and women's movements were students in the 1960s. Other constituents, such as those with backgrounds in family planning, had direct experience through their work with the problems of women seeking abortions. Many of these activists became involved in giving women referrals for abortions, an activity that radicalized participants and helped to mobilize the movement.

The Population Movement

A number of individuals who became active in NARAL were also active, previously or simultaneously, in population organizations like the Association for Voluntary Sterilization (AVS) and Zero Population Growth (ZPG). Lawrence Lader, for instance, had served on the executive committee of AVS and on the board of ZPG (Lader, 1973). Other early NARAL activists, including Ruth Proskauer Smith and Beatrice McClintock, had previously worked together in the Association for Voluntary Sterilization as well as in the Association for the Study of Abortion (Nathanson, 1979:48) and in Planned Parenthood. While population groups like AVS contributed some activists, others, notably ZPG, became active participants in the repeal campaign.

ZPG was organized in 1968 and took an abortion repeal position in 1969, after the founding of NARAL and possibly as a result of overlapping memberships. Although a repeal position on abortion was considered consistent with ZPG's goal of bringing down the birthrate, there was some internal debate as to how active ZPG should be on the abortion issue. ZPG's leadership consisted of both individuals concerned primarily with family-planning issues and persons who identified primarily with the environmental movement. The former pushed ZPG's involvement in the repeal effort, whereas the latter were concerned that ZPG maintain a broader perspective. For example, former ZPG executive director Hal Seielstad was an environmentalist who expressed concern in 1972 that "many people think of ZPG solely as an advocate of abortion" even though "the question of abortion is a minor one in the entire program of achieving zero population growth in this country" (ZPG *National Reporter*, June 1972).

But despite one executive director's warning that ZPG should "not neglect the other goals and become largely identified in the public mind with this one issue" (ZPG *National Reporter*, June 1972), ZPG was fairly active in the repeal movement before legalization for several reasons. First, as already noted, in this period there were a number of activists among ZPG's leaders concerned mainly with family planning. Because organizations like Planned Parenthood were not heavily involved in the abortion movement at the time, these activists had few other organizations through which to work for abortion repeal. Second, the movement for legal abortion was very small during this period and so needed ZPG's help. Third, and probably most important, ZPG's real strength at the time was in its local chapters, many of which had student constituencies. It was the local ZPG chapters that became the most highly involved in the abortion repeal movement, in some areas as the only organized representatives of the nascent abortion movement. It also is noteworthy that the local chapters were completely autonomous from the national organization, allowing grass-roots activists to influence organizational activities.

In Chicago, there were ten or more area chapters, many of them university based. Although documentation of these chapters' activities is scant, the chapters based at the University of Chicago and at the University of Illinois at Chicago were definitely working on the abortion issue. The University of Illinois chapter worked with a student women's liberation group to set up an abortion loan service to provide students with funds for abortions (see ZPG *National Reporter*, May 1970, February 1972). After 1971, when a Chicago-area ZPG office was opened to help coordinate area chapter activities, ZPG worked very closely with ICMCA on abortion repeal activities. Chicago-area ZPG involvement in the abortion movement was facilitated both by overlaps in membership with ICMCA and by the fact that ZPG and ICMCA shared office space provided by a nonprofit clinic, the Midwest Population Center. The Midwest Population Center was founded by population movement activists who were also members of ZPG and ICMCA, including Dr. Lonny Myers and Rev. Don Shaw, and it became important as a "local movement center" (cf. Morris, 1984) that brought together population activists who were also interested in the abortion issue. Thus, grass-roots constituents of the population movement played a critical role in the mobilization of the repeal movement.

The Women's Movement

At the same time that the single-issue "abortion movement" was beginning to take shape, the women's movement was also reemerging. The National Organization for Women (NOW) was founded in 1966 and endorsed abortion repeal at its second national convention in 1967. The endorsement was not a foregone conclusion and, in fact, provoked considerable conflict within the "older branch" women's movement organization.[7] At the time, abortion had not yet been defined as a "women's rights" issue, causing concern among a number of NOW members that the position would hurt NOW's credibility. However, NOW founder Betty Friedan, who was an old friend of Lawrence Lader's from their common backgrounds in journalism, strongly supported adoption of the repeal plank. According to Jean Faust, a NOW activist interviewed by Lader, Friedan was backed by younger NOW members:

> The professional women demanded we concentrate on economic goals—they were scared of harming the organization's dignity with abortion and sex. It was the kids, and not just the New York bloc, who led the fight. Kids from Michigan, Ohio, and Texas kept standing up and shouting, "We've got to have an abortion plank." We pushed it through finally, but a lot of delegates resigned. (quoted in Lader, 1973:37)

NOW's participation in the abortion movement was, for several reasons, limited in the early years. The abortion issue was controversial, and not all chapters were willing to tackle it. Moreover, many NOW members and chapters were preoccupied with economic issues in the 1960s and early 1970s. And perhaps most important, the national organization lacked the kind of structure necessary to promote grass-roots participation on the issue. The organization did form a national committee to deal with abortion, but, like other national task forces and committees, committee chairs had to operate with very few resources. Communication channels were not well established in the organization, and national coordinators had a difficult time getting in touch with the chapters. As Lana Clarke Phelan, who served as a coordinator of NOW's national task force on abortion prior to 1973, recalled in a 1984 interview:

> NOW was so loosely grouped at that time. There was no networking. There were phone calls for those that could afford them and plane tickets to meetings for those that could afford them, but no regular communication. And of course, as more members and chapters came into NOW, there were more internal factions. Now that NOW is a big organization, of course, everything has changed.

Some NOW chapters were highly involved in the repeal cause. The New York chapter was particularly active and spawned New Yorkers for Abortion Law Repeal in 1968 to coordinate NOW abortion repeal work. But other chapters took little interest in the abortion issue. Lucinda Cisler, another pre-1973 national NOW abortion committee coordinator, commented in an interview that she thought some chapters wanted abortion removed from NOW's "Bill of Rights for Women" because it made their work on other issues more difficult and that some chapters had a difficult time finding a coordinator for a local abortion committee.

Before 1973 the Chicago NOW chapter did have an abortion committee and did participate in some abortion-related activities. However, most of the chapter activities during this period were instigated by one individual, Madeline Schwenk, who was particularly concerned about the abortion issue and who also worked with the Abortion Counseling Service known as "Jane" that was affiliated with the Chicago Women's Liberation Union (CWLU), a "younger branch" women's movement organization. She was also, in her words, the "token housewife" in the NOW chapter, whereas the majority of Chicago NOW members were working women. In an interview, Schwenk reported having a very difficult time recruiting other NOW members for work on the abortion issue because most of the other activists in the chapter were personally more interested in employment issues. Because of the appeal of competing activities, Chicago NOW was not heavily involved in work on the abortion issue.

The women's movement, however, consisted of more than older branch organizations like NOW. If NOW's constituency was divided over the abortion issue in the late 1960s, that of the younger branch of the women's movement was not. All over the country, local women's liberation groups were highly concerned about abortion. The members of organizations like the Chicago Women's Liberation Union tended to be younger women, many of them students and former students with backgrounds in New Left student and anti-war groups, who saw themselves as part of a broader social change movement (cf. Freeman, 1975). And like the young NOW members who pushed the organization to adopt the abortion repeal position, young activists in the women's liberation movement were part of the generation attending college during the 1960s whose experiences help explain why abortion was of such great concern. As one CWLU activist observed in an interview:

> Even in the beginning, I feel, I have always felt, that one of the major issues was abortion, one of the reasons why women got together. My first year in college was '63, and it was a *major* issue. It was a *major* issue. And one friend got pregnant and what do you do and everyone is running around. Trying to get your friends abortions was an issue, [so] that when stuff started happening and people started getting conscious, it was *there,* it was the key issue, I really feel.

Thus from the start abortion was of paramount concern to the constituents of the younger branch of the women's movement.

Abortion Referral and Movement Mobilization

Not only did the emerging movement to legalize abortion have the advantage of preexisting organizational bases and constituents with immediately felt grievances, it also had a tactic. Although the movement's tactics before legalization will be considered in detail in Chapters 3 and 4, some discussion of abortion referral work is appropriate here because tactics are pertinent both as means of achieving goals and as means of gaining participants. Abortion referral services performed this latent function for the early movement, although not all participants viewed referral work as a tactic at all. For example, one early movement activist who engaged in referral work, Lana Clarke Phelan, stated in an interview that she never thought of referral work in strategic terms, but strictly as a means of helping individual women. Lawrence Lader, on the other hand, regarded referral work as a tactic for getting publicity for the movement (see Lader, 1973). But regardless of how abortion referral work was viewed, it helped mobilize grass-roots activists and build commitment to the cause.

Activists in both the women's liberation movement and the abortion repeal movement became deeply involved in abortion referral work. Some provided referrals for abortions as a result of their own experiences with illegal abortion, and some as a result of their experiences as family-planning practitioners. Persons who were visible as early advocates of change in the abortion laws often found themselves drawn into referral work when women contacted them for help. As early as 1961, Patricia Maginnis, a medical technologist who had herself undergone an illegal abortion, founded the California-based Society for Humane Abortion. Maginnis and associates such as Lana Clarke Phelan, who had also had an illegal abortion, became involved in providing abortion referrals. By the mid 1960s, several individuals had become nationally known by operating abortion referral services and attracting media attention to themselves. New York family-planning activist William Baird, for example, operated an abortion referral service in connection with his Long Island contraceptive clinic, the Parent's Aid Society, and earned a nationwide reputation through his public confrontation with the law (Lader, 1973).

Lawrence Lader was another individual who began operating his own abortion referral service in the mid-1960s. Lader's career as an abortion activist began with the publication of his book *Abortion* in 1966—preceded by an article in the *New York Times Magazine* in 1965—which presented his research on the large number of abortions being performed by licensed physicians in the United States. Having advocated legalization, Lader found himself inundated with requests for the names of doctors from women seeking abortions. At a national press conference held after the publication of his book in April 1966, Lader admitted to making referrals to hundreds of women and announced that he would continue to do so unless stopped by a district attorney. Crossing the line from writer to activist, Lader believed he had found an ideal strategy for publicizing the problem of abortion and creating public support. Using as a platform his opportunities for speaking engagements and lectures, Lader continued to operate and publicize a referral service for women, a strategy intended "to stir as much controversy and debate as possible while bringing the facts to the public" (Lader, 1973:xi).

By the late 1960s, abortion referral had become an important activity in the emerging women's movement as feminist abortion referral services cropped up across the country. In Chicago, the Women's Liberation Abortion Counseling Service that became known as "Jane"[8] was formed in 1968, a year before the formation of the Chicago Women's Liberation Union (document in CWLU papers, Abortion 1968–73, Chicago Historical Society). In fact, women involved in "Jane" were instrumental in forming the Union, so that there was never any question that abortion would be an important issue for the CWLU.

THE CLERGY CONSULTATION SERVICES AND
RELIGIOUS SUPPORT FOR THE MOVEMENT

One of the most important organizational outcomes of the referral strategy was the formation of a nationwide network of abortion referral services run by clergy members. Like other established organizations, the national Protestant and Jewish religious denominations did not become heavily involved in the abortion movement until after legalization. In sometimes explicit reaction to Catholic opposition to abortion reform (Sarat, 1982:128), however, in the mid-1960s a number of Protestant and Jewish religious institutions did endorse abortion law reform or repeal, and by 1973 about a dozen religious denominations and organizations were on record in support of the abortion movement (see Tatalovich and Daynes, 1981:66–67).

Religious support for change in the abortion laws was stimulated by the civil rights movement, which had generated social activism in many liberal churches and clergy in the 1960s. Some denominations, such as the United Methodist Church, became moderately active on the abortion issue through their social action arms. In 1972 the United Methodist Board of Church and Society began to distribute a packet of information on abortion supportive of repeal efforts (Balides et al., 1973:502). And throughout the country a number of Protestant and Jewish religious denominations and organizations were active in reform and repeal efforts.

In New York, the Judson Memorial Church lent its facilities to the first Clergy Consultation Service on Abortion (CCS). This organization was formed in New York in 1967 by Rev. Howard Moody, a minister at Judson Church, and other liberal clergy members previously active in the civil rights movement who had been urged by Lawrence Lader to become involved in making referrals (Carmen and Moody, 1973:21). After the clergy members received legal advice from the New York Civil Liberties Union, they agreed to provide the service and announced the formation of the Clergy Consultation Service on Abortion through an exclusive story given to the *New York Times* and published on its front page. The founders of the first CCS in New York originally had no intention of expanding the referral service "into what it ultimately and accidentally became—a nationwide effort involving thousands of ministers and rabbis" (Carmen and Moody, 1973:47). But the New York service was quickly swamped by requests for help from women all over the country, and clergy from different areas were expressing interest in setting up similar services (Carmen and Moody, 1973).

In Illinois, Rev. Spencer Parsons founded the Chicago Clergy Consultation Service in 1968 and the Illinois Clergy Consultation Service in 1970. As a result of his earlier involvement with Illinois Citizens for the Medical Control of Abortion, Parsons had received many requests for help from women seeking abortions. He was also a friend of Rev. Howard Moody, the founder of the New York Clergy Consultation Service, with whom Parsons had previously worked on other causes, including civil rights. For a while, Parsons referred women to the New York CCS but recalled Moody telling him, "You can't keep sending them to us; you've got to set up a service in Chicago." Rev. Parsons did so, recruiting about thirty Protestant ministers and Jewish rabbis into the service, about six of whom, according to Parsons's estimate, also became active in political work to repeal abortion laws (interview with Spencer Parsons, 1984).[9]

Activists in the New York CCS offered advice to Parsons and to other clergy who organized services in various cities (some of which were called Clergy Consultation Service for Problem Pregnancies), and in 1968 a national Clergy Consultation Service organization was founded as an umbrella group to coordinate the local referral services (Carmen and Moody, 1973). With the development of the Clergy Consultation Service network, a large number of clergy members were brought into the abortion repeal movement for the first time.

Beyond bringing clergy members into the movement, the Clergy Consultation Services and other abortion referral services played a critical role in mobilizing the abortion rights movement by attracting media attention to the cause and providing concrete tasks for activists. Many individuals initially became involved in the movement through referral work and later went on to other political activities. Lucinda Cisler, for example, was an early activist who worked with William Baird before going on to work with a number of groups, including New Yorkers for Abortion Law Repeal, NOW, and NARAL (interview with Lucinda Cisler, 1984). Sarah Weddington, the lawyer who argued the *Roe* v. *Wade* case before the U.S. Supreme Court, was drawn into the abortion movement when she was asked to serve as legal counsel for a referral service forming in Austin, Texas (see Faux, 1988:33–35). After making numerous contacts with other activists throughout the country through their abortion referral work, Lana Phelan and Patricia Maginnis both became active in NARAL, and Phelan became a national abortion committee coordinator for NOW.

Not only did the referral services provide concrete tasks for recruits to perform, they also brought grass-roots activists into immediate contact with aggrieved women seeking abortions. Whether or not they had personal experiences with abortion, activists who worked in abortion referral services gained firsthand understanding of what the movement to legalize abortion was all about. Moreover, abortion referral work kept participants motivated through the slow process of working for change in the abortion laws. As one New York–based activist told me in an interview, "Everybody was involved in doing referrals. It was a tonic; we couldn't have kept going in New York without the constant reminders of women who needed help."

Coordination and Coalition in the Movement

National Association for Repeal of Abortion Laws

By 1969, there were local reform and repeal groups, Clergy Consultation Services, women's movement groups, population movement organizations, and pockets of individuals in various parts of the country working for change in the abortion laws. Leaders of local abortion movement organizations and activists like Law-

A SA

rence Lader were soon in touch with one another, exchanging information and strategies. There was, however, no national single-issue movement organization to aid local efforts and bring together the various types of local constituents. The only organization concerned solely with abortion on the national level was the Association for the Study of Abortion. But, as Lader reported, there were problems with working through ASA:

> With an aggressive campaign of newspaper ads and radio and television programs, ICMCA soon built a membership of 10,000, and Illinois joined Maginnis' California group as the two most potent repeal bases in the country. Now a firm supporter of Myers' work, I urged, ASA's cooperation with the Illinois unit with no success. Ms. Ruth P. Smith, ASA's executive director, had already split with the board. ASA's constitution gave only twenty board members the right to vote. In 1968, ASA adopted a "rotation" policy which conveniently rotated a number of militants, including myself, off the board. This produced a turning point in the movement. When the militants eventually organized a nationwide coalition of repeal groups, Myers, Smith, and I were instrumental in putting the coalition together. (Lader, 1973:61–62)

Because of their perception of the need to coordinate local repeal efforts, and out of frustration with the limited role being played by ASA, Lader, Myers, and Smith formed a coordinating committee to organize what was billed as "The First National Conference on Abortion Laws." The conference was intended to gather together abortion activists from across the country and to launch a national organization to fight for the repeal of abortion laws. As Lader recalled in an interview, hundreds of invitations were sent to all kinds of women's groups, population groups, local abortion groups, Protestant and Jewish religious groups, and persons known to the organizers. Due to the intense interest in the abortion issue at the time, the conference, which was held in Chicago in February 1969, was well attended and the National Association for Repeal of Abortion Laws was born (cf. Lader, 1973; and Nathanson, 1979, for detailed accounts of the founding conference). ICMCA and other local reform and repeal groups became organizational members (rather than formal chapters) of NARAL.

NARAL

NARAL brought together a broad range of activists, including those with backgrounds in established organizations and voluntary associations and those with primary experience in social movement organizations. Even though the single-issue abortion movement had originated independently of the women's movement, and the impetus for the formation of NARAL came from single-issue activists with backgrounds in the family-planning and population movements, NARAL was strongly influenced by the women's movement. Not only did many feminists participate in the founding conference and join the organization, but the goals and rhetoric of NARAL also were shaped by the women's movement. Although there was originally some question as to whether the "R" in NARAL would stand for "reform" or "repeal" (see Lader, 1973), the strong feminist presence in the movement settled the question. Moreover, from the start, NARAL adopted a "women's rights" frame for the abortion issue rather than a more conservative frame (e.g., "population control") that might have been employed in the absence of the women's movement.

Coalition Organizations Before 1973

After 1970, when abortion was made legal in four states, including New York, single-issue coalition organizations were established on the national and local levels. On the national level, the Women's National Abortion Action Coalition (WONAAC) was formed in 1971 by members of the Socialist Workers Party (SWP), an organizational "entrepreneur" that hoped to use the abortion issue to bring potential recruits to the SWP.[10] Despite the conflict that occurred when the role of the SWP in WONAAC became known to other participants, WONAAC did enjoy some success in mobilizing. The coalition was able to secure endorsements from well-known individuals who supported repeal (a standard SWP tactic) and to gather a large number of people for nationwide demonstrations in November 1971 (mass demonstrations being another standard SWP tactic). Using SWP activists, affiliates were organized in cities across the country. And with financial backing from the SWP, WONAAC maintained a national office and carried out various activities, including an Abortion Action Week in May 1972, a petition campaign in support of the Abortion Rights Act in 1972,[11] and several national conferences. Because of the SWP's involvement, however, many autonomous feminist groups boycotted the coalition. WONAAC thus remained small in size and dissolved sometime after the Supreme Court decision in 1973.

In Illinois, a coalition organization called Total Repeal of Illinois Abortion Laws (TRIAL) was begun in 1970 at the initiative of the Chicago Women's Liberation Union (CWLU work group report, March 8, 1971; CWLU papers, Chicago Historical Society). Before the formation of TRIAL, the major movement organizations had been brought together for the purpose of forming a "coordinating group" by the American Friends Service Committee (AFSC) after an abortion reform bill was defeated in Springfield (*CWLU News,* June 1970). Although a formal coalition organization did not result from this initiative by the AFSC, it did put the major organizations in touch with one another.[12]

Shortly after this attempt at coordination in 1970, TRIAL was organized by CWLU activists "who felt that the passage of the New York abortion law was due in part to the activities of the New York abortion law repeal coalition, and who felt that a similar victory could be won in Illinois" (CWLU work group report, March 8, 1971; CWLU papers, Chicago Historical Society). When victory seemed within reach, CWLU activists decided they should become involved in coalition work on abortion repeal with other organizations to ensure that the women's liberation perspective would be represented. But because of differences in approach among participants in the coalition, TRIAL never developed into the statewide, multiorganizational coalition that it was intended to be.[13] In 1971, the Illinois Women's Abortion Coalition (IWAC) was formed as a local chapter of WONAAC. Organizations like ICMCA ceased active participation in TRIAL soon after its formation, and membership in the two coalitions soon became identical. TRIAL remained in existence for about a year until, in the words of one participant interviewed, "TRIAL kind of faded into IWAC." IWAC, like WONAAC, was kept alive by the SWP until shortly after the 1973 Supreme Court decision.

What is surprising about these ideologically diverse coalitions is not that they were short-lived but that they were created at all. One impetus for their formation was certainly the climate of expectation created after the 1970 state victories. At this point, legalized abortion throughout the United States seemed increasingly possible and there was a strong incentive for diverse groups of movement constituents to work together to achieve this goal. Another factor was that abortion repeal organizations prior to 1973 were relatively small and were not so concerned with their own organizational maintenance that they felt threatened by a new organization. Although NARAL was present to play a coordinating role in the movement, it was still small enough that its leaders were quite willing to work with whatever other groups were available. As Lana Clarke Phelan commented in an interview when asked about cooperation with WONAAC, "There were so few people working in the movement at that time, you couldn't afford to pick and choose who to work with." It was a movement in which persons with experience in traditional politics and organizations joined forces with feminists, socialists, and whoever else was willing to help challenge the abortion laws.

Conclusion

The history of the emergence of the movement to legalize abortion reveals the limitations of models that focus solely on the origins of movements from *within* the established political system or on movement actors as *outside* challengers. Examining the case that the movement arose from within established institutions, with elite support, we see that there was some support from established organizations and influential persons such as doctors and other professionals. The scope of that support, however, was quite narrow. Professional associations tended to back only limited reform of the abortion laws. Some churches became involved in the movement, but it was more typically individuals, like the clergy members who formed the Clergy Consultation Services, rather than institutions, that provided support. Organizations such as Planned Parenthood were more helpful in creating communications networks than in providing direct organizational support for the early movement.[14]

One constituency of the movement did have ties to established organizations with access to power holders. In addition to these connections they also had skills and experience in conventional methods of political influence that they brought to the movement. But the lack of sufficient support from established organizations forced these activists to form coalitions with such "outsider" constituencies as the women's liberation movement. Movement organizations like NARAL and NOW did not have the resources and organizational structures necessary to generate grass-roots support—as they would later be able to do—but they could compensate for their organizational deficits by joining forces with the grass-roots activists who were part of the cycle of protest under way in the 1960s. Before 1973, it was an expanded social movement sector, rather than established interest groups or authorities, that was the principal source of political opportunity for the abortion movement.

One reason for the movement's successful mobilization was the prevalence of immediately felt grievances. Contrary to the professional model of movement mobilization (McCarthy and Zald 1973, 1977), the "entrepreneurs" of the abortion rights movement were not career movement leaders looking to "create" an issue; rather, they typically were volunteers who had strong feelings about abortion rights. Moreover, it was unplanned events like the thalidomide and rubella crises rather than manufactured grievances that brought the abortion issue to public and media attention. Although many of the movement's early activists were "conscience" constituents rather than potential beneficiaries of legal abortion, as a result of their backgrounds in areas like family planning they often had direct experiences with the grievances of women in need of abortions.

Another reason for the movement's success was that it combined the strengths of constituents with experience in traditional voluntary organizations and institutionalized politics with the energy and skills of activists from grass-roots movements. The following chapters will show how early tactics were shaped by the dual origins of the movement as well as by constraints of the political environment. Chapter 3 describes the use of institutionalized tactics, made possible by the know-how and connections of seasoned activists in the single-issue branch of the movement. Chapter 4 examines direct-action tactics, which were a product of both the political climate and the backgrounds of young constituents of the movement.

3

Collective Action Through
Established Means

The social movements of the 1960s are associated with confrontational direct-action tactics. As we shall see in Chapter 4, the movement to legalize abortion was no exception; as the women's movement spread, feminists took the abortion battle to the streets. But there was also another side to the movement. Much of the early activity on behalf of legal abortion consisted of teas held at churches to discuss change in the laws and endless trips to the state legislatures by middle-aged women with long volunteer "careers" (cf. Daniels, 1988). Despite the fact that the word "abortion" could barely be mentioned in public when the movement began, the movement did use conventional channels of influence from the start. Even after women's liberation activists began demonstrating for "women's control of their bodies" and "free abortion on demand," abortion movement organizations continued to work through the "system" by lobbying their legislators and supporting litigation to test the abortion laws. What enabled movement actors to adopt institutionalized means of influence, and how successful were they in using the tactics of political insiders?

The organizational state of the movement prior to 1973 was not such that one would expect easy access to authorities through conventional channels. Few large established organizations lent their support to the movement before the legalization of abortion. For their part, movement organizations lacked the professional staff and formal organizational structures that would facilitate institutionalized tactics in later years of the abortion conflict. The movement as a whole was also quite decentralized, so that there was no way for national leaders to control the tactics of local activists, many of whom were oriented toward confrontational direct action. Although the National Association for Repeal of Abortion Laws provided some resources for state efforts throughout the country, before 1973 NARAL was quite a small organization and was limited in the extent to which it could coordinate a campaign of lobbying and litigation.[1]

The movement was able to compensate for its organizational deficits, however, with the skills of individuals who donated their time to the movement. Although not all activists possessed all of the necessary skills, and many learned these skills as a result of their participation in the abortion movement, organizations like

29

NARAL and ICMCA had access to many skills and resources which facilitated institutionalized types of mobilizing activities and persuasive rather than confrontational collective-action tactics. They had leaders who knew how to lobby their legislators, and they had members who belonged to voluntary associations that could be lobbied for support. Some leaders and members were professionals who had connections to other professionals and professional associations. Some had public relations experience that enabled them to get media coverage through means such as contacts with reporters. And many volunteers were women who knew how to put on fund-raisers to attract wealthy donors to the cause. To some extent, activists in the abortion movement were political "insiders."

In many ways, the backgrounds of these activists were well suited to a hostile political environment: They were persons who were accustomed to compromise and incremental gain. They were willing and able to frame their demands in a nonthreatening manner calculated to win support from conservative legislators and mainstream Americans. Nevertheless, they encountered severe difficulties in trying to pursue change through established means. Despite their resources and tactics, they met with strong resistance among legislators, particularly after the anti-abortion countermovement picked up steam in reaction to the abortion movement. In addition to their own organizational limitations, pragmatic single-issue abortion activists also had to deal with new activists, particularly feminists, who were becoming involved in the movement and introducing their own ideological approach and repertoire of collective-action tactics.

The Politics of Persuasion

The approach to change in the abortion laws taken by the early groups was decidedly nonconfrontational. Although the National Association for Repeal of Abortion Laws did engage in some confrontational tactics, the abortion movement routinely used persuasion, rather than coercion, in its attempts to win support for abortion law repeal. This approach was in some ways out of step with the pattern of protest in the decade in which the movement took shape—which had already seen the dramatic use of direct-action tactics in the civil rights movement—but it was consistent with the backgrounds and experiences of abortion movement leaders and with the political environments in which many local movement organizations operated.

Although the cycle of protest under way in the 1960s was important to the mobilization of the movement to legalize abortion, local abortion movement organizations tended to be more attuned to the political environment in their states than to national political trends. Not only were many movement organizations trying to bring about change in some very conservative states, but in some cases, such as Illinois, the abortion movement emerged before the women's movement became highly visible. By the mid-1960s there was certainly an encouraging trend toward approval of legal abortion in public opinion, but hardly a mandate for repeal.[2] Consequently, abortion activists felt they had to build on whatever sources of support were in evidence, however conservative they may be. To do so, a cautious approach seemed necessary and useful.

In Illinois, ICMCA initially looked to medical and legal professional associations, which were at least interested in limited reform, as a source of support. In fact, the name Illinois Citizens for the Medical Control of Abortion was suggested by its founder Dr. Lonny Myers as a means of appealing to the professional interests of doctors. As Myers wrote to Lawrence Lader in 1970, the early tactics were based on persuasion rather than confrontation:

> I repeatedly tried to get my opponents to be logical, come out and fight the decent fight. I wrote the Am[erican] Law Institute politely asking them the premise on which they based their model abortion law. I asked what was the nature of the crime and why did they advocate that abortion by a licensed physician be a crime? I wrote the AMA committee on human reproduction long before they came up with their first abortion statement (in this century) and asked them to consider similar questions, but based on the "sacred patient–doctor relationship" and they answered: The AMA House of Delegates does not see fit to answer your questions. (Of course, the ALI never answered me). I wrote to the Bar Association. I pleaded with the Department of Religion and Medicine of the AMA explaining that this was the area where religion MOST affected the practice of medicine. . . . and no recommendation from the department; and on and on and on. . . . WASTE of time. (letter, circa July 1970; Lawrence Lader papers, New York Public Library)

Although in this reflection on early ICMCA tactics Myers was calling her attempts at persuasion a "waste of time," it seemed logical at the time to assume that doctors and lawyers would be most sympathetic to appeals that highlighted their professional interest in abortion reform.

In other states as well, abortion movement organizations adopted mobilizing tactics calculated to win support from mainstream Americans and established organizations. In Iowa, in striking similarity to ICMCA in Illinois, the main abortion reform organization was not a medical organization but "astutely called itself the Iowa Association for the Medical Control of Abortion" to attract the support of doctors (Mohr, 1989:76). Members of an abortion movement organization formed in Dallas, Texas, in 1969 were quite concerned about presenting the issue in a nonthreatening manner in response to the conservative local political environment and so selected the name Dallas Committee to Study Abortion, similar to that of the national Association for the Study of Abortion, in a deliberate attempt to avoid antagonizing people (Faux, 1988:109).[3]

Interestingly, ICMCA pursued a nonconfrontational strategy for securing support but nevertheless adopted the radical goal of repeal, rather than reform, of the abortion laws, at least for the first trimester of pregnancy.[4] The explanation for this is that, although the backgrounds of ICMCA leaders in established organizations had taught them the politics of persuasion, their numbers included persons involved with family-planning work. These activists were quite familiar with the size of the demand for abortion; that is, they knew that if reforms along the lines suggested by the American Law Institute were adopted, abortion would remain available only to the wealthy. Consequently, ICMCA founders were in strong agreement on the need for repeal of the abortion laws from the criminal statutes.

On the other hand, ICMCA did not attempt to link its demand for repeal to a broader set of issues such as women's rights. ICMCA leaders were very careful to present legalized abortion as a change that would be an extension of existing contraceptive practices, which had gained widespread acceptance, rather than a radical social change. They continually attempted to present the abortion issue, and themselves, in as nonthreatening a manner as possible. For example, executive director Helen Smith described in an interview how she typically introduced herself in public debates on abortion: "Whenever I did one of these engagements I always tried to start out by saying something about myself—like 'I have three children, I've been married to the same man for 20 years, and I've never had an abortion.'" Whenever opponents were debated, ICMCA reported using these opportunities to combat the "emotional" tactics of the anti-abortionists (ICMCA newsletter, January 1972).

Activist Backgrounds and Institutionalized Channels of Influence

Mobilization Through Networks

In all of its activities, ICMCA took advantage of the connections of its leaders and supporters to voluntary associations and other organizations. Lack of response from both the state legislature and professional associations did lead ICMCA to mount a broader public education campaign, but established channels were used to carry out much of the educational program. The conventions of various organizations, particularly those of professional associations and health-oriented service groups, were used as an opportunity for ICMCA to conduct workshops on the abortion issue (ICMCA newsletter, June 1970). Members of ICMCA who were active in established voluntary associations, such as the Chicago-Region Parent–Teachers Association, worked to secure the endorsements of these oganizations (ICMCA newsletter, November 1970). ICMCA actively sought speaking engagements at organizational functions. In January 1971, three thousand letters were sent to various organizations asking for permission to speak and, significantly, requesting the groups to invite their legislators to attend (*Chicago Sun-Times,* January 24, 1971). ICMCA also filled numerous requests for speakers to debate opponents at various organizational functions.

In addition to using organizational channels, ICMCA employed the mass media for educational purposes, but the means used were a far cry from the dramatic direct-action tactics that created media coverage for the civil rights movement and the anti-war movement. Rather, established means of obtaining media coverage were systematically exploited by ICMCA, which benefited from the experience of leaders such as longtime executive director Helen Smith, who had had extensive experience in voluntary organizations, politics, and public relations work before joining ICMCA.[5] Smith cultivated contacts with sympathetic reporters to get coverage of ICMCA activities such as fund-raisers (usually in the "women's" section of newspapers). She also wrote numerous letters to the editors of newspapers and magazines, often using the names of other ICMCA activists, and with good results; in 1972, for example, Smith reported getting an average of several letters per month published in major newspapers throughout Illinois (ICMCA newsletter, January 1972; and personal interview with Helen Smith, 1983). When radio or television stations aired anti-abortion editorials, Smith never missed an opportunity to ask for equal time to respond. She also secured numerous engagements for ICMCA leaders to appear on radio and television shows to debate opponents.

The National Association for Repeal of Abortion Laws similarly took advantage of its leaders' skills and access to established organizations to mobilize support. Part of the reason for the similarity in tactics was that ICMCA leaders like Lonny Myers and Don Shaw were also involved in the formation of NARAL. Other early NARAL activists were also persons with experience in voluntary associations who had connections to sympathetic organizations such as population and family-planning organizations, women's groups, and Protestant and Jewish religious organizations.[6] NARAL executive committee members and other board members used their contacts to recruit organizations that had already taken repeal positions into NARAL and to persuade other organizations to take repeal positions. Local repeal groups and individuals interested in forming repeal groups were given the names of established organizations that had either endorsed repeal or were likely to be sympathetic to the cause, and local groups were encouraged to seek resources, including members, from these organizations (e.g., see a 1970 strategy document entitled "How to Organize a Repeal Group," Special Collections Department, Northwestern University library).

The approach to fund-raising taken by both ICMCA and NARAL in the early years also reflected the connections and resources of their leaders and members. Rather than seeking funds through such "mass" means as direct mailings, both organizations relied in the early 1970s on substantial contributions from wealthy supporters. Such contributions were easy to locate because NARAL and ICMCA leaders were active in other organizations that routinely received large donations; for example, longtime contributors to Planned Parenthood were successfully tapped as a likely source of support for the abortion movement. ICMCA also used the social skills of its more affluent members to put on a number of fund-raisers designed to attract wealthy donors at fashionable places like the Drake Hotel and the Playboy Mansion in Chicago.[7]

The experience and connections of ICMCA leaders like Helen Smith were evident in the skillful and systematic way in which they elicited endorsements and contributions from organizations and wealthy individuals. Lists of organizations and prominent citizens likely to contribute to ICMCA were compiled through referrals from members, and letters requesting donations were sent that began, "I am writing at the suggestion of _____." Follow-up letters were always sent to past contributors, and any requests for information were carefully answered. After speaking engagements, a skillfully crafted follow-up letter was routinely sent to all organizations, asking for support from its members with the plaintive phrase, "We honestly expected more response"—regardless of how much money ICMCA had received in contributions through the organization! (documents in NARAL of Illinois Records, University of Illinois at Chicago library).

The importance of the skills and connections of ICMCA and NARAL leaders, as well as their pragmatic approach, for obtaining resources through established organizations is apparent when contrasted with the experiences of organizations like the Chicago Women's Liberation Union, which lacked such assets. The CWLU did have a speakers' bureau that supplied speakers to talk to various organizations from a feminist point of view on a range of topics, including abortion. This was done frequently because there was a big demand for speakers on controversial subjects like women's liberation and abortion and because the fees earned by the speakers were one of the Union's main sources of revenue. Despite the demand for their speakers, however, the Union was not effective in its appeals to mainstream organizations for financial contributions. The Union lacked ties to such organizations, and the approach of the CWLU activists was too confrontational. In an address to the United Presbyterian Church convention in 1970, for example, CWLU members sharply condemned the church for its stand against legal abortion and then requested a year's worth of financial support for a proposed women's health clinic. After the predictably poor reception of the group by the church, CWLU members did debate whether or not it was worth addressing such conventions and, if so, whether a less confrontational style should be adopted (*CWLU News*, June 1970). But the organization never resolved this strategic dilemma and so remained ineffective at obtaining financial resources through established organizations.[8]

Collective Action Through Institutionalized Channels

Just as they mobilized support through established channels, single-issue abortion movement organizations, aided by groups like NOW and ZPG, proceeded to change the abortion laws through conventional means of influence, engaging in legislative lobbying and litigation. Because of the influence of the American Law Institute model, and largely at the initiation of professionals and individual legislators (see Luker, 1984:71), abortion reform laws began to be introduced in state legislatures in the early 1960s. Between 1962 and 1966, five states considered, and rejected, ALI-type abortion reform bills (Francome, 1984:102). Mississippi did, in 1966, pass a bill more limited than the ALI bill, allowing abortions to save the mother's life or in the case of rape (Tatalovich and Daynes, 1981:25). In 1967, Colorado—followed by North Carolina and California—passed abortion reform bills modeled on the ALI bill.[9] After these reform victories, nine more states passed reform bills through 1970, and in that year four states—Hawaii, Alaska, Washington, and New York—passed what amounted to repeal bills (at least for the first trimester of pregnancy).

By the mid-1960s, abortion movement participants had become active in lobbying for abortion reform and repeal legislation. They organized lobbies in states like Illinois where little or no progress was made through the legislature as well as in states like New York and Hawaii where critical victories were won. ICMCA leaders spent a great deal of time testifying for abortion reform bills, paying visits to legislators, and generating mail from constituents throughout the state of Illinois. NARAL leaders, including President Carol Greitzer, a New York City councilwoman, engaged in a lot of behind-the-scenes lobbying and political maneuvering on behalf of the New York abortion bill that was passed in 1970. NARAL also gave advice and some financial support to repeal campaigns in other states, using the NARAL leaders' skills and connections to individuals willing to donate large sums of money to the cause.

In response to these movement activities, anti-abortionists began to form "right-to-life" groups in the late 1960s. State anti-abortion groups began to organize in 1967, and the National Right to Life Committee was formed in 1971 as a national coordinating organization to provide educational material and information to these various groups, which nonetheless remained independent of the national organization (cf. Balides et al., 1973:513–14). By mid-1972 there were, according to one estimate, about 250 state and local groups loosely affiliated with the National Right to Life Committee (Potts et al., 1977:363).[10] In Illinois, the Illinois Right to Life Committee was formed in 1968 in response to the abortion reform movement. In Minnesota, one of the largest anti-abortion groups, Minnesota Citizens Concerned for Life, attracted a membership of ten thousand by 1973 and served as a model for other state groups (Balides et al., 1973:512–13).

Although many abortion activists were willing to work through the slow legislative process of repealing the abortion laws, they also turned to the courts for support. The success of the anti-abortion forces in blocking efforts to pass reform legislation provided one incentive to use litigation as an alternative to legislative lobbying. The opposition grew rapidly after 1970, when New York and three other states passed liberal abortion laws. Between 1970 and 1973, only one more state, Florida in 1972, reformed its abortion laws. In 1972, the New York law survived overturn only by the governor's veto after vigorous opposition to the law was generated by the Catholic Church (see Lader, 1973). The strength of the anti-abortion movement was revealed in a 1972 Michigan referendum campaign to repeal the state's abortion laws when anti-abortion troops armed with pictures of fetuses converged on the state, mounting a massive public relations campaign that resulted in the defeat of the referendum previously expected to pass (Francome, 1984:112).

Although countermovement activities in the state legislatures were one "push" toward the use of the courts by the abortion movement, the use of litigation cannot be interpreted solely as a response to blocked opportunities in the legislative arena. Movement activists often pursued litigation and legislative lobbying strategies simultaneously (cf. Lader, 1973; Faux, 1988). Favorable precedents in the courts created a "pull" toward litigation as an attractive means of bringing about social change. Civil rights groups were important pioneers in the use of litigation to achieve movement goals, providing a successful model for other social movements.[11] Not only did the landmark 1954 Supreme Court decision *Brown* v. *Board of Education* provide evidence of a trend toward "judicial activism" (Sarat, 1982), but the family-planning movement had won a number of victories through the courts. Most directly important to the abortion repeal movement, in 1965 the Supreme Court in *Griswold* v. *Connecticut* had struck down restrictions on the distribution of contraceptives based on a "right to privacy" (see Rubin, 1987; Sarat, 1982). Subsequent court rulings striking down the California and Washington, D.C. statutes in 1969 further encouraged repeal activists regarding the likelihood of substantial progress through the courts (see Lader, 1973).[12]

As early as 1966, movement activists began exploring the possibility of generating a test case to challenge state abortion laws (see Lader, 1973:12). The physician involved in the Washington, D.C. case, Dr. Milan Vuitch, was openly performing abortions, and movement activists referred hundreds of women to him with the expectation that he eventually would be arrested. As Lawrence Lader pointed out:

> I don't think the Supreme Court could have refused to hear a case [on abortion] with public opinion, the state laws, and the Vuitch case. . . . Dr. Vuitch was a friend of mine, and I referred women to him. . . . We had him keep a very careful record of each woman patient in terms of health, mental health, physical health, etc. So when we went into court we went in with very good documentation of the women's health, and we got a good case. (interview with Lawrence Lader, 1984)

Although none of the abortion repeal movement organizations had the kinds of financial resources needed for extended litigation, NARAL leaders did have network connections to civil liberties organizations and individual lawyers as well as to the Association for the Study of Abortion. Lawrence Lader helped recruit Cyril Means—whom he knew from Harvard University where they both had been students (interview with Lawrence Lader, 1984)—to work on a litigation strategy. Roy Lucas, a lawyer who wrote an important article making a constitutional case for abortion rights (see Rubin, 1987:44), was also at one time a member of NARAL's legal committee.[13] A number of lawyers, including Cyril Means and Sarah Weddington, who argued the *Roe* v. *Wade* case before the Supreme Court, worked together on a legal strategy (interview with Lawrence Lader, 1984; Faux, 1988).

The litigation strategy was not, then, strictly a movement initiative, but was carried out by a combination of support from established organizations, movement organizations, and individual abortion rights lawyers.[14] Organizations such as the New York Civil Liberties Union and the Law Center for Constitutional Rights lent valuable resources to the development of a legal strategy (see Lader, 1973; Rubin, 1987). As noted in Chapter 1, the Association for the Study of Abortion was important in funding Means's work on the legal question of abortion, which was cited in the 1973 Supreme Court decision, and in providing access to expert advice on abortion litigation. The abortion movement was critical, however, in nourishing support for bold initiatives in the courts at a time when organizations like the ASA favored a more cautious approach (see Faux, 1988).

It addition to supporting the initiatives of others, NARAL also became more directly involved in litigation in coalition with the ACLU, which supported the movement partly as a result of its ties to NARAL activists. In 1970, NARAL initiated a lawsuit that was handled by the ACLU against D.C. General Hospital in Washington to force the hospital to offer abortions after the court ruling striking down D.C. abortion laws in November 1969. In addition to filing lawsuits against other hospitals, NARAL also submitted court briefs and provided resources, including legal expertise and some financial aid, to other legal efforts to prove abortion laws unconstitutional. In Illinois, ICMCA was not directly involved in filing lawsuits, but lawyers on the organization's legal committee worked closely with the ACLU in preparing legal challenges to the state abortion law. The Illinois ACLU challenged the Illinois abortion law in *Doe* v. *Scott,* and one of the ACLU lawyers in the case was also active in ICMCA.

By forming alliances with established organizations like the ACLU, movement organizations were able to play an important role in bringing about the 1973 Supreme Court decision. Between 1969 and 1973, a large number of abortion cases were brought to the courts, resulting in petitions for hearing to the Supreme Court (cf. Rubin, 1987; Sarat, 1982). In 1971, the Supreme Court agreed to hear two of the state cases, the Texas *Roe* v. *Wade* case and the Georgia *Doe* v. *Bolton* case. Lower court cases, many of which were generated by the movement, played a pivotal role in educating the Supreme Court on the abortion issue, as did *amicus curiae* briefs filed by movement supporters (Rubin, 1987:47).[15] After a number of delays, the Supreme Court decided the cases on January 22, 1973, a ruling that struck down in one blow all of the state abortion laws (see Faux, 1988, for a detailed account of the decision).

It was important that the victory was achieved by movement participation in an arena in which the countermovement was comparatively weak. The relative strength of the movement and the countermovement in the judicial arena is evidenced by the fact that a wide range of movement and professional groups filed friend-of-the-court briefs in favor of legal abortion in the *Roe* v. *Wade* and *Doe* v. *Bolton* cases, whereas only a few briefs were filed in support of the anti-abortion laws (see Sarat, 1982:134–35; Tatalovich, 1988). This was no accident, as briefs in favor of legal abortion were actively solicited, in contrast with the absence of such a strategy on the part of anti-abortion forces (Faux, 1988:224–28).

Organizational Deficits and Movement Diversity

Despite the skills and connections of many individuals working in the abortion movement, the movement's capacity to bring about change in the state abortion laws through insititutionalized means was certainly limited. Organizations like ICMCA and NARAL lacked certain types of organizational resources, and the movement as a whole remained quite decentralized. Although NARAL did play a coordinating role in the movement, the national organization was informally organized and did not control its local affiliates, which were completely autonomous "members" rather than official chapters of NARAL. Feminist allies were even more independent than were local abortion groups, and there were a number of differences in approach within the movement, particularly between feminists and single-issue abortion activists.

Although NARAL had the know-how and connections to pursue an organizational mobilization strategy, the movement organization lacked the money and staff needed to attract a large number of individuals. Moreover, when NARAL was formed in early 1969, its leaders were uncertain about the extent of public support for legal abortion. At this point even the women's liberation movement was not highly visible to those outside its networks. Consequently, NARAL leaders had no confidence that they would be successful in attracting a large individual membership. As Lawrence Lader recalled:

> In the beginning, we thought our strength was in building organizations. We couldn't really handle large numbers, and we weren't even sure we could get large

numbers—[we thought] that it would look better on the stationery to have organizations. Because if you talked about [say] fifteen thousand members, it doesn't
look terribly impressive.... For some time, we just had four or five hundred
members—we were a very small operation, and to handle a huge membership
was not an easy thing. We didn't have the money in those days. (interview with
Lawrence Lader, 1984)

In the absence of an individual membership that could be called upon to write
letters and provide financial support for staff, NARAL depended on its state
organizational members to carry out local programs. The national organization
advised the state abortion groups, and its leaders also helped raise money for state
organizations, but they did not make strategic and tactical decisions for them. In
1972, for example, movement activists in Michigan decided to depart from legislative lobbying tactics and to use the state referendum to try to legalize abortion.
As noted above, the result was a stunning victory for the countermovement.
NARAL leader Lawrence Lader helped raise money for the referendum campaign, despite his doubts and those of other NARAL leaders about the tactic:

I can remember flying down to a very rich family in Pittsburgh [to solicit a con-
tribution]. Michigan had a popular referendum—we were somewhat afraid of ref-
erendums. We weren't sure we could win them, number one, and number two,
we felt what was right constitutionally and morally should not be voted on. I
mean, it sounds kind of undemocratic, but we felt it was right constitutionally
and morally. If you took a vote on slavery, the abolitionists might have lost. But
Michigan insisted they could win—so I ended up flying to Pittsburgh, and the
money was raised. It was very much a personal thing. (interview with Lawrence
Lader, 1984)

NARAL had individuals who could raise money and exert a certain amount of
influence, but the organization was not strong enough to implement its own strategic program throughout the country.

Because NARAL and other single-issue abortion organizations lacked sufficient resources for many tactics, they often sought help from multi-issue movement organizations. NOW and ZPG were particularly important sources of support on both the national and local levels. NOW's task force on abortion
attempted to encourage local volunteers to work in legislative campaigns to win
repeal. The national ZPG organization provided information about the abortion
issue and reported on local developments in the ZPG *National Reporter,* encouraging its activists to write letters whenever appropriate. In the case of the Michigan
referendum campaign to repeal the state abortion laws in 1972, ZPG aided
NARAL by soliciting funds and volunteers for the campaign through its newsletter. The Chicago-area ZPG affiliate helped ICMCA with a drive to send workers
from Illinois to Michigan for the referendum campaign. Chicago NOW assisted
ICMCA's lobbying efforts by regularly printing information on reform bills in the
chapter newsletter and urging members to write letters to their state
representatives.

But multi-issue movement organizations also suffered from resource limitations, as the abortion issue had to compete with other issues on their agendas. In

Chicago, the chair of the NOW chapter's abortion committee, Madeline Schwenk, continually urged NOW members to write letters on behalf of abortion bills before the state legislature, but she had no way of knowing how many members actually did so. She was certain of the lack of interest in lobbying among other members of the NOW chapter, recalling in an interview that "no one cared to beat their heads against the wall in Springfield! . . . I remember going down to Springfield for some show of support on an abortion bill, and I couldn't get anyone else in NOW to go." Because of the staunch opposition to abortion among Illinois legislators, there was little reward for such tactics, and most of the active Chicago NOW members, who numbered only about twenty before 1973, were busy with more rewarding activities concerning other issues. In the view of the chapter abortion committee chair, the work being done on employment at that time was generally regarded as more rewarding than the activities—outside the work with the Abortion Counseling Service—that were the staple of the abortion repeal movement. As she explained in an interview:

> When you look at what people were doing about abortion—you know, you could lobby, write letters, or rally—working on abortion was different, unless you were working with Jane, from working on employment, because there what they would do is help people file EEOC [Equal Employment Opportunity Commission] complaints. That was a concrete task that you did, something that taught you a skill, that made you feel good about yourself, that made you feel like you were changing reality—the same with Jane.

Consequently, Chicago NOW was severely constrained in its adoption of legislative lobbying tactics, despite the interests of its abortion committee chair.

In the area of litigation, other issues also competed with the abortion issue for scarce movement resources. The National Organization for Women had some volunteer lawyers in the pre-1973 period, but they were working on employment discrimination cases rather than on abortion litigation (cf. O'Connor, 1980). In 1971, the national NOW board did vote to participate in a lawsuit challenging the tax-exempt status of the Catholic Church as a result of its anti-abortion activities, a case in which the NOW legal vice-president was an attorney (*Do It NOW,* April 1971). NOW did not, however, participate in litigation to win repeal in the way that NARAL did, as NOW's legal resources were tied up with equal employment opportunity cases.

The Electoral Arena

It was perhaps in the area of electoral politics that the movement's ability to participate in the established political process was most limited. As a result of opposition to changes in the abortion laws in the state legislatures, single-issue abortion movement organizations and women's rights organizations like NOW recognized the value of work in the political arena. In the absence of sufficient resources, however, their ability to pursue various political tactics was limited. In 1971, NARAL adopted a policy of support for Catholic legislators favoring repeal in response to anti-abortion political activity by the Catholic Church (minutes of

Midwest Strategy Conference, January 9, 1971; NARAL of Illinois Records, University of Illinois at Chicago library), but the support was purely symbolic due to the lack of resources to pursue a political strategy. NARAL board members active in party politics did attempt, though unsuccessfully, to persuade the Democratic and Republican parties to adopt pro-repeal planks in 1972. NARAL also sent letters to the 1972 Presidential hopefuls asking them to state their positions on the abortion issue. NARAL did not, however, have the financial resources to make campaign contributions or the numbers to supply campaign workers to supporters before legalization as it would in the late 1970s and 1980s.

In Illinois, ICMCA became involved in political work in 1970 after the defeat of reform legislation in the state legislature (ICMCA newsletter, June 1970). ICMCA encouraged its activists to work in the reelection campaigns of state representative Leland Rayson, who sponsored reform bills for ICMCA in the state legislature. ICMCA also raised money for Rayson at a benefit dinner, a tactic easily employed because of the social connections of its organizational supporters. Besides these tactics on behalf of Rayson, ICMCA collected information on the abortion positions of other state candidates and endorsed those supporting reform or repeal of the Illinois abortion laws. ICMCA also urged its supporters to become involved in the campaigns of other pro-repeal legislators and described political campaign work as its "most important activity" after the defeat of a reform bill in 1972 (ICMCA newsletter, January 1972). However, ICMCA did not have the resources to coordinate this activity in the way that NARAL of Illinois would later be able to do.

Differences in Approach Within the Movement

Beyond the problem of organizational deficits, there were differences in approach within the diverse, decentralized movement to legalize abortion that affected the ability of individual organizations to pursue their strategies. In particular, differences between single-issue abortion movement groups and feminist groups were often intense, as organizations like ICMCA and NARAL were willing to make compromises that were not acceptable to some feminist groups. In New York, NARAL supported a bill that the feminist New Yorkers for Abortion Law Repeal opposed because it required licensed physicians, rather than paramedicals, to perform abortions (see Lader, 1973:130). ICMCA was willing to frame its demands in a nonconfrontational manner and even to pursue limited abortion law reform through the legislature because it was clear that a repeal bill could not be passed. Many feminist groups, on the other hand, were calling for "free abortion on demand." From the point of view of activists working in organizations like ICMCA, this approach was wildly unrealistic and harmful to their own attempts to present the issue in a nonthreatening manner calculated to win support from both state legislators and the public. As one highly pragmatic ICMCA leader argued in discussing her differences with feminist groups, "When you use phrases like that ["free abortion on demand"], it only helps the opposition."[16]

Political experiences, more than ideology, were apt to create such differences in strategy between single-issue abortion organizations and some women's move-

ment organizations. Although they had backgrounds in established organizations
and traditional politics, lobbying, and public relations work rather than in the
radical movements of the 1960s, NARAL and ICMCA leaders were not unsym-
pathetic to the idea of women's rights. In fact, one ICMCA leader that I interviewed remembered her own shock at the degrading manner in which Illinois legislators spoke of women, even before the issue had been framed by feminists as a
woman's right. But however sympathetic they might have been to the feminist cry
for "abortion on demand," ICMCA leaders were experienced enough politically
to know that the idea would not play in Peoria—or in Springfield. Moreover, the
legislative process, with all of its compromises, was attractive to early leaders like
Lonny Myers and Don Shaw, who had been successful in a prevous campaign
conducted through traditional channels to gain the legal right to make information on contraception available to public aid recipients. Members of younger
branch women's liberation groups, in contrast, lacked such experiences.

In Texas, the Dallas Committee to Study Abortion similarly had to fight the
association between abortion and feminist issues, which single-issue activists felt
hurt the abortion cause. Although the abortion group included women who supported women's rights, its members nevertheless worked to keep the abortion
issue separate in an attempt to win broad support. One key activist who was quite
sympathetic to feminism "firmly believed that radical politics alienated legislators
and that in a state like Texas they would not work" and "proudly viewed herself
as a behind-the-scenes worker." Another leader "belonged to both NOW and the
Junior League" but was "a firm believer in single issue politics" who sought to
appeal to conservatives as well as liberals on the abortion issue (Faux, 1988:
108–9).

There were also differences within the movement over which tactics were
likely to be most effective in bringing about change. For example, NOW's lack of
involvement in litigation may have been influenced by both resource limitations
and the fact that at least one national task force coordinator, Lucinda Cisler, was
not sure that the courts were an effective means of achieving a feminist version of
repeal. As she wrote in a nationally distributed report:

> It can be strongly argued that our most likely avenue for *actively* shaping events
> as *we* wish—and winning—is the tough, square, old legislative route.. . . . Ongo-
> ing, broad-based citizen action can achieve legislative change; after filing, court
> cases are finally in the hands of lawyers, and plaintiffs are relatively passive and
> powerless. We can never formulate judicial decisions, and even the most favorable
> tend to be ambiguous, narrow in scope, and avoid women's rights; also, the US
> Supreme Court has taken a distinct rightward turn lately. But we *can* draft our
> own repeal legislation quite precisely, and actively seek out legislative sponsorship
> of what *we want*. (National Task Force on Reproduction and Its Control, July
> 1971; National Organization for Women Chicago Chapter Records, University of
> Illinois at Chicago library)

In other cases, the differences were even more pronounced. For example, the
Chicago Women's Liberation Union did not lend its support to legislative lobbying tactics. As noted in Chapter 2, CWLU activists did initiate the Total Repeal
of Illinois Abortion Laws (TRIAL) coalition in 1970 in response to a perceived

opportunity to change the Illinois state abortion law after New York passed its liberal abortion law. But despite TRIAL's legislative target, it is striking that most of the activities of the coalition, which lasted only about a year, consisted of demonstrations and rallies, the tactics most familiar to CWLU activists. Not only were CWLU members ideologically opposed to institutionalized lobbying tactics, but in any case they lacked the experience to lobby effectively and had no interest in gaining such experience.

Conclusion

The involvement of abortion movement organizations in institutionalized strategies and tactics before the legalization of abortion was possible because one important element of the movement constituency had the skills and connections necessary to work through established channels. In this sense movement leaders were not "outsiders" lacking access to political power holders. But whatever routine access the movement had to authorities was due to its individual leaders, rather than to its organizational strength. Movement organizations did not have the kinds of resources and formalized organizational structures necessary to create a carefully orchestrated program for change, and more powerful established organizations had to be coaxed into providing support. The movement was not able to exert significant influence in all institutionalized arenas, as early forays into the political arena and obstacles to legislative victories demonstrated.

When support from established organizations proved insufficient, and when it looked like there were other sources of support available, abortion activists sought out coalitions with genuine "outsider" constituencies like that of the women's liberation movement and participated in "direct-action" tactics. These confrontational protest activities are examined in the following chapter.

4

Confrontation and Direct Action

By 1970, the women's liberation movement was a national phenomenon. Feminists were attracting media and public attention by staging demonstrations and raising controversial demands. Abortion was a central feminist issue that was dramatized through direct action: In New York in 1969 the feminist Redstockings held "counter-hearings" to protest the biased state legislative hearings on abortion reform. In Detroit in 1970 a "funeral march" was held by women's liberation activists to protest the deaths of women killed by back-alley abortionists while the legislature debated abortion reform. In Chicago, feminists disrupted the convention of the American Medical Association to protest the AMA's lack of support for abortion law repeal. Throughout the country, feminists staged street theater, "speak-outs," and other demonstrations for abortion rights (see Hole and Levine, 1971:294–99).

For all of its conventional pressure-group tactics, the movement to legalize abortion was very much a part of the protest cycle of the 1960s. Direct-action tactics such as demonstrations had become part of the repertoire of movement participants, and the grass-roots constituents of the population and women's movements could be mobilized to participate in such tactics. The opportunites for direct action and the strong obstacles to achieving legalized abortion through institutionalized channels alone ensured that no movement organization limited its activities solely to institutionalized arenas.

Use of the direct-action tactics of "outside" challengers was facilitated in part by the same organizational characteristics that limited the movement's capacity for influence through established channels. Although formalized organizational structures help movement organizations operate in the world of conventional pressure-group politics, such structures make it more difficult to take quick action and to bypass disputes over radical positions and confrontational tactics. The movement's informal organization in the years before the legalization of abortion allowed movement organizations to take advantage of opportunities for confrontation and direct action, which often involved an element of risk. This was possible in single-issue movement organizations like NARAL, where a small number of leaders maintained centralized control, and in women's liberation groups like the CWLU, which had decentralized structures in which subunits were able to act autonomously.

To understand fully the movement's strategies and tactics in these years, it is necessary to go beyond a strictly organizational analysis to an examination of the feminist approach to abortion, which was an important part of the movement. Women's liberation groups saw themselves as part of a larger movement that was challenging basic social, economic, and political institutions. Their goal was to create participatory democratic institutions that would serve human needs rather than corporate interests. The women's health movement that developed within the younger branch of the women's movement wanted to create a nonprofit, high-quality health care delivery system and to challenge the hierarchical doctor–client relationship, demanding that women participate in their own health care (see Ruzek, 1978). It was in this larger context that the women's liberation movement addressed the abortion issue.

The Creation of a New Consciousness

Although a movement's "success" is typically measured in terms of substantive reforms, movements can also succeed in bringing about changes in "collective consciousness" (Mueller, 1987). In the case of the women's liberation movement, changes occurred in the way in which women thought about their sexuality, their health, and their reproductive rights. To achieve this change in women's consciousness, the movement bypassed established organizational channels to reach women directly through new kinds of educational forums.

In Boston, a group of women—which became the Boston Women's Health Collective—began doing its own research on abortion, childbirth, and other women's health issues and offering an informal course to share the information with other women. In 1970, the group put together a book entitled *Women and Their Bodies* (later called *Our Bodies, Our Selves*) which was published by a local nonprofit press (Sanford, 1979). The book, which was distributed through women's centers and other movement networks, became the basis for "Women and Their Bodies" courses conducted by women's liberation groups across the country. Such courses were part of a larger "self-help" movement in which women sought to empower themselves by gaining access to information about their bodies and control over health care services.

In Chicago, a "Women and Their Bodies" course became part of the CWLU's Liberation School for Women.[1] Abortion was discussed in this course in the context of broader concerns about women's health care and women's control of their bodies. Moreover, the Liberation School was more than simply an educational forum. It exposed many women for the first time to the ideas of the women's liberation movement, and also helped recruit new women into the Union. On some occasions, women from the "Women and Their Bodies" classes even attended demonstrations for abortion rights and other CWLU activities as a group.

Another public forum for discussion of abortion created by women's liberation groups throughout the country was the "speak-out," a public event at which individual women talked about their own personal experiences with abortion.[2] In

Chicago, a speak-out held by the CWLU in 1970 "to provide a women's liberation point of view on a subject which has received so much media attention" (*CWLU News,* February 1970) was a key event for mobilizing activity on abortion (interviews with CWLU activists, 1983). This kind of educational activity was very successful for the CWLU because it relied solely on the willingness of activists to talk about their personal experiences, something they were quite prepared to do. Speak-outs were often genuinely moving events that served to recruit women to the movement and to attract media attention to the feminist perspective on abortion. These movement organizations were thus able to create their own means of reaching audiences with radical demands.

The feminist perspective that was articulated in such alternative forums was distinctly different from that of single-issue repeal groups. In contrast with the cautious approach of activists in groups like Illinois Citizens for the Medical Control of Abortion, feminists were publicly declaring the social acceptability of abortion and asserting an unconditional right to legal abortion. Participants in the women's liberation movement brought a different set of experiences to the abortion issue than did persons with backgrounds in family-planning organizations and traditional voluntary associations. Many CWLU members were students and former students who had participated in other protest movements and who had experienced something of a "sexual revolution" on college campuses in the late 1960s. Although some of my informants confessed a bit of embarrassment in looking back at their own rhetoric, at the time a "revolution" seemed to be under way. The rapidly growing women's movement appeared to offer an opportunity for bringing about far-reaching social changes.

Given their backgrounds—and the fact that groups like ICMCA were around to give a more moderate voice to the movement—CWLU participants saw no reason to limit their demands on abortion. Indeed, they saw their status as outsiders to the political establishment as an asset rather than a liability. The CWLU's activities were targeted mainly at women because part of the whole purpose of the Union was to build a larger and more powerful women's movement capable of bringing about radical social change. Based on their own experiences, CWLU activists thought that women would respond to more radical demands on issues like abortion and that controversial demands would help raise women's "consciousness." As a former CWLU activist explained when asked in an interview about the call for "abortion on demand":

> I think we felt that "abortion on demand" was the thing that would appeal to most people, most women . . . in the course of their lives, every single woman has probably had a chance or thought about an abortion. . . . We felt that that demand would bring more people in. . . . And part of it was just breaking out. Just changing something, breaking out from things. The most far-out thing was the one that you wanted to advocate because you felt that people would say, "You're right," you know, and break out—because everyone was feeling so repressed.

As this response indicates, there was an expressive element (cf. Lo, 1984) to the CWLU abortion demands, but there was also a belief that the expression of feelings would serve the more instrumental purpose of mobilizing more women. For women's liberation groups, legal abortion was not an end in itself, but part of a broader fight for "women's control of their bodies" and a responsive health care system (which was, in turn, part of a long-term challenge to other capitalist institutions). Although CWLU activists were concerned about the availability and legal status of abortion, the issue was also a means by which women could be mobilized and larger concerns raised. It seemed likely to CWLU activists that abortion would be legalized, especially after the progress made by the repeal movement in 1970, but they wanted more than just legalization. As another CWLU activist told me in an interview about the CWLU's approach to the abortion issue:

> Particularly after the New York stuff happened [including the emergence of for-profit referral services], we wanted to make it clear to people that although getting abortion legalized was a step in the right direction, it certainly wasn't the answer to any of the problems, because there were a lot of problems which have been *created* by legalization, and we wanted a situation where abortion was not only available on demand but ultimately where we had a health care system which did not allow profiteering on people's abortions, etc., etc., so it was couched in terms which would set up a debate which would allow all of these issues which we thought were consciousness raising to be elaborated.

An important reason, then, for the use of confrontational demands and noninstitutionalized protest tactics was that the women's liberation movement organizations had much broader social change goals than just legal abortion that required different kinds of strategies and tactics. Given the perceptions of the momentum of social change during this period, it did not seem unrealistic to expect that these broader goals could be achieved through confrontational tactics.

Feminists clearly played the most important role in creating alternative forums for education and mobilization and in fostering a new consciousness among women on a range of women's health issues, but other movement organizations also went outside established organizational channels to generate support for movement demands and to change the public's consciousness about abortion. Back in 1961 Patricia Maginnis's Society for Humane Abortion took the radical step of endorsing "elective abortion" and, in addition to distributing literature and filling speaking engagements, offered workshops on abortion techniques to doctors as well as referrals for abortions to women. Maginnis and her associates, including Lana Clarke Phelan, also taught public classes on self-abortion techniques, an intentionally confrontational tactic that resulted in their arrest in 1967 (Lader, 1973:32–33). Other tactics intended to attract public attention to the repeal position included a 1967 nationwide speaking tour by Maginnis and Phelan that began with a picket of the International Conference on Abortion in Washington, D.C., to protest the conference's lack of attention to the repeal position. In 1969, Phelan and Maginnis published a handbook on abortion techniques that was one of the first sources of such information available to women (Phelan and Maginnis, 1969). Although the Society for Humane Abortion did not build a broad base of support in the 1960s (Lader, 1973:34), its activists were pioneers who attracted media attention to the cause and who later hooked up with other activists in different parts of the country. As Lana Clarke Phelan stated in an interview about her early work:

> I'm not a confrontationalist; I always preferred lecturing, giving public educationals. I did give some of the first abortion lectures in my home in Long Beach, California. I would have some forty women attend sometimes—maybe one of whom was pregnant; the rest were police officers, social workers. It would be on abortion techniques—really how *not* to do it—but there was a lot of media interest. Really, our major accomplishment was in talking about abortion, saying the word out loud rather than using euphemisms. And from our little first meetings, there was such an influx of interested people. I would get more than five hundred letters a day asking for help. I had no budget, so I would do my own triage, answering the most desperate ones, sending others a xerox sheet. Then Pat Maginnis and I went across the country twice. . . . A few people can start a movement, but then at some point you have to reach out. I knew if we could just get it rolling that there would be more support sooner or later.

Whereas activists like Phelan and Maginnis employed such tactics as a way of getting the movement off the ground, single-issue groups like ICMCA turned to public education out of frustration with the lack of progress in institutionalized arenas. In 1967, after the defeat of a bill to establish a commission for the study of abortion in Illinois, ICMCA made a decision to spend the next two years on an educational campaign to convince the public of the need for repeal (ICMCA newsletter, November 1967). Similarly, after the defeat of a 1970 abortion reform bill, ICMCA decided to concentrate on educational work along with work in the political arena (ICMCA newsletter, June 1970). Although ICMCA worked through established organizations like churches, on numerous occasions the group also initiated public discussions of the abortion issue. These discussions were often held in settings such as university campuses, in order to reach the student constituency that was critical to both the population and the women's liberation movements. ICMCA also worked through women's rights organizations like Chicago NOW, which held an educational forum on abortion for its members in February 1970, with speakers from ICMCA and the Clergy Consultation Services participating (*Act NOW,* February 1970).

Like Lana Clarke Phelan and other early abortion activists, ICMCA activists felt that they were making an important contribution simply by discussing abortion openly in these various forums. This sentiment was also shared by Rev. Howard Moody, who recently reflected about the role of the clergy service in talking freely about abortion: "It was to free that word up. To free it from the silence, from the whispered things. People need to be able to say things. But abortion was so underground, so hidden, that to use that word openly—and then to explain it, what it really was—" (quoted in *Washington Post,* April 26, 1989).

Use of the Mass Media

Although not all public education tactics involved media attention, the mass media were frequently used to gain direct access to constituents, a strategy that encouraged dramatic presentations of confrontational demands. One of Chicago NOW's major activities on the abortion issue in 1970, for example, was a Mother's Day press conference at the city morgue—also attended by representatives from ICMCA, the CWLU, and Chicago-area ZPG—to dramatize the dangers of illegal abortion (*Act NOW,* May 1970). Although feminist groups attracted much of the media attention, single-issue abortion movement organizations were quite actively trying to get media attention for the cause. Both NARAL and ICMCA used the mass media to gain support for the repeal cause because they felt limited by established organizational channels.[3]

NARAL was able to attract a good deal of media attention as a result of both the controversial nature of its positions and the public relations skills of NARAL leaders. Lawrence Lader, a key architect of the NARAL strategy during this period, had already been making many media appearances and giving press conferences on the subject of abortion after the publication in 1966 of his controversial book *Abortion* (Lader, 1973). Under Lader's leadership, NARAL held several demonstrations and press conferences at which controversial announcements often were made in order to create publicity for the organization and win new advantages in the fight for repeal.[4] On many occasions, NARAL successfully combined the public relations know-how of its leaders with the willingness of feminists to participate in confrontational or theatrical kinds of activities.[5]

Like ICMCA, NARAL also spent a good deal of time debating the opposition, in part because this was a way to get media attention. For example, in the early 1970s NARAL developed materials, including a "Debating the Opposition" manual and a "Portrait of the Opposition" document, in order to train local activists and to expose the Catholic Church's backing of the anti-abortion movement. NARAL speakers debated "Right to Life" opponents on local television and radio shows across the country. The initial NARAL strategy, like that of ICMCA, was to respond to anti-abortion arguments and fetus pictures with "fact and reason" (NARAL "Debating the Opposition" manual; Special Collections Department, Northwestern University library). After advertisements employing pictures of fetuses were successfully used to defeat the 1972 abortion repeal referendum in Michigan, however, "militants" in NARAL used their influence to adopt a confrontational strategy similar to that of the opposition. As Lawrence Lader explained:

> Logic is not very powerful against those pictures. . . . We had to do something, so we decided we would come in with the same thing. . . . We were able to get highly documented [material] from sheriffs, hospitals; we were able to get these pictures together. We had a number of pictures of dead women on the floor in motels, killed during an abortion, from a hack doctor in prelegal days, and we had these blown up. So I would always call up a news station and say, "Look, we've got these pretty frightening pictures and we'll show them to you ahead of time if you want, but if they're going to come in with their pictures, we will demand equal right, and you've got to be aware of this. We prefer no pictures." So a lot of shows banned them. I can remember Channel 5 in New York had me on a show there, and they showed their pictures and I had a few horrible pictures and there were

all these gasps from the audience, and that's the last time I recall using them. They did their job. (interview with Lawrence Lader, 1984)

Overall, NARAL's mobilization tactics were more confrontational than those of ICMCA. Part of the reason for this was its greater use of the media to push proactive demands as well as to educate the public. Given the media's attraction to conflict, it was not difficult to get coverage by debating the opposition, but it was another matter to get coverage at press conferences. In order to do so, NARAL had to make "news." Another reason for the difference in strategy was that NARAL was formed later than ICMCA, with more input from feminists, and at a time when the women's movement was becoming increasingly visible.

Service Projects

Not only did the movement promote a women's rights perspective on abortion through the media and through the creation of new kinds of educational forums, but alternative institutions also were created as movement activists began offering abortion-related services to women, particularly abortion referrals. As described in Chapter 2, a number of individuals began making referrals to women for abortions in the 1960s, before the founding of most abortion movement organizations. By the late 1960s, their ranks were joined by feminists, clergy, and other activists who began organizing abortion referral services throughout the country.

NARAL leader Lawrence Lader viewed abortion referrals as part of a strategy of confrontation that would gain public sympathy for the movement and attract women to the cause (see Lader, 1973). Although NARAL as an organization did not run an abortion referral service, many of its activists were involved in referral activities, and after Lader and others received summonses from a grand jury in New York, the organization took a public position vowing financial and legal support for these activities (see Lader, 1973:104–8).[6]

For the women's liberation movement, projects such as abortion referral services were both responses to the immediate needs of women and part of a long-term strategy of creating alternative institutions that would empower women. In Chicago, the Chicago Women's Liberation Union had its hand in a number of abortion-related service projects, including the Women's Liberation Abortion Counseling Service, known as "Jane" (see Chapter 2). Like other referral services around the country, Jane began by providing referrals for abortions. But members of the Abortion Counseling Service ended up performing abortions themselves after learning to do so by assisting at abortions and after they learned that one of the abortionists they had been using was not himself a licensed doctor (cf. Addelson, 1988; Bart, 1987; Schlesinger and Bart, 1982). Thus, the women literally took control of the technology, creating a service that they felt was nonhierarchical and sensitive to the needs of women.

As part of the same strategy of empowering women with information and access to technology, the CWLU created pregnancy-testing services that were conducted at several locations in Chicago, including a working-class southwest side location. The first CWLU pregnancy-testing service came out of an unsuccessful attempt to form a free women's health clinic. Despite a great deal of planning work, this project failed largely due to a lack of funding. Another pregnancy-testing service was begun in 1972 as part of the CWLU Health Project formed in that year. At that point, a number of volunteers were recruited for pregnancy testing, and a service conducted at the CWLU office continued to operate until the mid 1970s (CWLU working papers in Jennifer Knauss private papers).

There were numerous debates in the CWLU as to the value of these service projects. Advocates of the projects argued that they were not merely providing services but also building alternative institutions that allowed women to control their bodies rather than rely on male-oriented, for-profit health care services. The Abortion Counseling Service, for example, made a deliberate attempt to create a supportive, female-oriented atmosphere for women having abortions. Supporters also contended that the services allowed the CWLU to reach minority, poor, and working-class women—and in fact the Abortion Counseling Service and pregnancy-testing projects did serve many minority and economically disadvantaged women, some of whom were recruited to the Union or at least were exposed to the women's liberation movement. Critics of the service projects complained, however, that they were not political enough and that they drained resources from other Union projects. There were also debates within the CWLU as to whether or not it was right for "Jane " to charge fees for abortions, as the collective did unless the woman was unable to pay.

There were several reasons why the Abortion Counseling Service and the pregnancy-testing services continued to function. In the case of Jane, it was abundantly clear that the service was needed by women who could not otherwise afford abortions. The risk in providing the service and the real needs that were so obviously being served created a strong sense of solidarity and commitment among the women in the Jane collective. Moreover, the decentralized structure of the Union (see Appendix A) allowed both the Abortion Counseling Service and the pregnancy-testing services to operate independently, despite whatever debate occurred within the Union. As with all CWLU work projects, women who were not official members of the CWLU could still participate in the projects, thereby making it easier to recruit enough workers. Both Jane and the pregnancy-testing services required little more than the commitment of activists, as both charged small fees that covered the costs of the services and required skills learned on the job. The attempt at establishing a free health clinic failed, on the other hand, because it would have needed far more resources than the Union was able to mobilize, particularly given the mixed feelings about service projects among CWLU activists.

Although the CWLU was the organization most deeply involved in abortion-related service projects in Chicago before 1973, other local organizations advocating repeal inevitably received pleas from women for help in obtaining abortions. Activists from Chicago NOW, ICMCA, and Chicago-area ZPG often found themselves counseling women and making referrals to the Clergy Consultation Service or to Jane.[7] Chicago NOW began helping the Abortion Counseling Service in informal ways because the chair of the chapter's abortion committee, Madeline

Schwenk, was a Jane member. Schwenk recalled in an interview that other NOW members supported Jane in various ways, some offering the use of their homes for abortions, which was a real risk. In 1972, after seven Abortion Counseling Service activists were arrested for performing abortions, NOW teamed up with the CWLU to administer an Abortion Defense Fund. According to several informants, the Chicago NOW chapter was very supportive of the "Abortion Seven," as were other abortion and women's movement organizations.

Feminist Mobilization and Direct Action

Given the limited support for abortion law repeal from established organizations, the presence of the women's movement was by far the most positive feature of the political environment of the abortion movement in the years following NARAL's founding in 1969. The women's movement was growing rapidly, and the news media were interested in both the abortion issue and the women's movement. In addition to tactics like referral services that were aimed at women, feminists initiated direct-action tactics such as demonstrations that were targeted at established power holders. They also provided support for direct-action tactics initiated by single-issue abortion movement organizations.

Demonstrations by women's movement activists sent a message of public support for abortion rights to established organizations and authorities and served an expressive function for participants. Organizations like the Chicago Women's Liberation Union organized a number of demonstrations that were targeted at representatives of the "establishment," such as the American Medical Association, as well as government officials. In 1970, for example, CWLU activists participated in a demonstration at the convention site of the AMA, and WITCH[8] activists, who were loosely connected to the CWLU, infiltrated the AMA convention to present a list of demands, including the demand for free legal abortion. When the AMA failed to respond, the WITCHes "hexed" the organization on the following day, and according to a CWLU report "the feeling of exhilaration and sisterhood was so rewarding that the WITCHes decided to hex the business establishment on a regular basis" (*CWLU News,* March 1970).

Women's movement activists were also critical to the strategies and tactics of a number of other organizations. Because of the visibility of the women's movement, NARAL leaders like Lawrence Lader became firmly convinced that the tiny abortion movement could succeed only by making confrontational demands and engaging in tactics that would attract young feminists as "troops" for the cause, stirring up sympathetic public opinion through the ensuing publicity (see Lader, 1973).[9]

NARAL frequently did take advantage of the availability of feminist groups to organize demonstrations. As a result of close ties between NOW and NARAL, NOW helped launch NARAL through strong participation in NARAL's first national action, a day of "Children by Choice" demonstrations held in conjunction with press conferences in eleven cities on Mother's Day in 1969. Because NOW was growing rapidly in terms of members and chapters in the early 1970s,

NOW was able to participate on a number of occasions in demonstrations for abortion law repeal in cooperation with NARAL. Chicago NOW joined other NOW chapters and local women's liberation groups in organizing or participating in demonstrations for abortion law repeal and related issues.

The adoption of confrontational demands and tactics by NARAL in response to the feminist presence in the movement was not inevitable, however. The conference at which NARAL was officially formed brought together abortion activists from across the country who represented a variety of approaches to changing the abortion laws. Many of the activists were feminists but there were also persons favoring a slower strategy of working for reform rather than repeal of the laws. Consequently, NARAL activists did not unanimously support the adoption of confrontational demands and tactics. The decision to publicly offer legal and financial support for referral services, for example, was a particularly controversial one in NARAL. Some NARAL leaders, including Lonny Myers, were concerned that its open connection to referral services left NARAL open to attack by opponents (Lader, 1973:96), and others were concerned about the financial obligations that might be incurred by activists providing referrals (interview with Lawrence Lader, 1984).

NARAL's adoption of radical demands and controversial tactics was due to internal organizational factors in addition to the influence of the women's movement. With regard to the organizational resources needed to advocate such positions, Lawrence Lader and other key leaders had experience in providing abortion referrals and knew the legal risks and public relations benefits of doing so. Moreover, Lader had published an article (in *Look* magazine in January 1969) reporting on the results of his study of women who had received nonhospital abortions as a result of referrals from abortion movement activists. According to Lader, the article gave the movement "documentary evidence of the high medical standards of in-office abortion" necessary for its position on free-standing clinics (Lader, 1973:93).

Most importantly, NARAL's organizational structure allowed those leaders of NARAL who advocated confrontational positions to push their strategies. NARAL was centrally controlled by its executive committee in the pre-1973 period, and its operating procedures were informal (see Appendix A). There was no system of rotating individuals off the executive committee every few years, thereby allowing the "militants" (Lader, 1973), who had a majority on the executive committee, to control the nominating committee. The NARAL board of directors, which was representative of a broader range of the NARAL constituency, may have chosen a more cautious approach, but it was an unwieldy body of up to ninety members that met only once a year and therefore did not control the real decision making in the organization. When those leaders on the NARAL executive committee who favored radical demands and confrontational tactics wanted to take action (e.g., call a press conference or a demonstration), they simply picked up the phone to obtain approval from a majority of the executive committee. In this way, action could be taken which bypassed bureaucratic procedures that might have limited NARAL to the adoption of less confrontational tactics. For these reasons, the informal, centralized NARAL organization facilitated the use of tactics favored by the "militants" in the leadership. For example, when leaders like Lader who openly provided referrals for abortions were indicted by a grand jury, they quickly pushed NARAL to provide support (see Lader, 1973:96).

The strategies of another major organization in the pre-1973 abortion repeal movement, Zero Population Growth, were similarly influenced by the growth of the women's movement in the late 1960s and the early 1970s and by internal organizational characteristics. Like NARAL and NOW, ZPG adopted the demand for repeal, rather than reform, of abortion laws, advocating legal abortion as a component of the "basic human right to limit one's own reproduction" (Statement Adopted by ZPG Board of Directors, September 30, 1969; document in Special Collections Department, Northwestern University library). ZPG's primary concern, of course, has always been overpopulation, and abortion was advocated, along with contraception and sterilization, as a "means of birth control" that would help bring down the birthrate. Sensitive to the concerns of feminists about its potential coercion of women, however, ZPG conspicuously stressed the voluntary nature of its demands for abortion, sterilization, and contraception and, from the start, expressed its support for women's rights.[10]

ZPG took a "women's rights" approach to abortion in part as a result of overlaps in the national leadership of ZPG and groups like NARAL and NOW. The organization was also influenced by its numerous chapters, many of which consisted of students who were strongly interested in abortion and women's rights. In the early years in Chicago, for example, a number of campus-based ZPG chapters were working for repeal alongside feminists. Although there was also a more conservative element in ZPG's local constituency (see Appendix A), the organization's decision-making structure allowed national leaders, who tended to be sympathetic to women's rights, to maintain control over ZPG's positions.

In general, the presence of the women's movement was a strong influence on the strategic and tactical choices of the abortion movement. Not only did women's movement organizations initiate many direct-action tactics, but various other kinds of organizations also sought to use both the energies of feminists and the repertoire of tactics associated with the women's movement and other movements of the 1960s. NARAL frequently mobilized feminist support for its actions. And in 1971 many feminist groups contributed to the success of the nationwide demonstrations organized by the SWP-backed Women's National Abortion Action Coalition (WONAAC), which received significant media coverage.

Even the more staid Illinois Citizens for the Medical Control of Abortion (ICMCA) engaged in demonstrations, although they were less confrontational than those in which feminists typically participated, and, significantly, they were targeted at legislators. In 1970, ICMCA sent a few busloads of women, accompanied by sympathetic reporters, to a small demonstration in Springfield to call attention to an abortion reform bill before the state legislature. And in 1971, ICMCA again bused supporters to Springfield for a demonstration in support of a repeal bill. Chicago-area ZPG supporters lent some needed bodies to these and other orderly ICMCA demonstrations, which were typically combined with more institutionalized tactics.

Conclusion

Before 1973, the confrontational direct-action tactics of political "outsiders" were as much a part of the movement to legalize abortion as were the conventional means of influence used by seasoned activists. The presence of the women's movement in the expanded social movement sector of the 1960s was an important factor prompting the use of these tactics. Feminists took to the streets to demand abortion rights, but they also worked to create a new social consciousness about women's rights to abortion. Although direct-action tactics did not have the direct impact that litigation had on the legalization of abortion, they helped bring the abortion issue to public attention and created an atmosphere of support for legal abortion. Moreover, the alternative institutions and cultural changes created by the women's health movement would have an important influence on subsequent collective action.

After abortion was legalized by the Supreme Court in 1973, there were significant shifts in the movement's political environment, resulting in changes in the movement's organization and in its strategies and tactics. The impact of the 1973 victory on the movement is the subject of the next two chapters.

II

SURVIVING THE VICTORY,
1973–1976

5

Movement Maintenance and Reorganization

Few abortion law repeal supporters had anticipated the sweeping changes in the abortion laws brought about by the January 22, 1973, Supreme Court decision. After a major success like *Roe* v. *Wade,* activists in the pro-choice movement might have been expected to savor the victory and fold up shop. Indeed, social scientists (see Luker, 1984:241; Tatalovich and Daynes, 1981:101; Zald and Useem, 1987) and popular commentators alike have made the mistake of assuming that this is in fact what happened. Reconstructions of the history of the abortion conflict have claimed that the pro-choice movement rested on its laurels while the anti-abortion countermovement suddenly mobilized in the wake of *Roe* v. *Wade,* and that it was not until the late 1970s (or early 1980s), in response to the shock of countermovement victories, that the pro-choice movement remobilized. Based on such a reconstruction, Zald and Useem (1987:249) employ the term "counter-countermovement" to theorize about the remobilization of the pro-choice movement, arguing that it should be considered a new social movement distinct from the earlier abortion movement.

Although there are germs of truth in this widely accepted account, it oversimplifies and distorts the history of the abortion conflict. The anti-abortion movement did receive a tremendous boost from *Roe* v. *Wade,* but countermovement organizations had begun to organize before legalization in response to state reform and repeal campaigns. There was some decline in local pro-choice movement organizations, but this did not occur immediately after legalization, and the movement never disappeared entirely. Nationally, the pro-choice movement remained organized and active throughout the 1973–76 period following the victory. The movement did expand greatly in the late 1970s and early 1980s in response to countermovement victories, but the organizational groundwork for this expansion was laid in the post-1973 period. Hence, there was no demobilization after legalization followed by remobilization in later years as suggested by the concept of a counter-countermovement.

After *Roe* v. *Wade,* changes in the political opportunity structure, together with internal organizational characteristics, made movement maintenance possible in a period in which demobilization might reasonably have occurred. First, countermovement activities created immediate threats to the newly won right to abortion that helped keep the pro-choice movement mobilized. Second, established organizations and interest groups, which had not been heavily involved in the abortion movement before legalization, became much more actively support- ive after 1973, and this involvement was an important source of resources and stability for the pro-choice movement. Third, the composition of the movement itself prevented its demobilization. Although the cycle of protest of the 1960s was waning, in 1973 there still were active multi-issue population and women's move- ment organizations that were able to assist single-issue pro-choice organizations in surviving the victory. Finally, the national pro-choice movement underwent internal changes in the direction of professionalization that affected its ability to remain mobilized for a protracted battle over abortion.

Countermovement Mobilization
and Movement Maintenance

If a period of savoring victory occurred after *Roe* v. *Wade,* it soon ended as it became apparent to pro-choice activists that the war was continuing on new fronts. Although anti-abortion groups had been active before 1973, the legaliza- tion of abortion provided a tremendous spur to the countermovement as it lob- bied to overturn or block implementation of the Court ruling.[1] Because of the impetus of *Roe* v. *Wade,* the countermovement was able to generate huge vol- umes of anti-abortion mail, creating real and perceived threats to the newly won right to abortion. On the national level, anti-abortion forces pressed Congress for a constitutional amendment to outlaw abortion and, by 1974, for riders to appro- priations bills to cut off federal funding for abortions.[2] On the state and local lev- els, supporters of legal abortion were faced with attempts to block implementation of the Court ruling through the state legislatures as well as resistance to the pro- vision of abortions by some hospitals.[3]

These activities of the anti-abortion movement were not offset by a ground- swell of public opinion in support of legal abortion following *Roe* v. *Wade.* Although the Court ruling did have some positive impact on public approval of abortion, most of the change in public opinion on abortion came before 1973. The increase in approval of legal abortion following *Roe* v. *Wade* amounted to an average rise of about 5 percent for all "hard" and "soft" reasons for having abortions, based on data from the National Opinion Research Center.[4] Between 1973 and 1977, approval of abortion leveled off, with an average approval rate of about 68 percent for all reasons (Granberg and Granberg, 1980:252). Whereas a majority of the public had previously approved of legal abortion for "hard" rea- sons, close to 50 percent now approved for "soft" reasons as well. In short, there was substantial support for legal abortion, but no public consensus on "women's right to choose" abortion for any reason.

In response to anti-abortion threats, single-issue abortion movement organi- zations did not disband but regrouped for the next round in the conflict. The National Association for Repeal of Abortion Laws changed its name to the

National Abortion Rights Action League (retaining the NARAL acronym) after it became apparent that the battle over abortion would continue for some time. Illinois Citizens for the Medical Control of Abortion (ICMCA) also carried on its work after the court victory, changing its name to the Abortion Rights Association of Illinois (ARA) in 1975. There was no real relaxation on the part of ICMCA's leadership following the victory because opponents of abortion immediately moved to block implementation of the Supreme Court ruling through the state legislature. As Helen Smith, ICMCA's executive director at the time, explained in an interview, the organization kept mobilized because "we had all those dolls in the legislature" such as Henry Hyde, then an Illinois legislator, who announced in 1973 that "the fight has just begun."

Support from Established Organizations
and Interest Groups

While the movement victory had the effect of increasing opposition to abortion, it also solidified support among some political "insiders." Perhaps because the Supreme Court ruling created legitimacy for the movement—which made participation less risky—single-issue movement organizations received more aid from established organizations and interest groups after *Roe* v. *Wade* than they had before 1973. Moreover, after legalization the movement relied less on direct-action tactics such as quasi-legal abortion referral services and turned more to institutionalized tactics such as Congressional lobbying, with which established interest groups were familiar. This tactical shift made it easier for established interest groups to join in, which in turn strengthened the movement's inclination to employ institutionalized tactics.

Among the established groups joining forces with the pro-choice movement were professional associations. Although the American Medical Association and the American Hospital Association acted mainly to protect the interests of their members and did not explicitly endorse *Roe* v. *Wade,* the American College of Obstetricians and Gynecologists did become quite active in support of abortion rights after 1973 (Lee and LeRoy, 1985:45–46). Even more critical was the post-1973 support of two other established organizations, Planned Parenthood and the American Civil Liberties Union (ACLU). Although neither organization had been greatly involved in the abortion movement before legalization, both became active participants in pro-choice lobbying after 1973, and the ACLU began a Reproductive Rights Freedom Project in 1974.

Mobilization of Religious Pro-Choice
Movement Organizations

Participation by established organizations in the pro-choice movement also increased with the founding of the Religious Coalition for Abortion Rights

(RCAR) in 1973, an organization of Protestant and Jewish denominations and other religious groups. The entry of these religious groups into the pro-choice movement at this point was in large part a response to the 1973 movement victory. As was the case for other established organizations, legalization decreased the risk associated with a public stand on abortion, making it easier to recruit religious denominations for visible activity in the abortion rights movement. The other spur to involvement was the activity of the Catholic Church in the anti-abortion movement, which began before legalization but escalated after *Roe* v. *Wade*. Protestant and Jewish groups with different theological positions on the issue believed that they had a duty to speak out on abortion and to prevent the public perception that the Catholic Church had a moral monopoly on the issue.[5]

Although it was the political environment after legalization that was most conducive to religious participation in the pro-choice movement, the social networks and institutional support established earlier were critical to post-1973 mobilization. As noted in Chapter 2, by 1973 a number of Protestant and Jewish religious denominations had endorsed abortion law reform, and individual clergy members across the country were involved through the Clergy Consultation Services (which did disband after legalization). Catholics had also become somewhat involved, as NARAL was constantly urging the formation of "Catholics for Abortion Repeal" groups, which were formed in some states before legalization. On the national level, Catholics For a Free Choice (CFFC) was founded in 1972, but it was not until after legalization, when the Catholic Church escalated its involvement in the anti-abortion movement, that CFFC was able to effectively get off the ground.

As part of the general trend toward social activism among liberal religious groups that intensified with civil rights activities, a few Protestant and Jewish denominations had been working to some extent on the abortion issue before 1973 through their social action arms. It was out of the activities of the social action agencies of the institutionalized denominations, particularly the United Methodist Board of Church and Society, that the Religious Coalition for Abortion Rights was formed. One of the founding members of RCAR, Jessma Blockwick, who was also a NARAL board member, was on the staff of the United Methodist Board of Church and Society before 1973 when the agency began to respond to the abortion repeal movement. Blockwick recalled in an interview that her office worked informally with other denominations (most of which were headquartered in Washington, D.C.) on the issue, engaging in some ecumenical activities such as a press conference and a letter in support of abortion rights signed by clergy members. According to Blockwick, "There was such interest among the denominations that the idea began to take hold to form a more formal coalition."[6] When the Religious Coalition for Abortion Rights was organized in 1973, it was legally a part of the United Methodist Board of Church and Society.[7]

Although RCAR's efforts were focused almost exclusively on Congress during this period of the abortion conflict, the national organization also helped expand the movement at the local level by doing some field organizing work. Initially, RCAR was trying to encourage the formation of local affiliates in states with large Congressional delegations in order to aid national lobbying efforts. Because the national organization had few resources for field organizing, however, early affiliates tended to be formed in places where the organization already had contacts.

The Illinois RCAR affiliate was officially founded on March 11, 1975, by persons who were, for the most part, already participating in the local pro-choice movement. Rev. Spencer Parsons, founder of the local Clergy Consultation Service and an early ICMCA activist, was one of the key organizers of the affiliate who brought together church activists, a few former CCS clergy, ICMCA activists, Planned Parenthood activists, and others interested in forming a religious pro-choice group. As a minister who had been involved in various social causes over the years, Parsons had connections to national RCAR activists, as did another Illinois RCAR founder, Phyllis Tholin, who had been a longtime activist in the United Methodist Church before her involvement with RCAR. Organizers of the local affiliate contacted national RCAR leaders who provided advice and sent a field worker from the national staff to help get the affiliate off the ground.

Multi-Issue Organizations and Movement Maintenance

In addition to the importance of countermovement activities and support from established organizations, the composition of the movement itself was important to its maintenance in the period immediately following the 1973 victory. Although it has been argued that the pro-choice movement suffered from a grass-roots "infrastructural deficit" (McCarthy, 1987), this assessment underestimates the role of multi-issue organizations, particularly women's movement organizations, in the movement. The pro-choice movement consisted of not only single-issue abortion movement organizations but also multi-issue population and women's movement organizations. These multi-issue organizations were important in keeping the movement alive in a period when the abortion issue had become less pressing to constituents.

It is true that the cycle of protest that had nourished the abortion movement before legalization was on the decline and, by the late 1970s, it was quite important that the pro-choice movement had organizational structures capable of generating grass-roots participation to compensate for this loss. But in the period immediately following legalization, there was enough activity among multi-issue organizations to buy time for single-issue pro-choice organizations until they became strong enough to play a leadership role in the movement. Moreover, women's liberation groups, which did decline by the mid-1970s, left a legacy of alternative women's health institutions that helped sustain the pro-choice movement.

Because they were fighting for a number of causes in various arenas, multi-issue movement organizations were better prepared than were single-issue organizations for the switch in battlegrounds that occurred on the national level in 1973. Both ZPG and NOW provided needed resources to the newly emerging pro-choice lobby in Washington.[8] ZPG was one of the few pro-choice organizations with an established lobbying operation in Washington in early 1973, and its lobbyist became involved in efforts to prevent anti-abortion forces from overturning *Roe* v. *Wade* through Congressional passage of a constitutional amendment banning abortions. The National Organization for Women opened a lobbying office in Washington in 1973 and, like ZPG, was one of the few pro-choice organizations in a position to join in Congressional lobbying efforts. Although NOW did not then have the resources necessary for a professional lobbying effort, the organization was able to use volunteers from the Washington, D.C., area to aid in the lobbying work during the difficult period for the movement following legalization.

On the local level, women's liberation movement organizations remained involved in the pro-choice movement to pursue a broader agenda beyond legal abortion. The Chicago Women's Liberation Union actually became somewhat more active on the abortion issue after January 1973 than it had been before the court ruling. Before legalization, the CWLU was involved in some service and educational activities on the issue but did not participate in the efforts to win repeal through the state legislature that absorbed much of the local movement. ICMCA was already covering that front, a battle in which the CWLU in any case was not ideologically inclined to participate. Legalization, however, opened up new battlefronts that were more appealing to the socialist-feminist organization. The medical establishment had to be pressured to provide abortions, including second-trimester abortions in hospitals, and it was necessary, in the words of one CWLU activist interviewed, "to control the takeover of the abortion scene by the profiteers." In short, the battles to be fought after legalization offered opportunities to relate the abortion issue to larger concerns about the capitalist health care system and male-controlled medicine, resulting in an expansion of CWLU activities.

There was some decline in the Chicago pro-choice movement by 1976, which can be attributed in part to the decline of immediately felt grievances and abortion referral work, both of which brought so many grass-roots activists into the movement before legalization (see Chapter 2). But the decline seems to have been more a result of internal organizational factors than a response to the 1973 movement victory. Abortion did become less of a priority for Chicago NOW following *Roe* v. *Wade*, but the chapter had not played a major role in the pro-choice movement before legalization.[9] ZPG chapters in Chicago and throughout the country, which had mobilized many college students in the early 1970s, began to dissolve prior to *Roe* v. *Wade*. The Chicago-area ZPG organization was not active in the pro-choice movement after legalization simply because it was in a state of almost complete decline (see Appendix A). By 1975, the Chicago Women's Liberation Union also began to fall apart as a result of internal conflict (see Appendix A) and consequently dropped out of active involvement in the pro-choice movement. However, an autonomous CWLU work group, the Health Evaluation and Referral Service (HERS), and two CWLU-connected women's health centers continued to participate in the movement. By the end of 1976 the Abortion Rights Association of Illinois was also having its problems, primarily as a result of a change in leadership in that year.

Organizational Changes and
Movement Stability

The organizational decline experienced by the Chicago movement[10] in the mid-1970s did not occur on the national level. Changes in the leadership and structures of movement organizations helped the pro-choice movement to maintain itself following the legalization of abortion, and, in this regard, local pro-choice organizations lagged behind national organizations. On the national level, movement leadership began to become more professionalized and movement organizations began to formalize their structures.[11] Paid staff, rather than volunteer activists, slowly began to assume leadership of pro-choice movement organizations. As they did so, the movement organizations gradually developed more formal divisions of labor and operating procedures (see Appendix A).

The cases of the most important national and local single-issue movement organizations, NARAL and ICMCA/ARA, are worth considering in detail to demonstrate the role of these organizational factors in movement maintenance.

NARAL

A number of internal changes occurred in NARAL as the organization struggled to deal with the new political situation following legalization. In response to anti-abortion activities, NARAL attempted to expand its own membership and to organize state affiliates. As a result, there were pressures for change in the organization's decision-making structure.

As described in Chapter 4, NARAL's structure in the pre-1973 years allowed for informal decision making by a small number of leaders. Although there were some disagreements among executive committee members in those early years, according to former executive director Lee Gidding, these differences were not extensive in retrospect (interview with Lee Gidding, 1985). The informal and centralized decision-making structure seems to have worked fairly well at a time when the movement was very young, abortion was illegal in most states, and it was necessary to act quickly to take advantage of opportunities for action and to meet crises.

After legalization, however, conflict over decision-making procedures began as new activists were recruited and more people wanted a say in the running of the organization. In 1974, the board members split into two factions, each running a slate of candidates for offices and executive committee positions. One faction, calling itself the "Feminist Activist" slate, consisted of some longtime leaders of NARAL (including Lader). The other group, which was endorsed by the nominating committee, called itself the "NARAL Women's Caucus" slate. The Women's Caucus slate objected to "power being concentrated in the hands of a few men in New York City" and supported having on the board persons "who are doing the work in the field—the State Coordinators." The Feminist Activist faction, in turn, accused its opponents of undemocratic efforts "to drop some of the most noted activists and feminists from the Executive Committee." The election was won by the "Women's Caucus" (documents in NARAL of Illinois Records, University of Illinois at Chicago library), resulting in a turnover of leadership on the NARAL executive committee for the first time and the adoption of somewhat more bureaucratic decision-making procedures to ensure that a few individuals did not control the organization. Although the executive committee remained the organization's decision-making body, practices such as the use of proxy votes were discontinued. Another major change was that for the first time in NARAL's history the executive director and other paid staff became more important than movement "entrepreneurs" like Lader as spokespersons for the organization.

In addition to the change in NARAL's leadership, the structure linking state and local members to the organization was altered. In the early years, organizations joining NARAL were only loosely affiliated, having their own organizational identities and developing their own programs. The national organization offered information and suggestions for strategy and coordinated regional exchanges (e.g., a Midwest Strategy Conference held in Chicago in January 1971). Representatives from some of the local organizations that were members of NARAL also served on the national organization's board of directors. But cooperation with the national program was purely voluntary, and local member organizations were autonomous from the national organization.

This situation gradually changed as NARAL became more involved in legislative lobbying work in Washington and realized that it was necessary to generate mail from the states to counteract the mail being received by Congress from the anti-abortionists. Steps toward developing state affiliates were taken in 1974 when a field coordinator began a more systematic recruitment of NARAL "state coordinators" from existing local organizations than had been done in the past. NARAL supplied strategy materials to the coordinators and organized some regional conferences to increase local communication with the national organization.

ICMCA/ARA

Illinois Citizens for the Medical Control of Abortion—which became the Abortion Rights Association of Illinois in 1975—did not make the same kinds of organizational changes as did NARAL in the 1973–76 period. Although countermovement activities kept the organization together after legalization, ICMCA continued to rely heavily on the abilities of its executive director, Helen Smith, as it had since she took over leadership of the organization in 1971. As executive director, Smith delegated certain organizational tasks to volunteers and did others herself, depending on the skills required. The performance of these tasks, however, was not the result of any formalized division of labor, but of Helen Smith's personality. By all accounts she had an extraordinary ability to recruit volunteers for various tasks. As one of my informants explained, "She was really effective at getting people to do things. She would keep after you so that it was easier to do what she wanted rather than have her continue to bug you." Another activist concurred, "There was nothing like having her call you at 7 A.M. and tell you what you were going to do that day!"

The highly personalized structure of ICMCA/ARA created difficulties for the organization after Smith resigned as executive director in early 1976. The new director hired to replace her was by all accounts inept, but regardless of her personal abilities, she was handicapped from the start in trying to take over an organization that was heavily dependent on Smith's abilities to recruit volunteers as needed and that had no established means of passing down information (e.g., lists of press contacts) that only Smith possessed. There was a board made up of long-time activists, but they had become accustomed to a self-sufficient director, and many of them were also active in other organizations (principally Planned Parenthood) that took time away from ARA. The result was a period of serious organizational decline for ARA, in terms of both its programs and its finances and general organizational maintenance.[12]

Conclusion

The contrast between NARAL and ICMCA/ARA illustrates the importance of organizational structures as well as changes in the political environment for movement maintenance. The move toward professionalization of leadership and formalization of organizational structures in NARAL helped create stability in the pro-choice movement. Consequently, when the abortion conflict heated up in the late 1970s, the movement was prepared to take advantage of its constituents' increased interest in the abortion conflict. These organizational strengths would help compensate for the decline of other social movements in the social movement sector that had previously supplied grass-roots support for the movement. In Chicago, where professionalization and formalization began later in single-issue organizations, "local movement centers" (cf. Morris, 1984; Staggenborg, 1989a) would be important in rejuvenating the movement in response to countermovement victories.

In sum, the 1973–76 period was one in which NARAL and other pro-choice organizations had taken some steps toward "polity membership"[13] as the movement maintained itself after the 1973 victory. Countermovement activities were forcing the movement into the national legislative arena. Support from established organizations brought the pro-choice movement closer to the political "inside." As a result, NARAL and other pro-choice organizations began to develop more formalized organizational structures, which were important in maintaining the movement after the 1973 victory and in making many pro-choice "movement organizations" more like established "interest groups." Although the movement did include local feminist organizations with broader agendas, these dynamics helped narrow the movement's post-1973 strategies and tactics. The following chapter describes the movement's activities in the 1973–76 period.

6

Defending *Roe* v. *Wade*

proactive and reactive forces — organizational shifts

Although the pro-choice movement remained mobilized, its tactical position changed after *Roe* v. *Wade*. Following such a decisive victory, collective actors might be expected to push for further advantages, but pro-choice forces soon found themselves on the defensive. Movement organizations like NARAL initially did make proactive demands regarding women's access to quality abortion services, but they soon became preoccupied with reactive tactics aimed at fending off countermovement attacks on *Roe* v. *Wade*.[1] Women's movement organizations, particularly local women's liberation groups, which had never viewed legalization of abortion as an end in itself, were anxious to push forward with their multi-issue agenda, but they too had to concern themselves with keeping abortion legal. Had there not been an anti-abortion countermovement, the pro-choice movement as a whole might have broadened its goals after legalization to encompass issues such as national health insurance. As it was, the movement became more and more narrowly focused on defending legal abortion, although some feminist groups continued to maintain broad concerns.

In addition to becoming more reactive, the movement's tactics also became more institutionalized in the period after *Roe* v. *Wade*. This occurred as a number of movement organizations opened offices in Washington, D.C., and began to develop a pro-choice lobby to protect legal abortion with the support of established organizations. In the process, the structures of these movement organizations were adjusted to facilitate participation in conventional interest-group politics. At the same time, local women's liberation groups, which were geared toward less orderly protest tactics, began to decline, thereby decreasing the proportion of "direct action" in the movement.

Proactive Actions Following the Victory

Did the victory in 1973 give the pro-choice movement any tactical advantages? There are indications that *Roe* v. *Wade* did in fact lead to some proactive actions by movement actors. The Court decision certainly encouraged the use of litigation as a tool for social change. Legalization also offered movement organizations the opportunity to employ tactics that they had used successfully in the past. As the following account shows, it was not only the victory but also the past experiences of movement actors that enabled them to take advantage of opportunities created by legalization.

After the successful use of the courts to legalize abortion, pro-choice groups aggressively used litigation to implement *Roe* v. *Wade.* NARAL teamed up with the ACLU to file lawsuits against public hospitals to force them to provide abortions (particularly second-trimester abortions) after local activists collected information for NARAL about the lack of such services.[2] In 1975 NARAL decided to send a mailing to public hospitals informing them of the favorable results of these lawsuits and urging them to provide abortions so as to avoid litigation (minutes of NARAL Executive Committee Meeting, April 13, 1975; NARAL of Illinois Records, University of Illinois at Chicago library).

Beyond implementing the Court decision, NARAL supported the establishment of free-standing abortion clinics, as it had in New York in 1970, and made some efforts to ensure that services were of high quality and accessible. NARAL used the expertise of the activists on its medical committee, in cooperation with Planned Parenthood, to provide nationwide seminars on how to set up these clinics. Here, its previous success in New York was important to NARAL's ability to take these proactive actions. The feasibility and safety of free-standing clinics had already been demonstrated in New York, and members of NARAL were knowledgeable and experienced about abortion procedures.[3] Legalization provided another opportunity to use this knowledge and experience.

The most vigorous attempts to maintain an offensive stance after legalization were made by local feminist organizations. As the Chicago Women's Liberation Union declared in response to the Court ruling:

> The Chicago Women's Liberation Union is pleased with Monday's Supreme Court decision on abortion, a decision due in large part to years of work by the women's liberation movement. The decision goes a long way towards recognizing woman's basic right to control her own body. We must now look to the issues involved in implementing the decision here in Illinois. It is not enough to have the qualified right to abortion. We must work to insure that women of all economic levels and races have access to safe, low cost abortions. Doctors must not be given the final word over whether women can have abortions—women themselves should be the ones to make the final decisions about what will happen to their bodies. Free or low cost abortions, in safe and clean local clinics, with sympathetic, supportive, pro-woman counseling services available—this is what we now must work for. (Chicago Women's Liberation Union press release, January 23, 1973; reprinted in *Womankind,* February 1973)

Through an Abortion Task Force (ATF), the CWLU engaged in a series of actions aimed at implementing and extending abortion rights. As a result of their experiences in "Jane" and other women's health projects before 1973, CWLU members had already developed what they considered a successful model of feminist health care. Immediately following *Roe* v. *Wade,* the CWLU's Abortion Task Force drew up a list of guidelines for abortion services with which to pressure abortion providers into adopting feminist standards.

Unlike other pro-choice groups that accepted medical interest groups as allies after legalization, women's liberation groups like the CWLU aggressively targeted their demands at these groups. CWLU activists wrote a skit attacking the medical establishment for failing to make abortions available in Illinois and performed it as "street theater" at the American College of Obstetricians and Gynecologists. This tactic attracted a good deal of desired media attention for the CWLU, and a few days after the "action" ATF representatives met with an official from the College and demanded implementation of the guidelines for abortion services that they had drawn up. Chicago NOW members active on the Abortion Task Force joined CWLU members in a 1973 meeting at the Board of Health (*Act NOW,* June 1973) at which ATF members became disruptive—in front of television cameras—after the Board of Health failed to respond adequately to the ATF's demands. And at an Illinois State Medical Society press conference, Abortion Task Force activists showed up to make their own press statement, with good press coverage. In other instances, ATF activists met privately with hospital and agency officials without engaging in demonstrations (Abortion Task Force Report, circa December 1973; CWLU papers, Chicago Historical Society).

One of the most important and enduring results of the CWLU's Abortion Task Force was the project that became the Health Evaluation and Referral Service (HERS). Following legalization, ATF began collecting information on available services, including second-trimester abortions at hospitals, with which to refer women in need of abortions to appropriate service providers. By withholding referrals to providers that did not meet their standards, Abortion Task Force members attempted to pressure service providers into meeting their guidelines. This project—initially called the Abortion Referral Project—became a subgroup of the Abortion Task Force and was then expanded in the summer of 1973 into the Health Evaluation and Referral Service. HERS, which operated a twenty-four hour abortion referral line, was successful in influencing the prices and standards of abortion clinics. When the Abortion Task Force dissolved in 1974, HERS survived as the major abortion-related activity of the CWLU.

In addition to HERS, the CWLU continued to offer pregnancy testing and in 1974 opened a feminist health center, the Emma Goldman Women's Health Center. In 1975, another health center, the Chicago Women's Health Center, opened at another location, partly in response to internal conflict among activists involved with the Emma Goldman center. In later years, HERS and the two women's health centers helped keep feminists active in the Chicago pro-choice movement. Thus, feminist groups played an important role on the local level in continuing grass-roots activities in the tradition of the pre-1973 abortion referral services.

Interestingly, Illinois Citizens for the Medical Control of Abortion, like the CWLU, also became involved in efforts to establish standards among abortion clinics and to monitor clinics. The difference was that ICMCA did so in order to eliminate potential targets for anti-abortionists rather than to set feminist standards for women's health care. In 1974, ICMCA attempted to investigate a Michigan Avenue abortion clinic that was charging illegal fees to Medicaid patients. Later the same year, in response to revocations of clinic licenses by the Chicago Board of Health, ICMCA was instrumental in setting up the Chicago Abortion Services Council. This was to be an organization of clinics and nonprofit referral agencies that would get together and agree on standards of care. Although neither effort was very successful,[4] the attempt at setting standards is interesting in that it shows that opposition can in some instances lead movement organizations to make proactive demands (in this case, demands for higher standards).[5] More frequently, however, countermovement tactics produce reactive responses from movement actors.

Movement Reactions to Countermovement Actions

As the victors, pro-choice activists at first did not expect to have to spend time reacting to countermovement tactics, but this changed rapidly as pro-choice leaders perceived that the countermovement was making headway in its attempts to overturn *Roe* v. *Wade*. Because countermovement forces took the battle to Congress, movement organizations had to learn how to act in this new arena. As we have seen, pro-choice groups already had some experience working through institutionalized channels, although they were hardly a fixture in the established political world.

There was no organized pro-choice lobby in place in Washington in early 1973, but pro-choice groups did have "inside" connections. NARAL had leaders who were in touch with legislators, and established organizations like Planned Parenthood and multi-issue movement organizations like ZPG had lobbyists who reported on legislative developments and the reactions of elected officials.[6] Through these sources, pro-choice leaders were warned that anti-abortion forces were flooding Congressional offices with mail supporting a constitutional amendment banning abortion. They also kept close track of legislative initiatives in Congress and in the states, including such developments as the passage of state resolutions (in early 1973) asking Congress to pass a constitutional amendment banning abortion and the Senate approval of a bill allowing health care providers to refuse to perform abortions without loss of federal funds. As NARAL reported to its members, this bill passed by a "staggeringly lopsided vote" of ninety-two to one (NARAL "Call to Action," April 5, 1973; NARAL of Illinois Records, University of Illinois at Chicago library).

As a result of these threats from anti-abortion forces, pro-choice organizations felt compelled to take defensive action. Although NARAL had declared a moratorium on debates with the opposition, so as to concentrate on its own initiatives immediately following the Supreme Court ruling, this decision was quickly reversed. Because anti-abortion activists were using the same graphic pictures of fetuses that they had used successfully before legalization, most notably in Michigan, NARAL responded by continuing the defensive strategy it had begun before 1973. A graphic slide show depicting the horrors of illegal abortion was made available for use by national and local activists in media appearances with the opposition (NARAL "Call to Action," April 5, 1973, NARAL of Illinois Records, University of Illinois at Chicago library).

Because the leaders of many pro-choice groups believed in the power of constituent pressure through the traditional means of letter writing, they urged their supporters to write letters of their own when it became clear that, in comparison with the opposition, the pro-choice side was making a poor showing in this area. NARAL also devised an abortion clinic letter-writing project as a strategy for increasing the amount of pro-choice mail to Congress. In this project, NARAL supporters and organizational members in different parts of the country, including Illinois Citizens for the Medical Control of Abortion, were asked to secure the cooperation of clinics in generating mail by requesting women who were having abortions to write letters to Congress in favor of legal abortion while they were recovering from their abortions (NARAL alert to organizational members and supporters, August 17, 1973; NARAL of Illinois Records, University of Illinois at Chicago library).

Even the Chicago Women's Liberation Union, which did not have much faith in such conventional methods of influence, was persuaded by countermovement threats to join in the effort to send letters to Congress. In August 1973, the CWLU newsletter published a warning issued by ICMCA on the need for more letters to Congress from pro-abortion forces to counter the large number of letters from anti-abortionists (*CWLU News,* August 1973). Soon afterwards, the CWLU steering committee proposed that the Union depart from its usual preference for direct-action tactics to help single-issue movement organizations with a letter-writing campaign:

> Since the anti-abortion groups are proceeding largely through conventional pressure group channels—lobbying, letter-writing, etc.—it seems reasonable for us in this instance to expend some amount of energy to organize a counter-letter campaign. The women's movement fought long and hard to win legalized abortion. It would be disastrous, even an insult to all the work that we and our sisters have done, to allow that victory to be taken away because of lack of organization and foresight!

The proposal called for letters to be sent by the CWLU to Illinois Senators and Representatives "demanding that they support the January 22 Supreme Court decision, and work against anti-abortion pressures." Copies of the letters were to be sent to the local news media as well. Individual CWLU members also were asked to send letters to their representatives in Washington and to get friends to do so as well (*CWLU News,* September 18, 1973).

Because of the intensity of anti-abortion efforts following the 1973 Supreme Court ruling, NARAL and other pro-choice organizations also felt compelled to go beyond tactics for generating mail to Congress. One important development was the beginning of an effective pro-choice lobbying coalition in Washington that consisted of both movement organizations and established organizations. NOW, ZPG, Planned Parenthood, RCAR, NARAL and other pro-choice organizations began participating in an informal "information exchange" to facilitate lobbying on the abortion issue.[7] In late 1973, NARAL opened a lobbying office in Washington staffed by two initially part-time lobbyists to create an ongoing NARAL presence on Capitol Hill and to participate more fully in the newly emerging lobbying coalition. By 1975, when NARAL moved its headquarters from New York to Washington, it was clear that institutionalized tactics in defense of legal abortion had become central to the pro-choice movement.

In Illinois, ICMCA/ARA continued its tireless monitoring of the activities of the staunchly anti-abortion Illinois legislature, with ICMCA leaders lobbying legislators and urging supporters to write letters in response to legislative activities. In 1974, ICMCA tried to prevent passage of a resolution by the state legislature memorializing Congress to pass a constitutional amendment banning abortions. After the legislature overwhelmingly passed the resolution, ICMCA doggedly urged supporters to write letters of thanks to the few legislators who voted against the measure (ICMCA newsletter, Summer 1974).

Although these lobbying efforts required extensive resources, pro-choice groups felt obliged to react to other countermovement tactics as well. NARAL even found itself defending the right of "Maude," the lead character in the popular CBS television program, to have an abortion. This occurred after the program became the target of anti-abortion attacks following an episode originally broadcast in November 1972, in which Maude chose to have an abortion (see Montgomery, 1989, for a detailed account). The countermovement, with the Catholic Church's support, successfully pressured sponsors to withdraw their commercial support from the show, causing a number of CBS affiliates to cancel a second episode dealing with Maude's abortion. In 1973, after the conflict resulted in the withdrawal of advertisers from the show when the episodes were rerun, NARAL felt compelled to respond with a picket and a boycott of the corporate sponsors of "Maude." As Lawrence Lader wrote to NARAL supporters in an action alert:

> With all our priorities in Congress, NARAL hesitated to launch a counter-attack until it became obvious that the official Catholic Church was determined to show that it could bend the media to its will, and at the same time, impress Congress with its power. Then NARAL Executive Director Roxanne Olivo and the small staff performed superbly in pulling together a coalition in a few days and organizing a picket line along with our old allies, ZPG, NOW, and other feminist, religious and population groups. We decided that the seven business corporations cancelling their sponsorship were equal partners in crime with the Catholic hierarchy in trying to destroy the freedom of the media, and that we had to meet force with force—to declare a boycott of all products of those seven corporations, announced at the picket line in front of the American Homes Products building on August 17. (August 17, 1973, NARAL memo to local organizational members and supporters; NARAL of Illinois Records, University of Illinois at Chicago library)

ICMCA participated in the NARAL boycott of "Maude" sponsors as well as in other direct-action tactics to counter anti-abortion activities. ICMCA was able to monitor rather easily the activities of anti-abortion movement organizations because of the propensity of local anti-abortion groups to use telephone "hot lines" to broadcast their strategies to callers.[8] Although it was not considered possible or worthwhile to respond to all countermovement activities, in a number of cases appropriate actions were taken. For example, if a hospital were to be picketed by anti-abortionists, ICMCA/ARA typically notified the hospital and, if supporters were available in the area, sometimes organized a counterpicket. Targets of anti-abortion letter-writing campaigns, such as magazines that had published articles favorable to the pro-choice movement, were informed that the anti-abortion effort was an organized one. And when the anti-abortionists boycotted the Upjohn Corporation for manufacturing an abortifacient, ICMCA urged its members to counteract the boycott by making a point of buying Upjohn products!

Quite a bit of pro-choice energy was thus used in reacting to countermovement tactics. Although pro-choice activists, particularly local feminist groups, did engage in some proactive tactics following the legalization of abortion, countermovement activities created overwhelming pressures to respond with defensive tactics. In this way, the countermovement destroyed some of the advantages of victory by competing with the movement for legitimacy with authorities. Because the battles were increasingly fought in institutionalized arenas, however, the countermovement also forced the pro-choice movement to develop organizational structures that would enable it to become more politically established.

Organizational Influences on
Collective Action

Pro-choice strategies and tactics in the period following *Roe* v. *Wade* were constrained not only by countermovement activities but also by characteristics of the movement itself. That is, the resources and structures of pro-choice movement organizations affected their ability to take the offensive after the 1973 victory and to react to countermovement initiatives. Changes in the organizational composition of the pro-choice movement thus led to changes in collective action. By the mid-1970s, some movement organizations with informal structures declined while others began to formalize their structures and professionalize their leadership. The trends toward formalization and professionalization, which accelerated in the late 1970s and 1980s, furthered the tendency toward institutionalized actions in support of *Roe* v. *Wade*.

The Chicago Women's Liberation Union, like many younger branch women's movement organizations, had a decentralized and informal structure (see Appendix A). This structure facilitated participation in direct-action tactics because it enabled activists to respond quickly to opportunities for protest.[9] It also led to a fair amount of innovation in tactics because the Union's work groups operated autonomously and were very inclusive with regard to membership. Within the work groups, interested individuals and subgroups with different ideological concerns were free to initiate a variety of tactics. However, the CWLU's structure reduced the staying power of its programs, as there frequently were not enough activists and other resources to support the many strategies initiated. The structures of the CWLU and other women's liberation groups also contributed to their demise because they made resource mobilization difficult and because their inclusiveness made possible infiltration by sectarian groups (see Appendix A; Freeman, 1975; Staggenborg 1989b). Consequently, there was a decline in participation in the pro-choice movement by organizations that were ideologically and structurally oriented toward direct action.

The willingness of the CWLU to initiate a number of tactics and the problems in doing so are evident in the post-1973 activities of its Abortion Task Force. As a result of political differences among women in the ATF, two subgroups formed to work on two different strategies. One group of women in the ATF began working to pressure "the Establishment" to comply with feminist guidelines on abortion services and ended up developing the Health Evaluation and Referral Service.[10] Another group of participants was more interested in organizing poor and working-class women around health issues, including abortion. Consequently, the second group began to research communities in Chicago and selected one, Lakeview, in which to begin a community-organizing campaign. The idea was to involve community organizations in efforts to pressure area hospitals and other health agencies to offer abortion and other health services. Beginning with one community, the activists hoped eventually to organize women's health groups in a number of Chicago communities. Although some efforts were made in Lakeview, the far-reaching goals of the organizing plan were never achieved because of the lack of resources for this type of work (CWLU working papers in Jennifer Knauss private papers). The Union's decentralized structure, which allowed multiple projects to flourish, no doubt contributed to the lack of resources for the community-organizing project.

Other movement organizations were also limited in their attempts to counter anti-abortion actions by their lack of appropriate resources and organizational structures. In contrast with local women's liberation groups like the CWLU, however, some of these organizations, particularly national groups like NARAL, began to make changes in the direction of greater professionalization of leadership and formalization of structure. They did so in order to make greater use of institutionalized lobbying tactics, but these organizational changes also had the effect of facilitating organizational maintenance.[11]

The influence of organizational structures and resources can be seen in NARAL's attempts to generate mail to Congress. Its clinic letter-writing program was not a huge success,[12] but the early use of this tactic reflected the backgrounds and experiences of NARAL activists. The project was the idea of a NARAL executive committee member who had been active in the Clergy Consultation Service and who operated a nonprofit abortion clinic. Knowing that women have to rest for a period of time following their abortions, he tested the letter-writing idea in his clinic before NARAL adopted the strategy. It was not until NARAL gained access to different types of skills that an alternative strategy for generating letters was devised. This occurred in 1974 when Beatrice Blair, who had experience in using direct mail to recruit individual members, was hired as executive director. She began to build the NARAL membership, which had previously consisted largely of organizations rather than individuals, by using mailing lists from sources such as *Ms.* magazine. Once the individual membership began to climb (from about two thousand in 1974 to about ten thousand by the end of 1975) as a result of the direct-mail tactic, it was possible to generate letters to Congress by sending alerts to the membership (interview with Beatrice Blair, 1984).

Pro-choice groups also struggled to make their resources cover the tasks of lobbying Congress and the state legislatures and in doing so began to make some organizational changes. To combat restrictive state legislation and to prevent state-level approval of a Human Life Amendment, NARAL moved to develop state affiliates.[13] The Religious Coalition for Abortion Rights followed suit in creating state affiliates, intensifying these activities as the Catholic Church increased its activities in the countermovement.[14]

The National Organization for Women also moved to tighten its ties with local chapters in order to defend abortion rights. Because NOW had only a very small staff in Washington in 1973, the organization's tactics for influencing Congress depended in large part on support from local chapters and members, NOW's most plentiful resource. Although at this point in its history NOW was still struggling to establish adequate channels of communication between its national and local units (cf. Freeman, 1975), the national newsletter did provide a continuing means of obtaining local support.[15] By 1974, regular coordination between the NOW office and local chapters and task forces was established through the use of Legislative Alerts, phone calls, and a "Right-to-Choose Kit" containing information and strategy instructions that was updated as needed.

Because of the small size of its Washington staff in the period following the legalization of abortion, NOW's strategy for influencing Congress relied on local volunteers who participated in the organization's Congressional District–District of Columbia Program, which was created in 1974. In this program, known as the CD–DC Program, volunteers from NOW chapters in areas around Washington worked with the NOW Legislative Office to set up volunteer teams that then visited Congressional offices to lobby for abortion rights as the authorized representatives of NOW chapters in other parts of the country (*Do It NOW,* March 1974). In this way, NOW was able to compensate for its lack of professional lobbying staff with the asset that it did have, volunteers. In the mid- to late-1970s, NOW began to develop a much more formalized national organizational structure and to rely more on paid staff (see Appendix A).

It was primarily the national pro-choice organizations that made changes in their organizational structures in the period immediately following the legalization of abortion as Congress became the principal battleground in the abortion conflict. In Illinois, most pro-choice groups did not develop formalized structures that would aid in organizational maintenance and the performance of institutionalized tactics in the 1973–76 period. ICMCA/ARA relied on its executive director, Helen Smith, rather than on a more formalized division of labor, to keep track of threats to abortion rights in the Illinois legislature. When emergencies arose, Smith and other leaders had to organize supporters, who did tend to turn their attention elsewhere after the Court ruling.[16] Fortunately (or unfortunately) for the leaders, the Illinois legislature was sufficiently hostile to be of help in the mobilization process. For example, in 1975, while the Illinois legislature was in the process of passing a highly restrictive anti-abortion bill, known as the "Kelly bill," over the veto of the governor of Illinois, Smith reported that there was more cooperation from members in ARA's lobbying efforts "now that they realize how close HB 1851 [Kelly bill] is to becoming law" (minutes of November 13, 1975, ARA board meeting; NARAL of Illinois Records, University of Illinois at Chicago library).

Other local movement organizations also struggled along in the post-1973 period. After its formation in 1975, Illinois RCAR (IRCAR) tried to assist the Abortion Rights Association in its lobbying work, but had trouble doing so because of its small size. The organization did respond to crises in the state legislature by calling on members of its Policy Council to testify at hearings and by alerting church and synagogue members to write letters and make phone calls to their legislators. IRCAR leaders would like to have created a formal state alert system to aid these efforts, but they were unable to do so. This was because it was difficult for IRCAR to keep its constituents continually involved in the pro-choice cause given their commitments to other social issues. Moreover, IRCAR was not well organized outside of the Chicago area as a consequence of the size of the state and the expense involved in bringing people together.[17]

RCAR and its affiliates were able to assist the pro-choice movement with public education tactics because the religious organization did have access to clergy members who were willing to be visible proponents of the pro-choice position when needed. However, Illinois RCAR was somewhat hampered here for the same reason that it had difficulty with lobbying work: Heavy involvement in a range of social causes limited the time of its volunteer leaders as well as that of activists in the denominations that joined the religious coalition. Consequently, it was difficult to organize aggressive educational programs such as a speaker's bureau. Instead of actively seeking out speaking engagements, therefore, IRCAR would find someone to fill an engagement when asked to do so, typically through referrals from organizations like Planned Parenthood. Illinois RCAR's educational tactics consisted mainly of a newsletter, some speaking engagements, and occasional "events" such as a prayer service on the January 22 anniversary of the *Roe* v. *Wade* decision. Attempts were sometimes made to write "letters to the editor" and to stimulate media coverage through press releases but, according to one activist interviewed, these attempts were "usually ignored" by the media. IRCAR did not have persons with strong public relations backgrounds (as did ICMCA/ARA) and did not have the staff or resources to develop connections with media sources.

The tactics of other movement organizations also were limited, by either their organizational structures or their attention to competing issues after legalization. As noted above, ZPG staff members in Washington contributed to Congressional lobbying efforts, but because ZPG chapters operated in a completely autonomous manner, the national organization could only suggest activities rather than implement programs at the local level. And although local affiliates had been quite active on the abortion issue before 1973, many, including Chicago-area ZPG, were floundering in the post-1973 period, in part because they had never developed the kinds of formalized structures that aid organizational maintenance.

Chicago NOW was also limited in the tactics that it could employ as a result of the chapter's decision to select fewer issue priorities in order to conserve resources (see Staggenborg, 1989b; Appendix A). Consequently, Chicago NOW's contribution to legislative lobbying after 1973 consisted largely of keeping its members informed of developments and urging them to write letters to oppose state and national anti-abortion bills. And this was done exclusively through the chapter newsletter rather than through the more organized methods that would be employed in the post-1976 period of the abortion conflict.

Conclusion

The history of the pro-choice movement in the period after 1973 reveals the ways in which social movements change following important outcomes such as *Roe* v. *Wade*. Just as the political opportunity structure changes as a protest cycle progresses, so does the political environment of a movement following important outcomes—including both victories and defeats—which typically occur over the course of a social movement (cf. Snyder and Kelly, 1979).

One of the lessons of the pro-choice experience regarding the effects of a major victory on a movement's fortunes is that the activities of its participants before the victory do matter. The 1973 Supreme Court decision created opportunities for proactive tactics, but in order to take advantage of those opportunities activists had to draw on skills learned in past actions. Thus, previous involvement in "Jane" aided CWLU activists in demanding feminist standards of service delivery, and the experiences of NARAL activists in New York helped them push for accessible abortion clinics after legalization. There were also opportunities to move closer to the political "inside" after the Court victory by joining forces with established organizations in institutionalized actions; again, the ability to do so depended on the past experiences and connections of many pro-choice activists.

Although victory may create certain tactical opportunities for a movement, the effects of the victory on its opponents have to be taken into account in assessing the advantages of success. Movement victories help mobilize countermovements and provide tactical opportunities to the opposition that constrain movement activities. Although in some instances countermovement threats may lead to proactive responses from the movement, reactive tactics in response to countermovement initiatives are more likely, as was the case for the pro-choice movement in the post-1973 period. Insofar as countermovement actors take the lead in initiating tactics, they also choose the battlefields on which the conflict takes place; after 1973, when the countermovement engaged in institutionalized actions, movement organizations were forced to try to follow suit.

The tactical choices of movements in the wake of a victory are also limited by their own organizational structures and resources. The decentralized structures of women's liberation groups like the CWLU aided the development of innovative tactics, but the dispersal of resources that resulted from this decentralization constrained their ability to engage in proactive collective action. The ability of pro-choice groups like NARAL to react to countermovement actions was limited by the fact that they did not yet have the organizational capacity to mobilize the resources needed for the new battlegrounds of the abortion conflict after *Roe* v. *Wade*. However, such countermovement attacks can provide an incentive for a movement's organizational development. The need to respond to countermovement initiatives forced national organizations like NARAL to begin creating organizational structures that would enable them to become players in institutionalized arenas. Countermovement attacks also led to the beginnings of a Washington lobbying coalition among pro-choice organizations.

The years between 1973 and 1977 can thus be viewed as a transitional period of the abortion conflict in which movement tactics became increasingly institutionalized as movement organizations began to establish themselves as political insiders. Women's liberation groups inclined to remain on the political "outside" and to press for more advantages were declining organizationally. Other pro-choice groups began after 1973 to build the structures needed to employ institutionalized tactics for a long-term battle with the anti-abortion countermovement, but, paradoxically, it was not until after the countermovement scored its first major victory that the movement made its most impressive advances toward the status of political "insider."

III

COUNTERMOVEMENT VICTORIES AND MOVEMENT EXPANSION, 1977–1983

7

Organizational Expansion and Transformation

The legalization of abortion in 1973 was a movement victory that fueled a growing countermovement and forced pro-choice organizations to defend abortion rights in new arenas. Had the anti-abortion movement failed to make any progress in the following years, it is doubtful that the pro-choice movement could have survived; threats to abortion rights proved to be critical to keeping the movement alive. But the countermovement won its first major victory in 1976 with Congressional passage of the Hyde Amendment banning federal funding of abortions. With this first important defeat, the pro-choice movement came to a second critical juncture.[1] Paradoxically, the anti-abortion victory on government funding of abortions, together with other threatening events in the post-Hyde period (e.g., the election of anti-abortion President Ronald Reagan), was a boon to the pro-choice movement. As pro-choice adherents became alerted to the threats to abortion rights, more resources became available, and an increasingly professional pro-choice movement became adept at mobilizing these resources.

New Threats to Abortion Rights

Following the victory on the Hyde Amendment in 1976, the anti-abortion movement underwent a second period of organizational expansion (the first having occurred after 1973). The partial victory, together with publicity gained during the 1976 election year,[2] reinvigorated the countermovement. New anti-abortion organizations, including single-issue political action committees, were formed, and new constituents, notably fundamentalist Christians and political conservatives, were attracted to the countermovement.[3]

Not only were countermovement forces visibly expanding, but other anti-abortion successes also followed passage of the Hyde Amendment. Most devastating to pro-choice groups were the first major anti-abortion victories in the courts. In the years immediately following *Roe* v. *Wade,* pro-choice forces had successfully used the courts to overturn restrictions imposed by state and local legislatures and to force hospitals to provide abortions.[4] In June 1977, however, pro-choice faith in the courts was shattered by the Supreme Court ruling that permitted state abortion funding bans.[5] In June 1980, yet another blow to the pro-choice movement was delivered by the Supreme Court when it decided *Harris* v. *McRae,* a class-action suit challenging the constitutionality of the Hyde Amendment. With this ruling, the Supreme Court settled the Medicaid funding issue as far as the courts were concerned by overturning the ruling of New York District Court Judge John F. Dooling that had declared the Hyde Amendment unconstitutional (see Rubin, 1987:171–74).[6]

The great majority of states responded to the 1977 Supreme Court rulings by refusing to fund all but therapeutic abortions (Tatalovich and Daynes, 1981:203). In Illinois, the state legislature passed a ban on state funding of abortions over the governor's veto. Like other states, the Illinois General Assembly also continued to consider, and sometimes pass, additional restrictive legislation, including parental consent requirements for minors in 1977.

In local communities, there were conflicts over the opening of abortion clinics (see Ginsburg, 1989), and city governments passed restrictive regulations on abortions through such means as zoning ordinances. The city of Akron, Ohio, passed one of the strictest of these ordinances in 1978, requiring, among other restrictions, a waiting period, parental consent for minors, and a lecture on the developmental state of the fetus to be given to the woman by her physician. In the late 1970s, other local governments passed similar ordinances modeled on the Akron law, and some emboldened local governmental agencies acted to close down public abortion facilities. In Chicago, the Cook County Hospital abortion clinic, which served poor women in the area, was closed in 1980 by order of the president of the Cook County Board of Commissioners. Although most of the Akron-style restrictions were struck down by the Supreme Court in a 1983 ruling (see Rubin, 1987:139–44), the laws, together with the closing of public facilities like the Cook County clinic, were real threats to abortion rights in the post-Hyde period.

Anti-abortion forces were also threatening in the political arena. In 1976, countermovement forces had succeeded in getting the Republican Party to include a qualified anti-abortion plank in its party platform (although the Democratic Party continued to support the pro-choice position).[7] After the 1976 election, anti-abortion forces increased their political activities and in 1978 claimed credit for the highly publicized defeats of several pro-choice supporters, including Iowa Senator Dick Clark (see Vinovskis, 1980). By 1979, single-issue anti-abortionists were joining forces with the New Right to produce a "hit list" of pro-choice supporters targeted for defeat, including Senators George McGovern and Birch Bayh (Sarat, 1982:141). Perhaps because anti-abortion forces received more credit from the media than they deserved for their influence in the 1978 elections (Traugott and Vinovskis, 1980), they were taken very seriously in 1980. Whereas the Democratic Party platform contained a pro-choice plank, the Republicans took a firm position in favor of a constitutional amendment banning abortion, a plank strongly supported by candidate Reagan.

Anti-abortion threats in the post-Hyde period climaxed with the election of anti-abortion President Reagan (and a Republican majority in the Senate) in 1980. Following his election, anti-abortion forces had high hopes, and pro-choice groups strong fears, that Congress would favor a ban on abortion. Moreover, anti-abortionists in Congress came up with a new strategy: a "Human Life Bill" that would circumvent the long process of passing a constitutional amendment to outlaw abortion by having Congress vote that human life begins at conception and that the national legislature has the right to protect that life by outlawing abortions (see *New York Times,* March 13, 1981).

By 1982, the period of extraordinary threat by anti-abortion forces, which began with the passage of the Hyde Amendment in 1976, was showing signs of decline. In the 1982 elections, the anti-abortion movement had little success in defeating pro-choice candidates. In Congress, the Human Life Bill, which was being pushed by North Carolina Senator Jesse Helms and Illinois Representative Henry Hyde, turned out to be a divisive strategy for anti-abortion forces. Because of questions about the bill's constitutionality, other Congressional abortion foes continued to favor various constitutional amendments.[8] In September 1982, in response to this division, the Senate delivered to anti-abortion forces a well-publicized blow by voting to table both Helms's legislation and an anti-abortion amendment. In 1983, anti-abortion legislation was again defeated in Congress, and the Supreme Court struck down most of the restrictions on abortions that had been passed by state and local governments. These defeats spelled the end of a period of highly visible threats to abortion rights, but the actions of counter-movement forces before the events of 1982 and 1983 produced an unprecedented mobilization of pro-choice forces.

Pro-Choice Growth and Development

As the anti-abortion countermovement became more heterogeneous and active in new arenas, so did the pro-choice movement. In response to the countermovement's successes, new pro-choice organizations were formed to attract a broader assortment of constituents, and existing organizations took advantage of the concerns raised among pro-choice supporters to increase their resources and expand their operations. The movement was in a position to respond to renewed concerns about abortion rights in the post-Hyde period because it had not demobilized after 1973 (although there were differences in national and local preparedness). Both the environment of threat and internal organizational factors were important to the expansion of the pro-choice movement in the late 1970s and early 1980s.

National-Level Expansion

On the national level, the pro-choice movement was in relatively good shape at the time that the Hyde Amendment crisis hit. Because the primary battle over legal abortion had shifted to Congress after legalization, the major pro-choice groups had established headquarters in Washington and were working together to lobby Congress. After passage of the Hyde Amendment through Congress for the first time in 1976, coalition work intensified among stunned pro-choice organizations. The informal "information exchange" was formalized as the Abortion

Information Exchange and greatly expanded.[9] Participation by established organizations and interest groups, which first became significant after legalization, was further increased as the variety of organizations belonging to the Exchange was expanded to include medical organizations, professional associations, labor unions, and environmental groups in addition to pro-choice movement organizations. NARAL was by this time in a position to play a leadership role in coordinating pro-choice coalition work. As former NARAL director Karen Mulhauser recalled in a 1984 interview:

> I guess it was in about the mid-1970s, or the last half of the 1970s, that it really became clear, through our membership growth, through our budget, through the kinds of information that we were able to distribute, and through our organizing on the local level, that we were the biggest single-issue group, so, more and more, media and legislators and other groups were turning to us for leadership. But . . . we were able to play that role once others were asking us to—we didn't impose it on them.

The resources conserved through coalition work on Congressional lobbying enabled pro-choice organizations to step up their efforts to protect abortion rights in other arenas. In response to political activities by the countermovement, pro-choice groups began to gather the resources necessary to participate in electoral politics. In 1977 NARAL created an affiliated political action committee, NARAL–PAC, and both NARAL and RCAR were able to raise more money and to expand the number of their local affiliates. Because of anti-abortion threats, pro-choice leaders found their constituents receptive to calls for support,[10] as RCAR's national director reported in 1978:

> I feel lousy about what's happening in the issue, but I feel great about what's happening in RCAR. With the escalation of anti-abortion efforts at the national, state, local and even precinct level, and in light of significant losses on the legislative front, one can hardly be encouraged by the current status of abortion rights in this country. But concomitant with, and undoubtedly because of, this unhappy state of affairs, we are experiencing an unprecedented upsurge of concern and activity on the part of the pro-choice religious community. (*Options,* November–December 1978)

New single-issue pro-choice organizations were also formed on the national level in the post-Hyde period. These included an organization of clinics and other service providers, the National Abortion Federation—which was formed in 1977 with the encouragement of NARAL (interview with former NARAL director Karen Mulhauser, 1984; and Encyclopedia of Associations, 1985). Also included were two independent, single-issue political action committees (PACs)—Friends of Family Planning (FFP) and Voters for Choice (VC)—which were founded in the late 1970s to counter anti-abortion PAC activities.[11]

Although some multi-issue movement organizations, notably ZPG, became less active in the pro-choice movement in the late 1970s, other multi-issue organizations joined the movement.[12] Most important were "reproductive rights" organizations that attracted feminists who disdained the single-issue approach of many pro-choice groups but who were similarly alarmed by new threats to abortion rights (cf. Clarke and Wolfson, 1985). These included two nationally known organizations: the Committee for Abortion Rights and Against Sterilization Abuse (CARASA), which was created in August 1977 in response to the Supreme Court ruling upholding state abortion-funding bans, and the Reproductive Rights National Network (known as R2N2), which was formed in 1978 in response to right-wing activities.[13]

Illinois

In contrast with movement developments on the national level, the pro-choice movement in Illinois was in a state of collapse at the beginning of the post-Hyde period of the abortion conflict. The Abortion Rights Association of Illinois, which had begun to decline with a change of leadership in 1976, had all but dissolved by 1977. Chicago ZPG experienced a brief and very limited revival beginning in 1977, and some of its members, who were also active in ARA, were pro-choice activists, but the organization itself was not in a position to contribute anything to the pro-choice movement beyond the use of its name. At this point, Chicago NOW was almost totally absorbed by the ERA struggle. The Chicago Women's Liberation Union formally disbanded in the spring of 1977, after several years of internal conflict. An exclusive study group was formed, however, by some former CWLU members and other women's health activists, and this new group eventually became the Chicago Women's Health Task Force (CWHTF). Illinois RCAR was active but, as a small organization, was unable to assume a leadership role in the pro-choice movement.

The movement in Illinois was kept alive, however, by the urgency of the abortion issue. Following passage of the Hyde Amendment, the Supreme Court was expected to rule on the issue of state funding in June 1977. The Illinois General Assembly had already passed a number of restrictive abortion bills and was moving to pass a bill cutting off state funds for Medicaid abortions, along with another bill to impose a parental consent requirement on minors. The legislative threats, particularly the state-funding cutoff (Illinois House Bill 333, as my informants recalled vividly), renewed interest in the abortion issue among many pro-choice supporters.

Despite a decline in local social movement organizations, other forms of organization aided mobilization efforts during this period of crisis (cf. Killian, 1984). Pro-choice activists were still tied together through social networks and through their participation in the service organizations that served as local movement centers.[14] One individual, Jean Robinson, who had been active in both ARA and Planned Parenthood, was employed at the time by the Midwest Population Center. This nonprofit birth control clinic, which had been founded in 1970 by ZPG and ICMCA activists, had long been a center of movement activity that provided office space as well as other support to ICMCA/ARA/NARAL of Illinois. Robinson and other staff at the clinic began to contact people about starting a coalition to fight the anti-abortion legislation that was continually being introduced in the Illinois General Assembly. Representatives from a variety of organizations, including the Midwest Population Center, the Abortion Rights Association,

Planned Parenthood, the ACLU, and several local chapters of NOW, were brought together for an initial meeting in late May 1977 (document in Jean Robinson private papers).

Feminists also remained connected to one another through social networks and alternative institutions that maintained the women's health movement in Chicago despite the demise of the Chicago Women's Liberation Union. While pro-choice activists with backgrounds in the population and family-planning movements were working through the Midwest Population Center, former CWLU members concerned about women's health care were working on various issues with activists from two feminist movement centers, the Health Evaluation and Referral Service and the Chicago Women's Health Center.[15] They were, of course, concerned about the current threats to abortion, particularly the cuts in Medicaid funding, because this was an issue of access to the health care system that provided an excellent opportunity for socialist–feminists to, as one informant put it, "deal with class and abortion together." It happened that the news about passage of HB333 by the Illinois Senate broke on the very day that a party had been planned for the purpose of raising money to pay off the debts of the Chicago Women's Liberation Union. As Jenny Knauss, a former CWLU member and participant in the Chicago Women's Health Task Force, remembered in a 1983 interview:

> That morning, the news about HB333 came out. I xeroxed something about it on a piece of paper, and we passed them around at this party which was really big because people had wanted to help with the Union [debt]. And we said, "Listen, we've got to do something about HB333," and from that, within a week, we organized a demonstration at the State of Illinois Building which was actually very successful.

The demonstration was attended by some of the people connected to other organizations who were trying to get a coalition together, and at the demonstration someone from the Midwest Population Center made an announcement about a meeting to form a coalition. The organizers of the event, unaware that an effort at forming a coalition was already under way, were taken aback at the announcement and were more than a little concerned that the funding issue, which they saw as *their* issue, was being stolen by groups of a different ideological persuasion. However, the group of women calling themselves the Chicago Women's Health Task Force recognized that there was a real urgency to the issue and that their organization was not able to fight the battle alone, so they attended the coalition meeting held at the Midwest Population Center. As a result, a loosely knit coalition group, called the Ad Hoc Committee for Abortion Rights, was formed in June 1977.

The Ad Hoc Committee played an important role in keeping alive the local pro-choice movement during a crucial period when none of the major pro-choice groups was in a strong enough organizational position to provide leadership to the movement (with the exception of Chicago NOW which was busy with the ERA campaign). The coalition group was most active during the summer of 1977 when participants mobilized support for various activities in opposition to HB333 (see Staggenborg, 1986, for further discussion of the coalition effort). After the summer of 1977 there was no longer the strong focus provided by HB333 to hold the coalition together, and it became less active, formally dissolving in 1978.

The local movement, however, did not decline after the coalition group fizzled out. The Abortion Rights Association, which became NARAL of Illinois in 1978, was revived by a new director and became, along with Illinois RCAR, Planned Parenthood, and the ACLU, highly active in lobbying for abortion rights. In 1979, another coalition organization, the Illinois Pro-Choice Alliance, was formed. The Chicago Women's Health Task Force also remained active, although not exclusively on the abortion issue, until it disbanded after the formation of a local reproductive rights group, Women Organized for Reproductive Choice, in 1979. Chicago NOW also increased its involvement in the pro-choice movement in 1979, making abortion a chapter priority issue for the first time since 1973.[16]

An independent political action committee called Personal PAC was also founded in Illinois in 1980 to respond to anti-abortion political activities. Its founder, Marcie Love, was a longtime pro-choice movement leader active in Planned Parenthood, ICMCA/ARA/NARAL, and Illinois RCAR. Before forming Personal PAC in order to raise money for pro-choice candidates in Illinois, Love investigated the possibility that NARAL of Illinois might form an affiliated PAC for this purpose. It was only after NARAL decided that this was not feasible and after the countermovement threat became acute that Personal PAC was founded.[17] As Love recalled when asked about her motivations for forming Personal PAC:

> I had been waiting for someone else to do it, but it became clear that no one else would, so I started this in 1980 because there was so much need for it in that election year. You know, you talk to legislators and they say, "Yes, I'm pro-choice, but what are you going to do for me in this election?" I have always been very much against single-issue PACs, but the horror of what was happening in 1980 with the New Right and their PACs made me realize it was necessary. (interview with Marcie Love, 1984)

Professionalization and Formalization of Pro-Choice Movement Organizations

Countermovement threats galvanized both national and local pro-choice organizations. Important internal organizational changes were also occurring in the movement in this period of the abortion conflict as many pro-choice organizations became more professionalized in their leadership and formalized in their structures. As a result, they were better able to obtain the resources necessary to act in institutionalized arenas. Reproductive rights organizations, which attempted to rely on volunteer leadership and informal organizational structures, were the major exception to this trend.

NARAL

In order to counter anti-abortion activities, NARAL needed to find additional resources, including both money and active participants. The trend toward professionalization of leadership and formalization of structure that began in NARAL after 1973, together with the threatening political environment of the post-Hyde period, enabled the organization to greatly expand its resources. And its increased resources allowed NARAL to hire more professional leaders who created an even more formalized or bureaucratic organization in which staff members took responsibility for more differentiated functions such as public relations work, lobbying, and political campaign work.

One of the most important developments was the use of sophisticated direct-mail techniques for raising money. In order to attract members and contributions, NARAL had begun a direct-mail campaign in 1974 that, although a modest operation implemented by a small staff, had stabilized the organization financially. In 1977, after forming an affiliated political action committee (PAC), NARAL embarked on a more professional direct-mail program. The decision was made to form an affiliated PAC, which is limited to raising money from an organization's members, rather than an independent PAC, which can raise money from the public at large. This decision cut administrative costs and allowed NARAL to use its nonprofit bulk mail rate in raising money. But the choice "only made sense," according to former NARAL director Karen Mulhauser, "if we were also increasing our membership through direct mail and through local organizing" (interview with Karen Mulhauser, 1984). Consequently, NARAL began to expand its recruitment efforts by hiring a professional direct-mail firm as well as by using local organizing tactics.

NARAL's direct-mail drive was a resounding success that greatly increased the organization's membership and financial resources. The movement's political environment no doubt contributed to the success of the direct-mail drive: Constituents mailed their checks in record numbers in response to visible threats to abortion rights in the post-Hyde period. But it was also important that NARAL employed professional know-how to implement the drive. In contrast, the Reproductive Rights National Network (R2N2) received a donation of money to undertake a direct-mail campaign during this period, but its attempt to raise money and recruit members in this manner was unsuccessful because R2N2's tiny staff did not have the experience to carry out the program correctly and no one else was around to take responsibility (interview with former R2N2 coordinator Margie Fine, 1984).[18]

The influx of resources allowed NARAL to expand and formalize its ties to local activists. NARAL's attempts to strengthen its ties with state groups began after 1973, but it was not until the post-Hyde period that the organization had the resources to aggressively recruit state affiliates. At that time, a formal process for affiliation was instituted, and more professional staff were hired to organize affiliates. NARAL initially recruited affiliates by offering training for local leaders and such resources as information on national legislative developments, low-cost professionally produced NARAL literature, "how-to" manuals, and audiovisual aids.

The national organization soon began to offer financial aid as well, which made affiliates more accountable and allowed the national organization to exert more control in implementing its strategies on the state and local levels.

NARAL's increased resources, together with its strengthened ties to local affiliates, also led to changes in the structure of NARAL's board of directors. As a result of the emphasis on grass-roots organizing, activists pushed to increase the involvement of the board of directors in running the organization. When the size of the board was reduced from ninety to thirty members to make it a working board, the greater financial resources made it possible for NARAL to pay travel expenses so that board members could attend at least four meetings per year. Moreover, terms on both the board and the executive committee began to be rotated systematically so that a larger number of NARAL activists could be brought into the decision-making process.

At the same time that these structural changes were made to enable the greater involvement of volunteer board members, NARAL was also expanding its professional staff, and NARAL's full-time paid executive director became more central to the organization. Although there was at first some conflict between the executive director and the board as NARAL adjusted to its new status as a large, professionalized movement organization,[19] a division of labor was gradually established, and the professional staff continued to maintain and expand the organization.

ARA/NARAL of Illinois

The Abortion Rights Association did not begin the post-Hyde period with the same organizational advantages as did the national NARAL organization. ARA had not created a formal division of labor and did not have a full-time professional staff to ensure ongoing maintenance. After its highly competent director, Helen Smith, resigned in 1976, the organization went into a severe decline under the leadership of a less competent part-time director.[20] It was not until October 1977 that the ARA board finally realized the seriousness of the situation and asked the executive director for her resignation.

Shaken by the reality of ARA's organizational situation, the board at last gave some thought to the role of the executive director. As one board member noted in a memo to the other board members, the problem with the director who was asked to resign was that she did not perform basic tasks like keeping lists of legislators and an up-to-date mailing list. But the problem with Helen Smith was that she had kept everything "in HER head" (document in Jean Robinson private papers). The ARA board decided that it needed to hire someone who was experienced as both an administrator and an organizer in order to get the organization back on its feet.

The board made a lucky choice in hiring Cindy Little, then a history Ph.D. student, who turned out to have strong organizational skills. Little stayed with the organization for two and a half years, during which time she succeeded in organizing and reactivating chapters throughout the state, rebuilding the membership of the organization, and stabilizing it financially. One of the reasons that the new executive director was able to revive ARA was the organization's decision in 1978 to become a local affiliate of NARAL.

Previously, ICMCA/ARA had been an organizational "member" of NARAL, with ICMCA activists having played a key role in organizing NARAL. Close contact with NARAL was maintained until the Abortion Rights Association began to decline around 1976. As Cindy Little explained in an interview about the decision to become a NARAL affiliate:

> Luckily at the time national NARAL was getting its act together and trying to make contacts with people in the states to organize state affiliates. I got a call from them one day—luckily I was there because I only worked part time—saying they were trying to set up state affiliates and that they knew there was an organization here, that at one time there had been a lot of contact between the local group and national NARAL. . . . Anyway, they said they'd pay my way to fly out to Washington; they were trying to get people in organizations in different states they had contacts with and individuals from other states to come and talk about affiliating with NARAL. Well, when they said, "We'll pay your way," that sounded good to me, so I went. Affiliating with NARAL was beneficial at that time because they were offering training for me as executive director and updated information on what was going on nationally. . . . We also got a bunch of literature free initially, then later more at cost. That was important because you have to have something to give out, and I always thought that NARAL had very high-quality literature. Also, they gave us booklets on how to do this and that, which were really very helpful.

Shortly after affiliation, the Abortion Rights Association of Illinois changed its name to NARAL of Illinois to reflect its new status.[21]

Not only did affiliation help stabilize NARAL of Illinois, but its new director, Cindy Little, was highly motivated to find a stable source of financial resources for the organization. Although she was not making a career out of movement work, Little did need the money from the job because, unlike her predecessors, she did not have a husband who made enough money to support her while she volunteered her time. And, unlike previous directors, Little did not intend to work as a volunteer when there was not enough money to pay her salary (about $11,000 a year for part-time work). Consequently, she set about trying to figure out how to bring a stable income to the organization.

Little knew that in the past some of the abortion clinics had contributed small amounts of money, and she also heard through her participation in national NARAL that other local affiliates in different parts of the country received some income from clinic contributions. She decided to pursue this strategy and was successful in doing so, in part because she established a personal friendship with Sheri Walker, an owner of the Concord Medical Center, one of the largest (and reputedly one of the best) abortion clinics in Chicago. Because the clinic owner was impressed by the abilities of the NARAL director and liked her personally, and because she herself had been active in organizations such as Planned Parenthood and ZPG, she agreed to make a monthly contribution to NARAL of Illinois (initially $100 a month, later $250 a month, and at one point as much as $400 a month). Little subsequently made contacts with the owners of other major clinics and was able to convince three others to contribute as well (between $100 and $250 per month). As a result, the organization had a stable income for the first time (interviews with Cindy Little and Sheri Walker, 1984).[22]

Thus, it was important that the leader of Illinois NARAL was someone who, though not a career activist, did need to be paid and therefore was motivated to make the organization financially stable. However, this financial stability was based largely on Cindy Little's personal appeal. After she left Illinois NARAL and a new director began in the fall of 1980, the organization went through a period of budget tightening resulting from the loss of contributions from the clinics, particularly Concord. This loss occurred because the contributions were contingent on the personal relationships established by Cindy Little, and when she left, the contributions stopped. Although the owner of Concord, the largest clinic contributor, had complete faith in the leadership of Cindy Little, she did not know the new director, who was younger and had a different style of organizing; consequently, she was unwilling to continue contributing a monthly sum, although Concord did continue to provide small amounts of money earmarked for special projects as well as some in-kind contributions such as help from the Concord staff in sending out mailings (interview with Sheri Walker, 1984).

Despite the loss of clinic funding, NARAL of Illinois was still in a relatively stable situation as a result of its affiliation with national NARAL. However, it was not until a director looking for a professional career in movement leadership took over that NARAL of Illinois became more formalized and less dependent on the personal characteristics of its leaders. In the fall of 1980, Jan Ryan, a young woman with a background in community-organizing work, was hired. Unlike her predecessor, Ryan wanted a career in "organizing." She did not have any experience working on the abortion issue before being hired as the director of Illinois NARAL, but she saw the job as a good experience for her, a way to develop her own skills and enhance her career objectives. Like other leaders, Ryan was highly committed to the goals of the movement, both because she held pro-choice views before directing NARAL and because her experiences in working with NARAL deepened her concerns about abortion rights. But it was Ryan's orientation as a professional organizer that led her to make some important changes in the structure of the organization.

Until Ryan took over as executive director, Illinois NARAL's board of directors was selected from the same pool of longtime activists, many of whom were highly involved in other organizations like Planned Parenthood, ZPG, and the Illinois Religious Coalition for Abortion Rights—a situation described by one activist involved in multiple organizations as "incestuous." Consequently, these longtime members were not very active in ARA/NARAL, and there was little division of labor in the organization, making it heavily reliant on the abilities and personal initiative of its executive director. After she was hired, Ryan recruited a number of very active new volunteers. She also insisted that the board selection procedures be revised so that they could serve on the board and the terms of service on the board could be systematically rotated. This procedure was implemented in 1980, resulting in a board composed of active volunteers and some longtime board members who continued to serve on a rotating basis to provide experience to NARAL.[23] The result was that a formal procedure for bringing "new blood" into the organization's decision-making structure was established for the first time. This change helped make the organization less dependent on its executive director for leadership. It also made volunteers more available to the executive director for use in organizational maintenance activities, such as the NARAL "house meeting" program, which was an important source of funds in the early 1980s (see Chapter 8). This professionalization of leadership thus helped stabilize Illinois NARAL, and after Ryan left in 1983 the formalized structure that she had created remained in place.

Conclusion

Paradoxically, the pro-choice movement actually became much stronger after its major victory, the legalization of abortion, had been won. It was after the countermovement won its first major victory, passage of the Hyde Amendment, that the movement expanded greatly. The Hyde Amendment and other partial anti-abortion victories did spur opponents as well, but as the countermovement expanded its organizations and activities and became more heterogeneous, so did the movement. The organizational dilemma for both movement and countermovement, therefore, is that victories are necessary to keep supporters from losing faith, but they also mobilize opponents.

Although countermovement threats aided the growth of the pro-choice movement after 1976, internal organizational developments also were critical. Local movement centers facilitated a quick revival of the pro-choice movement in Chicago in response to the new attacks on abortion rights. National movement organizations began the period of threat with the advantage of relatively stable organizational structures developed after 1973, which helped them take advantage of constituent concerns and attract more resources. NARAL then professionalized its leadership and further formalized its structure, enabling the major single-issue movement organization to expand greatly. As a result, NARAL was able to coordinate coalition work on the national level and to provide support for state-level organizations such as NARAL of Illinois, which went through a similar process of organizational change.

Pro-choice groups thus positioned themselves as contenders capable of fighting in institutionalized arenas. NARAL and a number of other movement organizations had developed the kinds of structures that made them similar to more established organizations and interest groups, many of which were working in coalition with the movement. Moreover, abortion service providers were interested parties that began to participate more actively in the movement in this period of threat to legal abortion. In short, the pro-choice movement was becoming more institutionalized. Chapter 8 shows how these organizational trends were reflected in the strategies and tactics of the post-Hyde period.

8

Single-Issue Politics

The tactics of the pro-choice movement had already become increasingly reactive in response to countermovement activities after the legalization of abortion in 1973. This trend continued in the post-Hyde period, but with some important changes. While movement organizations continued to engage in legislative lobbying and litigation, the political arena became the central battlefield of the abortion conflict. The pro-choice movement became increasingly involved in single-issue political tactics and more narrowly focused on defending legal abortion than ever before. Countermovement victories dictated pro-choice responses, but they also enabled the movement to obtain far more resources than had been available in earlier periods of the abortion conflict. National pro-choice movement organizations had already started to become more professionalized in their leadership and formalized in structure, and the increased resources accelerated these organizational trends. Formalized movement organizations with professional leaders were at the forefront of post-Hyde battles, but these trends did not preclude grass-roots mobilization. In fact, grass-roots mobilization was furthered by professionalization as well as by the threatening events that helped arouse pro-choice constituents.

Grass-Roots Organizing and Political Action

Until June 1977, when the Supreme Court ruled that the states do not have to fund "nontherapeutic" abortions, the pro-choice movement had been relying on the courts to strike down anti-abortion legislation.[1] NARAL leaders reported being "surprised, shocked and outraged" (*NARAL Newsletter*, July 1977) at the ruling, and it was at this point that NARAL's strategy underwent a major change. Having been disappointed by the courts in a major way for the first time, the organization told its membership that "we can no longer depend on the courts and must expand and mobilize NARAL's political action networks to guarantee abortion choice through legislation" (*NARAL Newsletter*, October 1977). RCAR's reaction to the Supreme Court ruling echoed that of NARAL:

> However much we may disagree with these latest decisions, we must now come to a full realization of their effect on the activities of pro-choice organizations. No

93

longer can we depend on the Court to nullify legislation designed to impede access to legal abortions. (*Options,* August 1977)

Pro-choice groups did not give up on the courts completely, even after 1980 when the Supreme Court gave anti-abortion forces another victory by upholding the constitutionality of the Hyde Amendment.[2] They also continued to fight an uphill battle in Congress against anti-abortion initiatives. But organizations like NARAL increasingly turned their attention to the electoral arena.

Pro-choice groups had taken some tentative steps toward involvement in electoral politics before passage of the Hyde Amendment, particularly after the National Conference of Catholic Bishops issued its "Pastoral Plan for Pro-Life Activities" in 1975[3] and after anti-abortion forces became visibly involved in the 1976 Presidential election. Nationally, both NARAL and RCAR began to direct educational efforts at political candidates while, locally, the Abortion Rights Association of Illinois and Illinois RCAR did the same. The National Organization for Women, meanwhile, was also moving toward greater involvement in the political arena as a result of its campaign to pass the Equal Rights Amendment.[4]

It took the anti-abortion victory on the Hyde Amendment and the 1977 Supreme Court ruling, however, before pro-choice organizations entered the political arena in force. Once it became clear that the courts would no longer reverse all anti-abortion gains, pro-choice groups recognized that certain issues (e.g., Medicaid funding) would have to be resolved in the legislative arena. Because anti-abortion groups were already becoming politically active, pro-choice groups had no choice but to follow suit. But in order to influence legislators as decision makers, pro-choice groups first had to influence them as politicians.

Because of the growing desire to become a political force, "grass-roots organizing" became the byword of pro-choice movement organizations. In a direct response to the growth of local anti-abortion groups and their success in lobbying Congress, national pro-choice organizations that did not have strong local constituencies began creating local units capable of pressuring authorities through visible collective action. As a result of their efforts, pro-choice organizations created a new pool of constituents, many of whom became participants in institutionalized politics for the first time.

NARAL took the lead in designing a new political-action strategy that was adopted by its affiliates, including NARAL of Illinois. The influx of financial resources into NARAL that began in 1977 enabled the organization to hire additional staff to coordinate the local organizing work, including a campus-organizing program, and to train local coordinators. By 1978, NARAL was in a position to provide special aid to affiliates in states with large Congressional delegations, including some financial help. It was also recognized that local activists could play an important role as workers in state-level political campaigns (*NARAL Newsletter,* January–March 1978). Within a year, NARAL had formulated an ambitious new strategy of local organizing intended to turn the organization into a political force.

The goal of the new "Impact '80" strategy, as it was called, was to activate members of the public already sympathetic to the pro-choice cause in order to convince political candidates that there was a single-issue pro-choice vote to match the single-issue anti-abortion vote. This strategy was based on a reading of public opinion that stressed the pro-choice majority, and, in fact, surveys did show a consistent majority of the public as supporting legal abortion in the years following *Roe* v. *Wade* (see Granberg and Granberg, 1980; Sackett, 1985). That public opinion on the abortion issue was also quite complex did not enter into the NARAL strategy at this time.[5]

NARAL's grass-roots organizing strategy was explicitly modeled on that of anti-abortion forces: To counter the National Conference of Catholic Bishops' Pastoral Plan for Pro-Life Activities, which called for the creation of "pro-life committees" in parishes and political districts across the country, NARAL would create its own network of local political units (*NARAL Newsletter,* May–June 1979). NARAL–PAC was formed in the same year that two major anti-abortion PACs, the Life Amendment Political Action Committee (LAPAC) and the National Right to Life Committee's National Pro-Life Action PAC, were created.[6]

Whereas the broad outlines of NARAL's strategy were determined by the nature of countermovement threats, specific tactics were the result of internal organizational assets and structure.[7] Chief among NARAL's assets were its local affiliates, including some that were just beginning to be organized in the late 1970s, and others that were well-established organizations. Affiliates supplied leaders for the national organization and ideas for the national strategy based on local experiences. A critical component of the Impact '80 program, a version of the "house meeting" organizing technique that has been used by the farm workers' movement and other movements (see Walsh, 1988:86), was introduced to NARAL by activists in its Massachusetts affiliate, one of the organization's oldest and strongest affiliates. After the model, based on a social network principle of recruitment,[8] was successfully employed in Massachusetts, it was further developed by the national organization through NARAL organizers who introduced the house meeting tool to other affiliates on a trial basis. Once the tactic was proven successful in a sample of affiliates, it was introduced to remaining affiliates through training sessions conducted for local organizers.

Many of the local organizers were hired with funds donated by the national NARAL organization. As discussed in Chapter 7, large increases in membership and contributions in the post-Hyde period enabled NARAL to give financial and other resources to affiliates as well as to use professional staff to train local organizers to run house meetings, conduct political skills workshops, coordinate lobbying efforts, and so on. By the early 1980s, NARAL affiliates were signing formal contracts in exchange for national funds to carry out the political action program created by the national organization (interview with former NARAL director Nanette Falkenberg, 1984).

There was not complete agreement within NARAL on the Impact '80 strategy. An informant on the NARAL board of directors admitted that some of the older board members were initially uncomfortable with the new tactics because "it was not their way." But by that point, changes had been made in the NARAL decision-making structure to ensure that new persons joined the board. Because terms on the board were rotated and because the affiliates were now more closely tied to the national organization, NARAL attracted board members with different types of experiences, including women with backgrounds in women's movement organizations who were familiar with "grass-roots organizing" activities. Consequently, there was support for the new strategy on the board and, after it began to produce favorable results, opposition to the new tactics vanished.

Although the 1980 election was considered a "disaster" by NARAL, the "Impact '80" program was not (*NARAL Newsletter,* December 1980). NARAL analyses revealed successes in state and local races in which NARAL had been able to place a substantial number of pro-choice campaign workers. Moreover, the election of Ronald Reagan brought another flood of donations to NARAL, allowing the organization to continue to expand its program. NARAL's "Political Strategy for the 80s" (the theme of the organization's 1981 national conference) called for a continuation of PAC contributions, the channeling of local activists into campaign work, postcard campaigns, and house meetings.

The election of an avowedly anti-abortion President and a Republican Senate did, however, affect NARAL's mobilization strategy. The threat of a constitutional amendment banning abortion seemed very real at this point, and so NARAL began to put a major share of its resources into selected states, which were chosen on the basis of whether or not NARAL thought it had the ability to organize the state to prevent passage of a constitutional amendment. As former executive director Karen Mulhauser explained:

> The board agreed that to organize against a constitutional amendment, we should learn from the ERA effort, that we don't need to organize everywhere; we need to organize in enough states so that there would not be thirty-eight states to ratify a constitutional amendment against abortion. So that was the reason that we decided to target our resources into, I think, seventeen states, rather than spread all of our resources evenly over fifty states. (interview with Karen Mulhauser, 1984)

Consequently, the national organization took an active role in organizing and supporting affiliates that carried out NARAL's political strategy.[9]

In Illinois, the NARAL affiliate began to implement the national NARAL Impact '80 program in 1979. "I'm Pro-Choice and I Vote" postcards were distributed to supporters and placed in clinics, then collected and sent to legislatures. A few house meetings were held, and a speakers' bureau was activated. Members were urged, although not actively organized, to work in the 1980 campaigns of pro-choice candidates. It was not until the early 1980s, however, that NARAL of Illinois became committed to tactics endorsed by the national NARAL organization as part of the "grass-roots organizing" drive for political influence. The postcard campaign entailed setting up tables in public places and at organizational functions, giving the organization exposure as well as a mailing list, in addition to a substantial number of signed postcards to deliver to Springfield and Washington. Numerous house meetings were held (a total of 121 in 1981), resulting in significant increases in membership and income for the organization. Political skills workshops also trained volunteers to work in the campaigns of pro-choice candidates. In 1982, NARAL of Illinois instructed 185 campaign workers who worked for candidates in eighteen state legislative races in the November election (NARAL of Illinois newsletter, December 1982).[10]

One reason why the switch in mobilization tactics occurred after 1980 was that the national NARAL organization had by this time become much better at implementing the grass-roots organizing program through training and grants to local affiliates. The other reason was that a new executive director, Jan Ryan, was hired in the fall of 1980 to replace Cindy Little, who had served as executive director since 1978. As pointed out in Chapter 7, the two directors brought different backgrounds and skills to the organization. Moreover, the shape of the organization was different in 1978 than in 1980.

When Cindy Little was hired in 1978, she was confronted with an organizational disaster. As she recalled in an interview:

> It was as if the organization had been shut up for months; you can't imagine what a mess it was—literally. Papers everywhere, checks uncashed. Not much had been done for two years. And the organization was in debt, not really a large debt, but substantial for an organization that size.

Given the state of the organization, Little spent much of her time in administrative tasks: securing funding, renewing contacts with members, and organizing the office. Because of her organizational skills and attractive personal style, Little was highly successful at reviving the organization. She consequently won the loyalty of NARAL board members, who gave her a free reign in designing organizational strategies.

Little's approach was pragmatic and instrumental. Rather than concentrating on bringing large numbers of activists into the organization, she recruited volunteers with particular skills, including her many friends, for specific tasks such as writing "letters to the editor." Tactics were aimed less at gaining exposure for NARAL than at accomplishing specific objectives. For example, when Chicago Alderman Edward Burke moved to introduce an "Akron-style" ordinance restricting the availability of abortions into the city council, the NARAL director worked to have the measure killed through quiet, behind-the-scenes maneuvers. In this instance and in lobbying work in the state legislature, Little used the skills and influence of seasoned activists.

Based on her background and success with such conventional tactics, Little was not sold on the NARAL's "Impact '80" program. In accord with the national organization's wishes, she began to conduct a limited number of house meetings, but remained unconvinced of their effectiveness. As she admitted in a 1984 interview:

> I hated those things. I started doing a few even before I had the training by reading a book they gave us. Then I had the training program, I think around February or March of 1980, and it was really a very good training program. . . . But, I don't know, I just thought that more energy went into those house meetings than they were worth. I was better at raising larger sums of money—rather than this kind of Tupperware-for-choice approach. It was very embarrassing to ask friends for money. . . . I think too, that I had given a lot by that time—I hated asking my friends. . . . The best meetings were when people [outside her network of contacts]

got their friends to come. . . . The people I talked to were people who knew their Congressmen or who were politically involved—an older, more moneyed group which was more politically sophisticated. They just found this house meeting stuff hokey.

Little had similar objections to other parts of the national NARAL grass-roots organizing program. When I asked her about the political skills workshops, she replied:

I refused to do those political skills workshops. I didn't have time, I said [to national NARAL]; I'm doing the house meetings program—that's enough. I really just didn't think they were necessary—there are enough organizations like the League of Women Voters which do political skills training. From an organizational point of view, I guess it's good to do your own skills training to show that the organization is really involved.

Although she recognized the organizational value of such tactics, Little was not principally concerned with organizational expansion, but with more specific goals, such as defeating particular pieces of anti-abortion legislation. She was accustomed to using individual skills for this work rather than turning out large numbers of activists. When asked about campaign work, she noted:

I always encouraged people to get involved in campaigns—even two years before that in 1978, I did that, like in public speeches. But a lot of people, especially our older members on the newsletter list, were people who were already involved in politics. I do think the "I'm Pro-Choice and I Vote" was important in getting the message across to legislators and candidates in a public way. I put a lot of emphasis on clinics for postcards because there was a ready-made setting for getting people to sign them. . . . As far as the campaign work, it was clear to me at the time that Reagan was going to be elected. It was too late in 1980 to make a difference. And, on the local level, there are already liberal groups that almost always support pro-choice candidates anyway. And groups like the AAUW [American Association of University Women] and the League of Women Voters. I'm just not that much on duplicating efforts which I think NARAL is doing with the campaign work.

In talking about the grass-roots organizing program in general, Little, who had worked on some national NARAL committees, commented:

I also think that, with this Impact '80 approach, NARAL is not really using the skills of some of the organization's older constituents, people who have political experience and connections. They could be more effective in other ways. [Like how?] That would depend on what was needed, maybe behind the scenes in state caucuses or something like that. Some of the more experienced people in NARAL didn't like all of the rah-rah stuff; they were put off by all this grass-roots organizing. You know, that stuff definitely appeals to a younger age group. And I'm not sure national NARAL networked effectively with traditional women's organizations like the AAUW and the League of Women Voters. I think they missed out on attracting some of those people by adopting the Saul Alinsky–type organizing strategy.

In all of these comments it is clear that the Illinois NARAL director who served from 1978 to 1980 preferred instrumental tactics rather than organizing tactics. She saw the house meetings as an inefficient form of raising money and, correctly, saw that they did not appeal to more sophisticated persons.[11] Little recognized that political skills workshops and campaign work were good for organizational visibility, but she was not convinced of their effectiveness for achieving movement goals—her principal concern. She used the "I'm Pro-Choice and I Vote" postcards as a signal to legislators rather than as an organizing tool. Because of Cindy Little's influence, then, most of Illinois NARAL's activities during her tenure were instrumentally targeted at state legislators. There were exceptions, however, because all organizations have maintenance needs, and organizations that rely on volunteers have to give their activists some kind of reward. For example, when asked why NARAL began in 1978 to have a booth at the state fair each year, Little explained:

> For one thing, because the opposition always has a booth. Plus NARAL people enjoyed doing it. You need to do things that are fun for people, to keep them going. Not that sitting at the table for hours was fun, but you make contacts with other people downstate and you're at the fair, which was a new experience for some people from Chicago. Also the fair booth gives NARAL visibility. And there are funny things that happen. Like I remember the first year, we had this really nice booth—it was a really nice color of blue, with flowers and everything, really the only tasteful one there. And this whole pack of nuns came over, dressed in their habits, and smiling. They said, "Oh, what a nice booth" and "We're so glad you're here." I just looked in disbelief, then said "Oh really, do you know what cause we're working for?" They said, "Yes, abortion," and I said, "Yes, but I think we're your opposition." They just turned and took off; it was so funny.

Although all movement organizations engage in some such activities to attract and maintain members, it was not until 1980 when an executive director with experience in community-organizing work was hired that the Illinois NARAL affiliate enthusiastically carried out the national NARAL grass-roots organizing program. Like her predecessor, Jan Ryan was able to exert a strong influence on the organization, but for different reasons. Although initially hired on a part-time basis, Ryan was able to convince the NARAL board to make her position a full-time one, as the organization was now in a stable financial condition. She also succeeded in introducing rotating turns on the board, a structural change that allowed younger and more active members who were newly recruited to replace some of the old-time board members. This created a board that was more receptive to the new organizing tactics than the older board might have been.

Ryan used the house meeting tool to raise money and to bring new activists into the NARAL affiliate. In this regard, her approach was quite different from that of her predecessor. Cindy Little had been reluctant to delegate the responsibility of public speaking, including speaking at house meetings, to volunteers because she was concerned that they might make mistakes as representatives of the organization. As she commented, "Even at house meetings, they are still representing the organization, and I was leery of letting volunteers do it" (interview with Cindy Little, 1984). Jan Ryan, in contrast, was armed with her past experience with community organizing and a professional interest in organizing techniques. She was highly successful at training volunteers to conduct house meetings and, with funds raised from the meetings and some financial aid from national NARAL, was able to hire an organizer to run the house meeting program. When the program was employed systematically, NARAL was successful in tapping into different networks of women and recruiting many new women as active volunteers. As Ryan remembered:

> We had some pretty diverse networks to draw on, and we got referrals from people who came to the meetings, so we got a lot of different types of people. It would go in trends or waves. Like at one point we went through all these Greek women, then they ran out and we had all these public relations people, then we had women in insurance. It seemed like it took about six months to tap all the women in a particular group. What I was really impressed with was the age span we were able to get to house meetings—the whole range from teenagers to senior citizens. (interview with Jan Ryan, 1984)

Just as the house meetings were used as an organizing tool, so were the NARAL postcards. As the NARAL director explained:

> The best thing about the postcards was that they gave us new contacts. We would set up tables in different places, and people would come up and sign and say things like "I'm really glad someone is doing something about this issue." And then we'd say, "Would you like to get more involved?" and we got a number of activists that way. We also got names for a mailing list. . . . So the postcards were good as a way of making contacts, a means of exposure for the organization. The actual effect of the postcards on legislators was, I think, minimal. I know some of the legislators never even opened the envelope; when we delivered an envelope full to Springfield, they'd just throw them away.

NARAL tactics did more than simply mobilize support for the pro-choice position. Campaign work was intended to have a real impact on the votes of state legislators in Illinois. But, beyond its instrumental value, Ryan believed that campaign work helped create solidarity among volunteers. As she explained:

> It's a social thing, and people like to work on them [campaigns]. Also, it's usually cold, and people feel a lot of solidarity going out together in the cold. Campaign work meets a lot of different needs—it's possible to have any amount of input into a campaign; you can do as much work as you have time to do, from being totally involved to just going into the office and volunteering a few times. And the social part is attractive to people.

Besides the organizing activities and campaign work, NARAL used other tactics that also helped keep activists mobilized. When asked about demonstrations, Ryan commented:

> Mostly, we'd just do that kind of thing for the media. Politically, things like pickets have zero effectiveness, but volunteers like them. So occasionally we'd do them for the volunteers, to rev people up when they need a boost. They really like pickets—I don't know why, I can't stand them myself. Usually, we tried to channel energies into more productive things like campaign work, which volunteers also like.

NARAL was also involved in lobbying work, particularly in nonelection years, but most of the real lobbying work was done in coalition through the Illinois Pro-Choice Alliance. Apart from this coalition work, NARAL's former director explained that lobbying work, like demonstrations, was sometimes done for the benefit of activists:

> We do some lobbying as part of our electoral work—we do it for the benefit of our members, not for its impact on legislators. Like sometimes we will get a member to visit a person who we know is completely intractable. They're so upset after the visit they can't wait to get into campaign work! You know, they think, "This person is representing me?" And doing lobbying work is also useful for newer people because nonpolitical people are sometimes intimidated by the idea of a public official. After visits, they have a different view; lobbying cuts down on the sense of awe and distance that a lot of people have and makes politics more real to them.

Tactics with ostensibly external targets can thus serve internal educational functions. With its grass-roots organizing program, NARAL was building support for the organization and bringing new people into active participation in the political process.

The Religious Coalition for Abortion Rights also increased its efforts to build state affiliates and expand its activities in response to the countermovement victory. Like NARAL, it met with significant success in doing so, for both internal and external reasons. The external environment of increased Catholic Church activity and countermovement success created a receptiveness to activity on the abortion issue among RCAR constituents. Although RCAR did not have a very large budget, the organization was able to capitalize on the concern created by countermovement threats by hiring some additional staff and increasing the number of its affiliates. Whereas previous efforts had been targeted mainly at Congress, the growth of its state affiliates allowed RCAR to engage in a greater variety of tactics designed to increase religious pro-choice visibility on the state and local levels as well.[12]

In contrast with NARAL of Illinois, however, the Illinois RCAR affiliate did not make major changes in its mobilization tactics in the post-Hyde period of the abortion conflict. The organization was restricted by its modest resources and by the fact that its constituents were religious organizations and denominations whose active members tended to be committed to various other social causes. The Illinois RCAR coordinators that I interviewed did report having an easier time mobilizing members of the religious community when the threats to abortion rights were most visible, but they did not have the resources for any all-out organizing campaigns like the NARAL Impact '80 program. Moreover, because of the tax-exempt statuses of its denominational members, RCAR could not involve activists in electoral politics.

The only major change in Illinois RCAR activities came about in 1983 with the hiring of a new coordinator, Barbara Moore, and the opening of an office in Springfield rather than Chicago. The new coordinator came to the organization with previous experience in organizing religious groups and began a major effort to get religious organizations and denominations outside Chicago involved on the abortion issue. She remained limited, however, by the tiny Illinois RCAR budget (about $10,000 per year) and by shifts in the political environment around 1983, which lessened concern about abortion, particularly among people, such as many RCAR activists, who were active in other causes. As former Illinois RCAR coordinator Barbara Moore commented in a 1984 interview when asked about the difficulty of expanding the organization:

> I've found that in the religious community here [in Illinois]—that the hunger issue is very important, that there is a lot of concern about Central America and nuclear disarmament. But abortion rights—a lot of people's feelings are that it's taken care of. It's really difficult to find people who are activist types, who are not already committed on other issues. The other thing is, in almost every community around the state, there is an anti-choice group, either a Catholic group or a fundamentalist group. Often, it's only a small group of people, but they are real effective. A lot of clergy are saying to me, "I'm with you, but I think there are a lot of anti-abortion people in my congregation." Ministers are very cautious about choosing issues with which to address their congregations. So it is something of an uphill battle. You really have to go after the support.

So Illinois RCAR was faced with the problem of trying to draw on a pool of already involved and overworked activists. In contrast with NARAL of Illinois, the organization did not have the resources to mount the kind of grass-roots organizing program that might bring in young new activists.

As a multi-issue women's movement organization, NOW had an easier time enlisting support in a period of high concern about abortion rights among pro-choice adherents. NOW's mobilization tactics did not undergo as radical a shift as did those of NARAL because NOW already had a strong grass-roots base, making tactics like house meetings unnecessary. As the organization noted in urging political work on the abortion issue after passage of the Hyde Amendment, "We have a pool of hard-working NOW members to work in campaigns" (*Do It NOW,* March 1977). Chicago NOW, similarly, had no need for an organizing program to recruit activists for tactics like campaign work because the chapter already had a base of active members (although Chicago NOW did try to continually expand). And, interestingly, a Chicago NOW leader interviewed was not so taken with the organizational benefits of campaign work as was the NARAL director, Jan Ryan. As former Chicago NOW executive director Karen Wellisch explained in a 1984 interview:

> We have gotten more involved in the electoral process. ERA taught us that it's better to try to replace legislators than to convince them. But it's an area that does not do much to build the organization. It does build credibility, but it takes money and volunteer hours away from other work. . . . We are putting a lot of time and money into campaigns because we feel we have to change the legislatures, and we want to get more women elected. But campaign work is a drain; you're doing the same tasks over and over—going door to door doesn't teach members new skills; it's just hard work.

The difference in attitude toward campaign work between the NOW and NARAL directors can be attributed to differences in organizational needs. NARAL of Illinois was recruiting a body of new activists and found campaign work useful in providing concrete tasks and solidarity incentives for its volunteers. NOW already had a pool of volunteers and was trying not only to expand its membership but also to increase women's skills in the hope that some NOW members themselves would seek public office or gain entry to other positions of authority. Nevertheless, both NOW and NARAL were developing constituencies of politically active women.

As Chicago NOW began to focus more on the abortion issue in the early 1980s, the chapter transferred to abortion work those methods of producing letters and telegrams used in the ERA campaign. According to former NOW director Karen Wellisch:

> Chicago NOW does weekly Tuesday evening workshops where we write letters and send public opinion messages. We have these pro-choice authorizations we use—we started doing it with the ERA campaign. It's really very clever; we get people to sign them. . . . We've gotten hundreds of people who've authorized us to sign their names and a lot of people who pay for telegrams more than once a month. Then on Tuesday evenings we pull names from legislative districts.

Through phone calls, chapter members were persuaded to volunteer their time at the weekly work sessions. As Wellisch commented:

> Our members love it when you make it possible for them to do something easily. You'd be surprised; we call people to help and they say things like, "I feel so guilty, I'm so glad this is something I can do." People love to do something like this that is already organized, that's easy for them to do.

Through this technique, Chicago NOW became extremely proficient at generating letters and telegrams which were sent to both national and state legislators as needed.

Institutionalized Tactics and Narrowed Demands

Perhaps the most remarkable fact about movement tactics in the post-Hyde period is the extent to which they were carried out through institutionalized channels of influence. Major national organizations like NARAL and NOW engaged in few real "direct-action" tactics. They did organize some demonstrations, but these tended to be ritualized "events" for the benefit of the media rather than collective actions aimed directly at decision makers or countermovement actors. As Chapter 9 will show, it was primarily the feminist reproductive rights organizations that attempted to buck this trend and initiate direct-action tactics in the late 1970s and early 1980s. Other pro-choice organizations were becoming established actors in the legislative and political arenas.

At the same time that pro-choice organizations became more involved in institutionalized lobbying and party politics, their demands became more narrow. This was due in part to the need to respond to the successes of the single-issue countermovement: As the countermovement made gains in Congress and the courts, movement actors felt they could not afford the luxury of anything beyond the defense of legal abortion. Moreover, new constituents recruited through "grass-roots organizing" were attracted by the single issue of legal abortion rather than by a larger set of ideological concerns. And even those with broader concerns found that a single-issue approach was a requirement of acting in institutionalized arenas.

Pro-Choice Lobbying Coalitions

Both nationally and in Illinois, the pro-choice movement managed to become a player in the legislative arena through coalition work. Although coalition work is generally very difficult to maintain because of interorganizational competition (see Staggenborg, 1986, for a detailed analysis of this problem), countermovement victories, beginning with the Hyde Amendment, provided a strong incentive for coalition work. In addition, changes in the movement's organizational structure facilitated coalition work. Professionalization helped stabilize pro-choice coalitions, as paid staff were available to coordinate coalition work around legislative lobbying. Established organizations and interest groups also lent critical support to coalition efforts, thereby easing resource strains on movement organizations.

Nationally, the Abortion Information Exchange became a cohesive lobbying coalition that involved many pro-choice organizations in varying levels of activity. Along with the established organizations Planned Parenthood, the ACLU, and the Alan Guttmacher Institute (AGI), NARAL and RCAR used their professional staff to organize the coalition. NOW was less active than were NARAL and RCAR, but it also had staff who worked with the coalition in lobbying Congress and helped coordinate constituent mail and home visits from chapters. NARAL and NOW also encouraged their chapters and state affiliates to lobby their state legislators to prevent passage of anti-abortion bills, and RCAR provided clergy members to testify at Congressional hearings.

Smaller pro-choice organizations and multi-issue organizations that were less active on a day-to-day basis were also available when needed to support the pro-choice coalition in Congress. Organizations such as the National Women's Health Network and Zero Population Growth followed the lead of NARAL and other highly active organizations in the Abortion Information Exchange. They contributed to the coalition by regularly printing in their newsletters information on legislative developments provided by organizations like NARAL and asking their members to write appropriate letters to Congress and other targets. ZPG, the NWHN, and other pro-choice groups also gave testimony at Congressional hearings when needed.[13]

In Illinois, legislative lobbying efforts were also made primarily through coalition work in the post-Hyde period. The organization that had previously taken most of the responsibility for legislative tactics, the Abortion Rights Association of Illinois, was in a state of organizational crisis at the start of the period and consequently was unable to make much of a response to the Medicaid funding crisis. Activists from ARA did work with the Ad Hoc Committee for Abortion Rights and were instrumental in persuading the coalition to supplement demonstrations with a letter-writing campaign to the governor of Illinois urging him to veto the state legislation banning funds for abortions.[14] Because it was a time of crisis, and because the battle was taking place in the legislative arena, other organizations in the Ad Hoc coalition aided the ARA in its institutionalized efforts to fight the Medicaid funding cuts. As one of a few movement organizations in stable condition in 1977, Illinois RCAR played a particularly important role in helping the ARA activists to generate letters. Even the Chicago Women's Health Task Force, which preferred direct-action tactics, participated in the letter-writing campaign during this crisis.

Following passage of the state ban on Medicaid funding over the veto of the governor of Illinois, other crises continued to occur in the state legislature (e.g., attempts to pass a call for a constitutional convention to outlaw abortion and numerous bills restricting the availability of abortion). After hiring a new executive director in early 1978, ARA/NARAL of Illinois put most of its energies during 1978 and 1979 into lobbying the state legislature. Illinois RCAR worked closely with the NARAL affiliate, aiding lobbying efforts throughout the state of Illinois with RCAR religious contacts. As a result, NARAL of Illinois was able to set up a legislative alert network system to get supporters to write letters and make contact with their legislators when crises arose in Springfield. NARAL supporters were asked to authorize the organization to send Public Opinion Messages to legislators when needed. Constituent visits to legislators were coordinated, and an extensive effort was made to organize support throughout the state of Illinois by reactivating NARAL of Illinois "chapters" outside Chicago. National legislators were also targeted with letter-writing campaigns and visits to their district offices. In 1979, the director of Illinois NARAL, along with activists from the ACLU, Planned Parenthood, and RCAR, helped form the Illinois Pro-Choice Alliance in order to step up lobbying efforts in Springfield.

The other local pro-choice organization that engaged in legislative lobbying tactics during this period was Chicago NOW. Because of the chapter's heavy involvement in the campaign to pass the Equal Rights Amendment through the state legislature, legislative lobbying work on abortion initially was limited. Until around 1980, Chicago NOW's legislative tactics on abortion consisted largely of providing updates on state and national developments to members through the newsletter along with encouragement to write appropriate letters. In the early 1980s, Chicago NOW began to use its impressive organizational resources to generate letters and telegrams on state and national abortion legislation through weekly work sessions and membership authorizations. Chicago NOW became more directly active in lobbying work in the state legislature in 1983 after the state NOW organization, Illinois NOW, hired a part-time lobbyist. At that point, the Illinois NOW lobbyist began to work closely with the lobbyists from Planned Parenthood and the ACLU, who were in close contact with the coordinator of the Illinois Pro-Choice Alliance. Consequently, both Illinois NOW and Chicago NOW began to be much more active in the coalition and to put more resources into lobbying work, the Alliance's principal activity.

Insider Political Tactics

Countermovement tactics increasingly pushed pro-choice organizations into the political arena during the post-Hyde period of the abortion conflict. Help from established organizations on litigation and coalition work on legislative lobbying allowed major pro-choice groups to use resources saved on litigation and lobbying to engage in political tactics, including financial contributions to the campaigns of pro-choice candidates, campaign work by activists, and educational programs aimed at politicians.

Both NARAL and NOW established affiliated political action committees in 1977, the year in which major anti-abortion PACs also were founded. NARAL made campaign contributions to supporters, including those on anti-abortion "hit lists," on a single-issue basis. NOW typically used candidates' stands on both abortion and the ERA as "bottom line" criteria for campaign contributions. Both NARAL and NOW were able to use this financially expensive tactic as a result of direct-mail campaigns. NOW also asked its state and local chapters to form local PACs to raise money for state races (*Do It NOW,* March 1977).

Neither NARAL nor NOW had unlimited resources, however, and both recognized that they could not achieve political influence through financial contributions alone. Consequently, both also adopted the tactic of placing local activists in campaign work. NARAL recruited and trained activists through house meetings and political skills workshops. NOW encouraged its chapters to hold political skills workshops to train their activists to participate in campaign work on the abortion issue (*Do It NOW,* March 1977), although many were already politically experienced as a result of the ERA campaign.

In Illinois, NARAL of Illinois began to use political tactics in 1978 by giving its members the results of a NARAL survey of candidates' views on abortion and urging them to work for pro-choice candidates in the 1978 elections. Representatives from NARAL also visited political candidates and supplied them with "educational kits" on the abortion issue. In the 1980s, NARAL of Illinois also adopted the national NARAL organizing strategy consisting of house meetings and political skills workshops. As a result of its organizing work, NARAL was very successful in placing workers in campaigns, a tactic that activists believe made an important difference in the attitudes—and votes—of Illinois legislators.[15] Chicago NOW engaged in similar political tactics. In 1978, Chicago NOW–PAC was formed (*Act NOW,* September 1978), and in 1980 chapter activists were working for candidates who supported the ERA and abortion rights.[16]

Single-Issue Demands

After the election of President Reagan in 1980, a narrow single-issue approach became particularly pronounced in the pro-choice movement. In the post-election political climate, the passage by Congress of a constitutional amendment prohibiting abortion seemed like a real possibility. NARAL reacted to the threat by narrowing its demands and consciously adopting a single-minded focus on the political arena. NARAL had always been a single-issue organization, of course, but beyond the demand for legal abortion, NARAL had previously fought for additional advantages such as free-standing clinics and services from public hospitals. At this point, however, a conscious decision was made to limit NARAL's concerns to the legal status of abortion. This decision was the result of an assessment of anti-abortion threats and of the strength of the pro-choice coalition. Other organizations, such as Planned Parenthood and the National Abortion Federation (an organization of clinics and other service providers), were now considered capable of handling these other concerns. As former NARAL executive director Karen Mulhauser recalled in an interview:

> After the 1980 elections, we had a several-day retreat with the board to develop a mission statement that clarified that our mission was a political one, that there were other organizations that were limited for reasons of educational tax-deductible money to carry on an educational program. We could do some of that through the [NARAL] Foundation, but that's not our primary purpose at NARAL. And we even spent several hours trying to decide whether or not part of our mission should include the phrase "keep abortion safe and legal" or just "keep abortion legal." There were other groups formed to keep abortion safe, and then we decided to exclude that word from our mission statement. That's not part of our mission to keep it safe.

Both NARAL and RCAR concentrated on preventing further losses during this period, but neither organization felt itself in a position to try to regain Medicaid funding, much less make further demands, when the legal status of abortion itself was in danger.

Many of the activists mobilized by NARAL's grass-roots organizing program were motivated by the single-issue goal of preserving legal abortion. In Illinois NARAL, a number of the new activists were younger women who had not been part of the earlier struggle to legalize abortion but who firmly believed they had a "right" to legal abortion. Not surprisingly, their demands were strictly reactive. As Jan Ryan, the young executive director hired in 1980, explained in an interview, "I was too young to remember the whole fight for legalization and so were most of the new people; to us it looked like this was the first round, and we were all fired up about protecting this right which was being threatened." For older Illinois NARAL activists, the fight was also a reactive single-issue one as a result of the political climate of the period. As a veteran board member commented in an interview, "None of us really wanted to treat abortion as a single issue, but that was the political reality. It wasn't a choice. Times were such that it was a single issue."

Women's movement organizations did have broader concerns, and some did try to maintain a multi-issue stance on abortion. Although the most strenuous attempts to develop a multi-issue perspective on abortion were made by reproductive rights groups, the National Organization for Women called in 1978 for an enlarged focus on reproductive "choice," including the rights to contraception and child care in addition to abortion, to counter the narrow focus on abortion pushed by "forced pregnancy" proponents (*National NOW Times,* November 1978). In practice, however, abortion tended to be treated as a single issue.

In the case of Chicago NOW, organizational factors, together with involvement in institutionalized lobbying tactics, led to a narrowing of political demands on the abortion issue. Like the national NOW organization, Chicago NOW was concerned about a broad range of women's issues. In practice, the chapter took what amounted to a single-issue approach to the abortion issue. It demanded only that abortion be kept accessible and legal, and did not try to connect the abortion issue to other reproductive rights such as economic rights and adequate day care. In part, this approach was due to changes that were made in the chapter's structure in order to conserve organizational resources (see Appendix A). This structural change—along with the ERA campaign—created a trend away from chapter work on multiple issues and toward work on one or two main issues, with subcommittees divided by skills rather than by issues. Another reason for the single-issue approach to abortion was that on this issue Chicago NOW tended to engage in institutionalized tactics; as chapter leader Karen Wellisch explained in an interview, "When you're lobbying, you have to talk about one issue at a time. Those arguments about other issues being connected are just not bought in the state legislature."

Conclusion

Significant countermovement victories and changes in the political climate, beginning with the Hyde Amendment and continuing with the Court rulings on Medicaid funding and the election of Ronald Reagan, created a new era in pro-choice strategies and tactics. Whereas the interaction between movement and countermovement before the legalization of abortion might be described as "loosely coupled" (Zald and Useem, 1987), by the late 1970s movement actions were tightly constrained by countermovement offensives. Because of the success of the countermovement, movement actors had little choice but to abandon their own initiatives and defend abortion rights on battlefields chosen by the opposition.

Despite its ability to dictate pro-choice tactics, however, the countermovement did not succeed in raising for the movement the costs of mobilization (cf. Zald and Useem, 1987:260). Rather, new threats to abortion rights actually helped attract new support to the pro-choice movement. New pro-choice coalitions were created and sustained by countermovement successes. In addition, many pro-choice movement organizations increased their resources and hired more professional staff to facilitate participation in the institutionalized arenas in which the abortion battle was being waged.

Professionalization resulted in important changes in the pro-choice movement. More attention was paid to organizational maintenance and expansion as career movement activists—who were committed to organizing work over and above specific goals—created more formalized structures for this work. As a result, a number of pro-choice organizations became larger and more stable. The leading national pro-choice organization, NARAL, and the leading single-issue movement organization in Illinois, NARAL of Illinois, developed formal procedures for rotating board members as part of this process, and this brought new participants into decision-making power.

The professionalization of leadership and the formalization of organizational structures did not, however, prevent grass-roots mobilization but, rather, facilitated involvement by local activists. NARAL and other pro-choice organizations engaged in grass-roots organizing to create a pro-choice political force, and many women became active participants in party politics for the first time. Pro-choice groups also placed more emphasis on legislative lobbying through coalition work. At the same time, movement demands were narrowed. In short, the pro-choice movement was becoming institutionalized as a single-issue political force.

Not all pro-choice groups agreed with this single-issue approach through largely institutionalized tactics. Reproductive rights groups, which also sprang up in response to the threats of the late 1970s and early 1980s, tried to maintain a multi-issue approach and a commitment to direct action as well as to informal movement organizations. Chapter 9 looks at this movement within the larger pro-choice movement.

9

The Reproductive Rights Movement

Feminists alarmed by threats to abortion rights in the late 1970s and early 1980s did not want to engage in reactive, single-issue politics. Nor did they want to create formalized movement organizations led by professional leaders. They wanted, instead, to reclaim the offensive and fight for reproductive rights in the tradition of the younger branch of the women's movement. As a founder of the Reproductive Rights National Network (R2N2) explained:

> There was no reproductive rights *qua* reproductive rights activity in the country at the time. . . . The debate on abortion was being framed narrowly and being framed by the Right, by reactions to the Right, rather than by the women's movement. You know, it used to be a positive fight when abortion was illegal, but then it became a negative issue. . . . The real impetus [for the Reproductive Rights National Network] was to reframe the debate, to talk about the conditions which would be necessary for women to be able to make a real choice [about whether or not to have children]. (interview with Marilyn Katz, 1984)

R2N2 and other reproductive rights groups that emerged did try to reframe the debate and maintain a proactive stance in a period when other pro-choice organizations were busily reacting to countermovement initiatives. The movement succeeded in mobilizing women throughout the country who were attracted to the reproductive rights perspective, but it met with significant obstacles in trying to advance its multi-issue agenda. Not only was the political climate hostile, but the informal structures of reproductive rights organizations also proved less suitable for generating sustained grass-roots activity than did the more formalized structures of organizations such as NARAL.

Origins of the Reproductive Rights Movement

Reproductive rights organizations had their roots in the women's health movement that formed within the younger branch of the women's movement. Since the 1960s, local women's health groups had been fighting for a broad range of changes in women's health care, including legal abortion, and in 1975, a national organization, the National Women's Health Network, was formed. Reproductive

110

rights groups built on the networks of the women's health movement, as well as other left-wing political bases, but what distinguished them from other women's health organizations was the critical role that threats to abortion rights played in their mobilization.

The Committee for Abortion Rights and Against Sterilization Abuse (CAR-ASA) formed in reaction to the Hyde Amendment and the 1977 Supreme Court ruling that permitted state bans on Medicaid funding of abortions. The particular combination of interest in abortion and sterilization was a result of both these new threats to abortion rights and previous concerns about sterilization abuse among women's health movement activists. The New York–based Committee to End Sterilization Abuse (CESA) and other groups that used the name CESA or a similar name had been organized in a number of cities between 1974 and 1978. CAR-ASA was founded before CESA disbanded, and many activists in CESA also became involved in CARASA (Shapiro, 1985:147–48). Although based in New York, CARASA gained a nationwide membership and reputation among younger branch women's movement groups. Since 1977, some branches of CARASA also were formed outside New York.

The Reproductive Rights National Network began in 1978 as a project of a Chicago-based socialist organization called the New American Movement (NAM).[1] The project was conceived in 1977 by NAM's national political secretary, Marilyn Katz, who had been involved with local women's groups and left-wing political groups in several parts of the country, including a group working on sterilization abuse in California. Katz came to the conclusion that local activists working on abortion, sterilization abuse, and other "reproductive rights" issues would accomplish more by working within a national organization with a broader orientation—a perspective that she perceived to be missing from the existing "pro-choice" movement, as shown in her comments quoted earlier.

The project was proposed to NAM as a response to right-wing attacks on abortion rights, which were seen "as part of a general onslaught by conservative and right-wing forces on social gains made in the last decade by women, minorities and the labor movement" (Proposal for National and Local NAM Work for Abortion Rights, November 17, 1977, in Jennifer Knauss private papers). The project's short-run strategy was to strengthen the "defensive movement" to protect abortion rights by coordinating the local efforts of abortion rights and women's health groups. The long-term goal was to develop an "offensive movement" that could fight for a more comprehensive set of demands as the conditions for "free choice," including child care, national health care, high-quality education, and a guaranteed income. The proposal was adopted by NAM in 1977 and implemented in 1978 through existing left–feminist organizational channels. Copies of the first issue of the *Reproductive Rights Newsletter* were distributed through women's groups, NAM chapters and other leftist political organizations, feminist bookstores, and women's centers.

According to Marilyn Katz, there was initially some resistance to the idea of a national network organization:

There was a lot of negativity about coalitions and national groups because of all the splits in the women's unions which had occurred. . . . We had to convince them of the need for a national reproductive rights organization. Also, there was some territorial turfing involved. People from CARASA had their own newsletter and were organizing their own network. They were franchising on the East coast and had their own supporters. They were doubtful the Reproductive Rights National Network would work—I think they may have seen themselves as providing the needed network. They didn't want to put the energy into it. But after it got started, they cooperated. (interview with Marilyn Katz, 1984)

Although these concerns about forming a national organization did affect the type of organizational structure created, the Reproductive Rights National Network got off the ground. R2N2's success was due in part to the availability of preexisting organizational bases. CARASA, in particular, offered the support of its staff, office space in New York, and the use of its membership network. It was also due to the fact that many women, including some who had been members of feminist groups that had broken up, were very interested in working on the abortion issue in the years following the passage of the Hyde Amendment. Not only had the Hyde Amendment raised the class issue of access to abortion, but the New Right had become a visible part of the countermovement. Socialist feminists and other leftists were anxious to respond to these developments.

In response to the formation of a national network organization, a number of new local reproductive rights organizations were created. In addition, a number of existing women's groups and some leftist political groups joined R2N2. By the end of 1978, the project was successful in creating a network of about fifty women's groups and leftist organizations across the country. The Reproductive Rights National Network had taken on an identity of its own even while a project of the New American Movement; in the spring of 1979, R2N2 officially split from NAM and became an independent organization.

One of the local groups formed in response to the creation of R2N2 was Women Organized for Reproductive Choice (WORC). The Reproductive Rights National Network originated in Chicago where the New American Movement was headquartered, and there were close ties between socialist feminists working in the Chicago Women's Health Task Force and members of NAM who were working on the reproductive rights project. In 1979, when the threat from the New Right was particularly visible, activists from the CWHTF began working with activists from the Chicago Women's Health Center, the Health Evaluation and Referral Service, and some leftist political groups in an informal kind of coalition to send demonstrators to a National Right to Life Committee convention in Cincinnati, an effort being coordinated nationally by R2N2. Through this experience, it became evident that there were many adherents of the R2N2 approach in Chicago who were willing to put their energies into work on the abortion issue. As a result, members of the CWHTF began to explore the idea of forming a new organization to mobilize such people. According to the activists I interviewed, there was more than a little hesitation about creating a more inclusive organization among CWHTF members who had endured the sectarian infiltration of the Chicago

Women's Liberation Union (see Appendix A). As a CWHTF activist recalled in an interview:

> It was a very scary time, I remember, due to a strong fear of takeover [by sectarians] within the Chicago Women's Health Task Force. But there was a recognition that we needed to get bigger, so there were ongoing discussions during the summer of 1979. Then in the fall, WORC was formed. So the Chicago Women's Health Task Force didn't really dissolve, it just changed into WORC.

Despite the experiences with sectarian infiltration of some CWHTF members who had been active in the Chicago Women's Liberation Union, the spirit of the time prevailed. The CWHTF disbanded and a new, larger organization, Women Organized for Reproductive Choice, was founded as a member of R2N2 in the fall of 1979.

Multi-Issue Demands

In part because organizations like NARAL and RCAR existed as strong organizations taking a more narrow approach to the issue, feminist organizations often expressed multi-issue concerns in connection with abortion rights. The National Organization for Women, for example, made some attempt to connect abortion rights to other issues. The National Women's Health Network adopted a "Position Paper on Abortion" in 1978 that placed the Network's concern for abortion within the context of the organization's other concerns about the availability of contraceptives, pregnancy disability rights for working women, access to infant health care and high-quality day care, sterilization abuse, and health care in general. The Reproductive Rights National Network (which the NWHN joined as an organizational member) put forth the most comprehensive "pro-choice" position, demanding not only the right to legal abortion, but also the right to child care, health care, an adequate income, and other conditions that would allow women a real choice as to whether or not to have children (see "Reproductive Bill of Rights," *Reproductive Rights Newsletter,* Summer 1979).

Beyond being concerned about more issues than just legal abortion (as are many women's movement organizations active in the pro-choice movement), women's health and reproductive rights groups have been concerned about the way in which the abortion conflict is framed.[2] For example, the NWHN's 1978 statement on abortion concedes a need for "legislative and legal work on abortion rights," stating that the NWHN "supports the single issue organizations which are leading the struggle at the federal and state levels" but opposes "population control" arguments for abortion rights:[3]

> [The NWHN] opposes the use of arguments and policies on the abortion issue which stem from an analysis which suggests that population control is an element in the movement for reproductive rights. Population control groups have tried to counter the attempt to prevent sterilization abuse through regulations, and have suggested that states should fund abortions as a way of keeping welfare costs

> down. The NWHN does not support the population control analysis. It takes its
> stand on the inalienable right of each woman to control her body and her life.
> (Position Paper on Abortion, adopted by the National Women's Health Network
> Board, June 4, 1978; *Network News,* June–July 1978)

The NWHN was thus unwilling to compromise its broader perspective by using
arguments that might be expedient in the single-issue battle for abortion.

Local women's health and reproductive rights activists also tried to promote a
multi-issue perspective. For instance, the Chicago Women's Health Task Force
began as a study group of women's health activists and students who were interested in a whole range of health issues beyond that of abortion. Abortion became
a focus of attention in the summer of 1977, with the threat of a state Medicaid
funding cutoff, the point at which the CWHTF became politically active and open
to new members. Although the political environment forced an initial concentra-
tion on abortion, the Task Force continually attempted to develop a broader analysis of abortion rights. In attempting to reach other activists, the CWHTF argued
that the cutoff of Medicaid funds for abortion discriminated against poor women.
Further, the lack of funding for abortion might increase the incidence of sterilization abuse among poor women and "have a detrimental effect on their overall
health and the health of the community," because of maternal deaths associated
with illegal abortion. They also argued that "if this cut-off is not resisted, cutbacks
in other health services may follow." The Chicago Women's Health Task Force
concluded:

> It is not only necessary to fight for safe and legal abortion but to work for improve-
> ments in the delivery of other health services. Women need more adequate pre-
> natal care, improved access to birth control counseling, better health care services
> for their children, etc. (letter from the Chicago Women's Health Task Force, Sep-
> tember 1977, in Jennifer Knauss private papers)

When the CWHTF disbanded and Women Organized for Reproductive
Choice was formed, the new socialist–feminist organization carried on the perspective that began with the Chicago Women's Liberation Union. The continuity
of membership from the CWLU to the CWHTF to WORC helped ensure this, as
did the connections between WORC and R2N2. Like the Reproductive Rights
National Network, WORC was begun with the idea of organizing women into a
movement to fight for a broad range of "reproductive rights." Although WORC
considered the right to legal abortion important in itself, the group also tried to
use the issue to make connections to other issues included in a comprehensive
notion of "choice."

Strategies and Tactics

Formulating multi-issue demands proved easier than finding the means to pursue
such an agenda. Reproductive rights movement organizations wanted to engage
in proactive, multi-issue, direct-action tactics, but found themselves limited by

both the political environment and their own organizational structures. Although there were some opportunities for direct action and consciousness raising regarding the multi-issue concerns of the reproductive rights movement, the political environment created strong pressures to engage in reactive, single-issue, institutionalized tactics in the electoral and legislative arenas. Organizationally, reproductive rights groups had difficulty finding financial resources and sustaining large memberships because they lacked professional staff and formalized divisions of labor to perform these tasks. And because of both the political environment and organizational considerations, they had trouble convincing stronger movement organizations to act in coalition to achieve proactive multi-issue goals.

Limited Political Opportunities

In the tradition of younger branch women's movement organizations, women's health and reproductive rights groups did try to initiate direct-action tactics whenever there were political opportunities to do so. Before the mobilization of new reproductive rights organizations, existing women's health organizations spearheaded some actions concerning abortion in the wake of the Hyde Amendment. In August 1977 the National Women's Health Network organized a day of demonstrations, including sit-ins at abortion clinics, to protest the Supreme Court ruling permitting states to deny funding for abortions. The NWHN persuaded NARAL, NOW, and Healthright (a New York feminist health journal collective) to co-sponsor the August 11 demonstrations, and mobilized local women's health groups to participate through the connections of NWHN board members.

The Chicago Women's Health Task Force participated in the NWHN sit-ins and other direct-action tactics in response to the 1977 Medicaid funding cutoff proposal in Illinois. The CWHTF was also influential in convincing the Ad Hoc Committee for Abortion Rights to engage primarily in demonstrations rather than in more conventional pressure-group tactics. Nevertheless, the demonstrations were aimed at elected officials, particularly the governor of Illinois, in reaction to anti-abortion gains in the legislative arena. This was a notable change from the tactics of the Chicago Women's Liberation Union, which were often intended to "raise consciousness" and recruit women to the movement, rather than to influence authorities. As one former activist in the CWLU pointed out in an interview regarding the women's liberation movement of the late 1960s and early 1970s, "None of use cared a fuck what happened in the state legislature." In contrast, by the late 1970s, those women's movement organizations descended from the younger branch of the movement were in the position of having to care what happened in the state legislatures as there was now an institutionalized abortion right to protect.

The Reproductive Rights National Network tried to capitalize on concerns about protecting the right to abortion to create a multi-issue movement. Because R2N2 wanted to build a movement, many of its tactics were aimed at publicizing the reproductive rights political perspective in the hope of attracting women to local affiliates. Beginning in 1979, the National Women's Health Network and R2N2 cooperated to organize several demonstrations at the sites of the National

Right to Life Committee's annual conventions. These demonstrations were important organizing tools in that they helped bring into R2N2 local reproductive rights groups like WORC. R2N2 also launched a petition campaign against the Hyde Amendment in 1979, which provided a means of mobilizing activists. But this tactic was not really expected to have an impact on legislators. As former R2N2 staff coordinator Margie Fine explained in an interview, "What we tried to do with the petition campaign was to set up tables, talk to people." This form of "outreach" also had the organizational advantage of giving R2N2 a mailing list.

As an affiliate of R2N2, Women Organized for Reproductive Choice frequently used "petitioning" as a mobilization tactic. Like other R2N2 affiliates, WORC collected names on petitions to protest developments such as the Hyde Amendment, the Human Life Amendment, and the closing of the abortion clinic at Cook County Hospital, more as a form of outreach than as a means of influencing decision makers, although the petitions also were delivered to the appropriate authorities. This tactic, like NARAL's postcard tables, allowed WORC activists to talk to women in various public places about issues of concern. It also provided an activity for would-be activists. When WORC used this tactic in the early 1980s, the organization began to offer training sessions for petition drives and was successful in attracting a number of women who were not regular WORC members but who wanted to do something about the issue. According to WORC coordinator Cathy Christeller:

> We have really talked about the issue at these sessions, and a lot of people raised their concerns about abortion and the whole pro-choice effort. A lot of women who came were women who don't want to come to our meetings, but they come forward to do petitions. Most are young women who want to be activists but who don't share our political views entirely. About fifty women came to a meeting to hand out the petitions. (interview with Cathy Christeller, 1984)

The difficulty with the petitioning tactic, however, was that it could not be used indefinitely; there had to be some fairly concrete threat or issue (e.g., the Medicaid funding cutoff) in order for it to seem legitimate.

Reproductive rights groups needed ongoing opportunities to raise wider issues and to use direct-action tactics. WORC had one such opportunity in 1980 when the president of the Cook County Board of Commissioners, George Dunne, decided to close down the Cook County Hospital abortion clinic, which served poor women in Chicago. This provided an occasion for petitioning and demands for public hearings to protest the closing. WORC became very active in this campaign and also began to cooperate with other groups in the Illinois Pro-Choice Alliance similarly concerned about the clinic's closing. Although some veteran abortion rights activists thought the hearings were a waste of time, because they knew that Dunne was determined to close the clinic, WORC valued the opportunity to raise publicly issues about poor women's access to abortions. As WORC's coordinator at the time commented:

> Our efforts were semi-successful—successful in the sense that we implemented our strategy. We got about one hundred women to show up to demand hearings, and then about two hundred people showed up at the hearings, which was really

good and we got good press coverage . . . of course, the problem with that strategy—we organized the hearings, and they [the opposition] came to speak too. So
that's the risk there. I'm still glad we did it, but of course they won the battle.
(interview with Cathy Christeller, 1984)

At the national level, there was an opportunity to raise public consciousness
in 1981 when Republican Senator John East held hearings on a Human Life Bill
that were biased toward the anti-abortion point of view. On this occasion, R2N2
activists calling themselves the Women's Liberation Zap Brigade disrupted the
hearings. Although R2N2 did not officially sponsor the illegal activity, the organization condoned the disruption by organizing a defense fund for its activists
following their arrest and claiming victory when the case resulted in a lot of publicity for R2N2 and a small fine for the women in the Zap Brigade (*Reproductive
Rights Newsletter,* Summer 1981 and Fall 1981).

Although R2N2 did not have many chances to use the commitment of its
activists in such a manner, the members of local R2N2 affiliates, along with local
NOW members, did engage in some other clever consciousness-raising tactics. For
example, in Cleveland and other cities, local activists attended the speaking
engagements of opponents like Phyllis Schlafly, posing as the barefoot, pregnant
members of organizations like "Ladies Against Women" and carrying signs with
slogans like "You're nobody till you're Mrs. somebody" and "Sperm are people
too" (see Van Kleef, 1982). Such tactics put some life into the movement and
helped attract activists, but there were only so many occasions for their use.

The problem for both WORC and R2N2 was that there were few tactical
opportunities for pressing multi-issue, proactive demands in the post-Hyde period
of the abortion conflict. Like other pro-choice groups, reproductive rights organizations found themselves reacting to countermovement initiatives and successes. Although there were some opportunities for direct-action tactics, the
actions were nevertheless reactive defenses of the right to abortion rather than proactive attempts to gain new advantages. For example, reproductive rights activists
set up escort services for women using abortion clinics in order to counter the
"street counseling" of anti-abortion activists trying to talk women out of having
abortions.

Moreover, because much of the abortion battle was being waged on institutionalized battlegrounds, R2N2 found it difficult even to maintain its commitment to direct action. Most notably, R2N2 could not totally ignore the fact that
the abortion conflict was shifting to the political arena. In 1980, several local affiliates of R2N2 became involved in electoral politics and presented proposals for
R2N2's participation in the 1980 elections. But owing to the biases of some members of the R2N2 steering committee against such institutionalized tactics, and to
fears that electoral activities would detract from the broader goal of building a
movement for reproductive rights (*Reproductive Rights Newsletter,* Summer
1980), the proposals were rejected. It was decided that the national organization
would not become directly involved in electoral politics through tactics such as
campaign endorsements. Some local R2N2 affiliates did engage in political activities, however, and the national organization did some educational work on the
candidates' voting records. As the staff coordinator of R2N2 in 1980 commented,

"Really, we didn't have much choice about whether to address electoral politics because that was the arena; that was where the battle was" (interview with Margie Fine, 1984).

Organizational Obstacles

Women's health and reproductive rights groups did try to create forums for advancing their own proactive goals, but they were limited by a lack of resources and by organizational structures that made resource mobilization difficult. In the case of the National Women's Health Network, the lack of local affiliates made it difficult to sustain any kind of direct-action campaign. A member of the NWHN board of directors who helped organize the sit-in demonstrations in 1977 said in an interview that she and others on the board would have liked the NWHN to spearhead more such actions, but that this was too difficult to do without "more lasting structures" at the local level. In the early 1980s, the NWHN began to establish state affiliates, but was limited in its ability to do so by insufficient resources for hiring staff such as field coordinators. In contrast, a more professionalized organization like NARAL could actively assist the formation of affiliates with staff and funding.[4]

After the Reproductive Rights National Network was formed, there was a pool of local activists, but R2N2's decentralized and informal organizational structure (see Appendix A) limited its ability to expand its membership and programs. Because R2N2 activists wanted to avoid creating a bureaucratic organization, there was only a steering committee consisting of regionally elected representatives and one national staff person to lead the organization. R2N2 relied on the motivations of its steering committee members to coordinate its programs. According to informants, there was a fair amount of turnover on the steering committee, and the national leadership did not always include the kind of highly motivated individuals the organization needed. The result, in the words of one informant experienced in the women's liberation movement, was "the classic leadership problem"; sometimes there were people around to coordinate projects and sometimes not, creating an uneven national leadership. In contrast with organizations like NARAL and NOW, there was no formalized division of labor to ensure that tasks would be performed regardless of changes in leadership.

Resolutions were passed at annual meetings, but in order for a program to get off the ground, someone had to take the initiative to organize it, and frequently no one did. R2N2 also did not have field staff to recruit new groups into the network. The organization particularly wanted to reach "women of color" groups, but there were organizational obstacles to doing so despite the fact that R2N2 did address issues of race and class. Such groups were invited to national meetings, and some financing was obtained from local New York foundations to enable them to come, but R2N2 had a difficult time getting activists from these groups involved.[5]

R2N2 also had difficulty performing tasks such as the fund-raising necessary to keep the organization afloat. With only one regular staff member,[6] professional leaders could not take over the maintenance of R2N2 as they did in many other pro-choice organizations. Consequently, R2N2 was unable to take advantage of opportunities for raising money through such means as direct-mail solicitation. Indeed, the organization's maintenance problems became so severe that R2N2 ended up dissolving in 1984, largely because of financial difficulties.

The local Women Organized for Reproductive Choice had similar problems, although it managed to survive the demise of R2N2. Although WORC's strategy was to use tactics that would build a movement capable of achieving long-term goals, what happened was that its activities were aimed at simply keeping the movement alive in the interval between whatever tactical opportunities there were to react to countermovement initiatives. The difficulty was that in the absence of a more bureaucratic organization capable of mobilizing more resources and dividing the labor among members, WORC activists literally wore themselves out just trying to keep the movement going. As a WORC activist explained in a 1984 interview when I asked her about the group's tactics:

> You've got to understand that there are two kinds of things we do: activities aimed directly at winning things and activities aimed at building a movement. You know, you've got to keep having events; we need to have actions to let people know we're still around; there is still a women's movement. We do those kinds of things on days like January 22 [the anniversary of the 1973 Supreme Court ruling] and October 3 which is Rosie Himenez Day—the day she died from the first illegal abortion after [the] Hyde [Amendment]. The problem is that we end up doing what we call "date hopping," which we hate. First there is January 22, then International Women's Day on March 8, then we do some summer outreach work, then October 3. It takes about two months to plan for each event; then everybody is out of energy.

The lack of more formal organizational structures in the reproductive rights movement thus created resource strains that complicated organizational maintenance. Although reproductive rights groups could survive on enthusiasm when the abortion issue was "hot," as it was in the late 1970s and early 1980s, they had a hard time remaining active after such threats had subsided. Movement organizations with more centralized structures and more formal divisions of labor are better able to maintain themselves while also pursuing instrumental tactics. For example, NARAL and NOW have developed the kinds of structures that allow them to carry out such activities as fund-raising and public relations work but still engage in tactics like lobbying and campaign work.[7]

The Limits of Coalition Work

Originally, the strategy of the reproductive rights movement was to take advantage of the organizational strengths of the single-issue abortion rights movement to build a broader pro-choice movement. R2N2 and WORC both joined pro-choice coalitions and tried to convince larger organizations to extend the work of the coalitions to address multiple issues, but they were unsuccessful in doing so. One source of this failure was the political environment. Countermovement activities forced pro-choice organizations to focus on defending legal abortion in the legislative and political arenas. In a period in which a Human Life Amendment seemed a real possibility, it was difficult for organizations like NARAL and RCAR to think about regaining Medicaid funding, much less joining R2N2 in the fight against sterilization abuse. Far from being able to sway single-issue groups to their perspective, reproductive rights groups often created conflict and resentment within pro-choice coalitions. As an informant from Illinois NARAL commented in an interview about WORC's participation in the Illinois Pro-Choice Alliance:

> It was really hard to take a group like WORC coming in and talking like we didn't care about sterilization abuse, like we didn't care about poor women. Other people in the coalition really resented their holier-than-thou attitude. It's just not true that the rest of us don't care about poor women or other issues. But it was like, first things first; right now we're fighting this battle.

Beyond the fact that external threats to abortion in the post-Hyde period created pressures for a single-issue focus on abortion, it was difficult for reproductive rights groups to win over other pro-choice groups to their perspective because coalition work tended to be oriented toward conventional pressure-group politics. Both the national-level Abortion Information Exchange and the Illinois Pro-Choice Alliance became almost exclusively focused on legislative lobbying tactics. This focus was organizationally useful to the coalitions because it helped overcome one of the major obstacles to coalition work: When individual movement organizations work in the name of a coalition, they forego the recognition and visibility that they achieve with campaigns of their own. However, groups that might otherwise compete with one another have an incentive to cooperate on a very expensive and necessary activity such as legislative lobbying because, by working together on that one activity, they save resources for other activities pursued outside the coalition (see Staggenborg, 1986).

In the institutionalized arena of legislative lobbying, pro-choice groups realized that a narrow, single-issue approach was most effective and that the many demands of the reproductive rights movement were out of place. Even in the Ad Hoc Committee for Abortion Rights, which was much more oriented toward direct-action tactics than institutionalized lobbying, some strategic differences appeared when the group tried to appeal to government authorities. For example, a meeting was arranged between the pro-choice coalition and a representative of the governor of Illinois to discuss the state Medicaid funding cutoff. As an Ad Hoc Committee participant from Illinois RCAR recounted in an interview:

> We put together a group of people to go talk to Governor Thompson. Thompson, you know, has been very supportive right down the line. Well, he couldn't see us, but he sent an aide. This was to talk about public funding. I remember a woman from the Emma Goldman Clinic—and I remember being very impressed with her, actually, the way she stood up—but she stood up and said, "What we want is for abortion to be free to all women"! Well, if you really pushed me to the wall I'd probably support that position because I believe medical care should be provided to all, but politically, it was just absurd to come out with that kind of thing at that meeting!

This informant interpreted differences within the Ad Hoc Committee as strategic rather than truly ideological:

A lot of those people were just not politically astute. Like they would say things like "voting is not the issue. I don't vote." The basic difference in that coalition was, I think, one of strategy. If you are going to have the strategy of appealing to the broad middle-class liberal-to-conservative wing, which can understand the abortion issue in a certain way, it just doesn't help to say "get your laws off my body." . . . The general difference in strategy was the strategy of going for the middle-of-the-road people versus making a statement without regard to the political implications.

Women's health and reproductive rights activists, for their part, did not see themselves as simply "making a statement" or as cutting off a middle-of-the-road constituency. Rather, they saw themselves as doing "political education" that would raise consciousness about issues beyond that of abortion, to potentially radicalize people. But this clearly is not the way conventional lobbying is carried out, and, as pro-choice coalitions became more involved in institutionalized arenas, it became more difficult for reproductive rights groups to influence their tactics.

The presence of organizations like NARAL also left R2N2 and its affiliates with no real role to play in an abortion battle fought primarily in institutionalized arenas. R2N2 was never intended to compete with NARAL or NOW. As founder Marilyn Katz explained in an interview, the idea from the start was that R2N2 would have a "symbiotic" relationship to groups that did the legislative work while R2N2 did "political education" to organize women into a broader reproductive rights movement. Once women were organized, however, they would need tactics to carry out, and R2N2 and its affiliates had neither the kinds of assets nor the ideological inclinations necessary for most of the institutionalized tactics that had become the mainstay of the pro-choice movement.

Conclusion *all*

The experience of the reproductive rights movement in the late 1970s and early 1980s reveals the importance of the political environment in creating and limiting opportunities for collective action. The rise of the New Right and other countermovement threats to abortion rights in the post-Hyde period provided the opportunity to mobilize feminists attracted to the multi-issue politics and the direct-action tactics of the reproductive rights movement. Reproductive rights activists were able to engage in some direct action in response to countermovement initiatives, and they did have some success in carrying out consciousness-raising activities to promote the reproductive rights perspective.

The reproductive rights movement was greatly limited, however, by its dependence on countermovement initiatives for opportunities to engage in direct action. And, like other movement organizations, reproductive rights groups were subject to external pressures to engage in institutionalized tactics or to be left out of the pro-choice movement. Moreover, whatever gains were made in terms of public education and movement mobilization, the reproductive rights movement could not win substantive victories in the absence of tactics for achieving proactive goals.

The problems of the reproductive rights movement were further compounded by its organizational choices. Although decentralized and informal structures can lead to tactical innovation because they encourage grass-roots participation (as was the case in the CWLU and other younger branch women's movement organizations), they also complicate organizational maintenance (cf. Staggenborg, 1989b). In the long run, the kind of grass-roots organizing carried out with the aid of professional leaders in organizations like NARAL and NOW may be more enduring than the grass-roots participation engendered by the decentralized and informal structure of an organization like R2N2.

The experience of the reproductive rights movement suggests that the strategy of capitalizing on concerns about a single issue to create a multi-issue movement will produce limited results in the presence of a strong countermovement that is making visible gains. This is seen clearly in the difficulties that reproductive rights groups had working in coalition: The multi-issue perspective of the reproductive rights movement was a luxury that other pro-choice groups did not feel they could afford in the face of mounting threats from the anti-abortion movement.

IV

THE
PRO-CHOICE MOVEMENT
IN THE 1980s
AND BEYOND

10

Victory and Survival, 1983–1989

On June 15, 1983, the Supreme Court reaffirmed *Roe* v. *Wade* by striking down most state and local restrictions limiting access to abortions.[1] And on June 28, the Senate rejected a constitutional amendment that would have allowed Congress and the state legislatures to restrict abortions (see *New York Times,* July 10, 1983). With these events, the years of heightened threat to abortion rights that began with the anti-abortion victory on the Hyde Amendment came to an end. The Supreme Court would later open the way for another period of intensive attacks on abortion rights with its *Webster* v. *Reproductive Health Services* ruling in 1989, but in 1983 the abortion conflict entered a new phase during which threats to abortion rights were much less visible than in the late 1970s and early 1980s.

As we saw in the period following *Roe* v. *Wade,* victories such as those of 1983 affect the political opportunity structure of a movement, creating both opportunities and obstacles for further collective action. On the one hand, victory may solidify the position of a movement as a respected player in established politics and present opportunities to engage in offensive, rather than defensive, actions. On the other hand, the removal of immediate threats may also demobilize movement support.[2] And, as was the case after 1973, countermovement activities are critical to determining the course of a movement following victory. If the countermovement is able to create new threats, the movement may be forced to drop its own initiatives to respond, but it will also benefit organizationally from threats that galvanize constituents.

Opportunities for Action

There was a definite recognition within pro-choice ranks that the victories of 1983 represented a critical juncture in the movement. Suddenly, pro-choice groups were no longer in the position of simply responding to countermovement initiatives but, instead, were asking themselves, in the words of a NARAL memo to supporters in July 1983, "Where do we go from here?" They also realized that the victories might create complacency among pro-choice constituents, while spurring the countermovement. NARAL's executive director argued that it was essential to *"continue to take the power of the opposition seriously"* (emphasis in original) by keeping up the pro-choice lobby in Congress and working against the reelection of an anti-abortion President who would have the chance to appoint more justices to the Supreme Court ("Analysis of Recent Pro-choice Victories, or: Where do we go from here?" memo to NARAL members, July 1983).

The 1983 victories did have a noticeable effect on pro-choice strategies and mobilization. Although mindful of the need to continue to fend off countermovement attacks, pro-choice groups began to think about recouping their losses, rather than only guarding against further incursions on abortion rights. As a 1983 report from the NARAL Foundation noted:

> The present circumstances provide a unique opportunity for pro-choice forces to take the initiative to reverse previous losses. Our state organizations can intensify activities to regain Medicaid funding in order to guarantee equal access to abortion for all women regardless of their economic circumstances. In addition, we can work to secure for pregnant teenagers the option of abortion, unencumbered by parental consent requirements. ("The Future of the Abortion Rights Movement: An Update Prepared by The NARAL Foundation," 1983)

In 1984, NARAL and other pro-choice organizations began lobbying Congress for a Reproductive Health Equity Act to restore Medicaid funding and federal employee insurance coverage for abortions. Although supporters of the bill did not expect it to pass in 1984, it is significant that pro-choice forces took this action following the 1983 victories.[3]

At the same time that the movement was beginning to take the offensive, the concerns of leaders about a potential decline in constituent support following the pro-choice victories were becoming a reality. Local and national informants reported a drop in financial resources and active participation as threats to abortion rights in the Reagan era seemed to subside.[4] As an Illinois NARAL leader recalled, "When we won on the national vote in Congress, and with the Court ruling, people started feeling the issue was settled and laid off on it" (interview with former Illinois NARAL director Jan Ryan, 1984). For the NARAL affiliate, this meant a cutback in staff and a drop-off in the number of house meetings held, due to both the reduction in staff and a lack of enthusiasm among potential constituents. However, large national organizations like NARAL had professional leaders who helped sustain movement activities despite changes in the political climate that made the abortion issue less pressing to constituents.

Although formalized organizations like NARAL and NOW were able to remain stable despite some membership losses, informally organized groups had a much more difficult time. For example, the Reproductive Rights National Network dissolved in 1984 when it ran out of money. According to a former R2N2 staff coordinator, its severe financial problems began after the 1983 Supreme Court ruling, when the local New York foundations that had previously provided the bulk of R2N2's funding began to neglect reproductive rights in favor of other causes such as the peace movement. R2N2 had never developed alternative sources of funding such as direct-mail solicitation because of its lack of formalized structure, and, in the view of its former coordinator, it was consequently "too dependent" on foundation money (interview with 1980–83 R2N2 staff coordinator Margie Fine, 1984). Although local R2N2 affiliates like Women Organized for Reproductive Choice remained in existence after 1983, many were barely alive. Not only was the abortion issue no longer "hot," but there also were few opportunities for the kind of direct-action tactics that helped attract reproductive rights supporters.

In the year and a half after the pro-choice victories of June 1983, it looked to many observers as if the abortion conflict was finally settling into a quiet stalemate. The anti-abortion movement was divided after its defeats (see Low, 1987), and the pro-choice movement was losing some of the financial and activist support that it had mobilized in times of greater threat. Pro-choice groups did want to regain Medicaid funding and complete access to abortion for teenagers, but even reproductive rights sympathizers recognized that these efforts had "less mass appeal than issues of legality" (Clarke and Wolfson, 1985). It was also difficult for local reproductive rights groups to continue to persuade activists to work on such problems when they were not making any progress. In Chicago, Women Organized for Reproductive Choice experienced this problem as the group continued its work on abortion access issues in the 1980s, including a campaign to reopen the Cook County Hospital abortion clinic that was closed in 1980 (see Chapter 7). As WORC's coordinator commented, "The problem has been how to keep going when we're not winning any victories, when nobody is doing anything. People after a certain point felt like there was not a lot more we could do" (interview with Cathy Christeller, 1990). Nevertheless, the pro-choice movement did survive in the 1980s, largely because the countermovement came up with new tactics and the Reagan and Bush Administrations continued to attack abortion rights, thereby creating new threats, albeit somewhat less visible ones, and tactical opportunities for the pro-choice movement.

Countermovement Initiatives
and Movement Survival

The Battleground Shifts

The situation of the pro-choice movement changed fairly quickly as the countermovement responded to its losses by shifting the focus of the abortion conflict away from the institutionalized arenas in which pro-choice forces were gaining the upper hand to the realm of public relations. The centerpiece of the new anti-abortion strategy was the film *The Silent Scream,* which was produced by the former NARAL activist turned anti-abortionist, Dr. Bernard Nathanson, and released in December 1984. *The Silent Scream* used sonography in its attempt to make its case that the fetus suffers pain in an abortion and to shift the debate on abortion to "scientific" issues. The film was distributed to members of Congress and received a great deal of media coverage, including network news coverage around the time of the anniversary of *Roe* v. *Wade* in January 1985, which was largely favorable to the anti-abortion movement (see Kalter, 1985).

After the public relations success of *The Silent Scream,* pro-choice groups were forced to respond. Although it diverted resources away from pro-choice initiatives, the countermovement tactic was also beneficial to the movement in that it aroused supporters and created tactical opportunities for local volunteers. National and local pro-choice groups mobilized throughout the country to respond to the countermovement initiative. Some organizations, including Planned Parenthood, employed their own experts to refute the "scientific" arguments of the film.[5] Others attempted to reframe the debate.

NARAL took the latter approach with its "Abortion Rights: Silent No More" campaign. This strategy employed a formalized version of the "speak-out" tactic begun by women's liberation groups. NARAL's use of this tactic, which had successfully raised consciousness and mobilized women before legalization, was intended to focus media and public attention on women and their lives rather than on the fetus. To accomplish this, NARAL asked women around the country to write letters about their experiences with abortion, addressed to President Reagan and other elected officials, and to send the letters to NARAL and its affiliates. Along with the NARAL message, "We are your mothers, your daughters, your sisters, your friends, and abortion is a choice we have made," the letters were read, often by their authors, at public forums on a scheduled day. Although this version of the speak-out was not the spontaneous public event of the early days of the women's movement, it was nevertheless effective in arousing pro-choice emotions and generating media publicity. For example, the letter of a woman who had been brutally raped by her illegal abortionist and then left near death received widespread attention.[6]

For NARAL, the campaign against *The Silent Scream* created some momentum in an otherwise "slow" period of the abortion conflict. Kate Michelman pointed out that when she took over as executive director of NARAL in 1986, it was a time when mobilization was difficult, "but NARAL had just come off the 1984–85 Silent No More campaign, which was very important as a galvanizing force. It had succeeded in reframing the debate—away from a complete emphasis on the fetus to the role of women" (interview with Kate Michelman, 1990). Many feminist groups were also energized as they participated in the NARAL campaign and organized to make their own responses to *The Silent Scream.* The shift in battleground temporarily reinvigorated Women Organized for Reproductive Choice, which was barely surviving when the opportunity to respond to the film came along. WORC urged women to write letters for the NARAL campaign and also sponsored a well-attended screening and discussion of *The Silent Scream* and a Planned Parenthood response film. Across the country, feminist groups developed responses, including some feminist films, to the anti-abortion strategy.[7]

Although the outrage and activism provoked by *The Silent Scream* could not sustain the pro-choice movement indefinitely, the film came along at a critical time. It provided tactical opportunities which utilized the energies of local activists and helped revive the sense of immediately felt grievances that had rallied activists before the legalization of abortion. The film also shifted the abortion debate to an ideological realm (cf. Petchesky, 1987) where many feminists who felt left out of institutionalized battles were quite comfortable.

Street-Level Tactics

Following the *Silent Scream* strategy, countermovement actors and their supporters continued to generate tactics that helped, in turn, to keep the pro-choice movement on the alert. The most important development in the abortion conflict in the 1980s was the increased use of direct-action tactics (cf. Hershey, 1986), which were often aimed at abortion services and their workers and clients.[8] Although these tactics included bombings of abortion clinics and other forms of harassment, anti-abortionists also drew on the repertoire of tactics employed earlier by the civil rights and women's movements and by the pre-1973 abortion movement. By engaging in direct action and bringing the abortion conflict back to the level of women's experiences, the countermovement helped revitalize the grass-roots pro-choice movement.

THE PROBLEM PREGNANCY INDUSTRY

One of the important developments of the 1980s was the growth of what Ginsburg (1989) calls the "problem pregnancy industry," consisting of various services to pregnant women as alternatives to abortion clinics. Although Birthright had been in existence since 1968 as a service that was intended to give women an alternative to abortion, many additional alternative services sprang up after 1983.[9] One reason for the growth of these services was the recognition among anti-abortionists after their 1983 defeat of "the reality that a human life amendment is not a viable remedy in the near future" (Wharton, 1986). Another reason was the concern of some countermovement activists to answer pro-choice criticisms that they had no concern for pregnant women (Ginsburg, 1989:97).

Although some of these services have been candid about their purposes, others have earned the label "bogus clinics" through their deceptive advertising practices. Based on a strategy devised by the St. Louis–based Pearson Foundation, many such clinics advertise themselves as "problem pregnancy" or "crisis pregnancy" centers, offering free pregnancy testing and giving no indication that they do not provide abortions. Once lured to these clinics, women are shown an anti-abortion slide show or film that sometimes includes pictures of bloody aborted fetuses (see *Newsweek,* September 1, 1986). These tactics have outraged pro-choice activists, who have mobilized against the bogus clinics.

In Chicago, Women Organized for Reproductive Choice undertook an investigation of problem pregnancy services reminiscent of the type of research activism pioneered by younger branch women's movement activists such as the founders of the Health Evaluation and Referral Service in Chicago. Through this activity, WORC recruited a number of young women activists, who were sent undercover to investigate the bogus clinics, armed with urine from pregnant women obtained from a women's health clinic. In addition to publicizing the findings of these investigations through leaflets and press work, WORC activists picketed bogus clinics and "abortion referral" services, which began cropping up in Chicago in 1986 (WORC newsletters, 1986–87; interview with former WORC coordinator Cathy Christeller, 1990). Throughout the country, pro-choice activists made similar efforts to expose such services, and in San Francisco and elsewhere pro-choice activists filed lawsuits to force the services to alter their practices (see *Newsweek,* September 1, 1986; *Against the Current,* 1989).

In addition to services aimed at women seeking abortions, anti-abortion groups also began to offer help to women "traumatized" by abortion. In 1985, two organizations, The American Victims of Abortion and National Teens for Life, were formed for this purpose (Wharton, 1986). Anti-abortion organizations, including an organization called the American Rights Coalition, have been promoting the existence of a "post-abortion syndrome" of physical and emotional effects following abortion[10] and have offered legal services to women wishing to file malpractice suits against abortion clinics. As Garb (1989a:3) notes, such tactics have pushed the abortion conflict "onto the pro-choice activists' own turf—women's health."[11] Although such tactics may prove effective, they also give pro-choice activists an opportunity to draw on the skills of women's health movement activists who have years of experience with their own self-help projects and battles with the medical establishment.

ATTACKS ON ABORTION PROVIDERS AND CLIENTS

Beyond offering alternative services, anti-abortion activists have used several other direct-action tactics aimed at preventing abortions. The most dramatic attacks on abortion services have been the bombings of abortion clinics, which began in the 1970s but increased sharply in 1984. In that year there were twenty-four bombings and arsons, compared with one such incident in 1981, eight in 1982, and three in 1983 (Donovan, 1985a). In 1985, abortion providers reported increased harassment of various types (see Forrest and Henshaw, 1987), and there was a great deal of media publicity about clinic bombings. Although bombings and other forms of violence have been disavowed by most anti-abortion movement organizations, and appear to be carried out by individuals and small groups on the fringes of the countermovement, such as the Army of God (Donovan, 1985a:6), they have helped spur pro-choice activities in defense of abortion clinics. For example, members of the National Organization for Women spent several nights in abortion clinics around the United States to protect them and protest the violence (*Chicago Tribune,* January 11, 1985). Longtime pro-choice activist William Baird organized clinic operators to track down bombers (*Newsweek,* January 14, 1985). And in Chicago, WORC formed a Clinic Defense Network that organized supporters to be on call for emergency pickets wherever there were bomb threats or other types of attacks on clinics (WORC newsletter, March 1985).

Besides bombings and arson, other activities targeted at abortion providers and clients also increased in the 1980s. The growing popularity of these tactics reflected the rise to prominence within the anti-abortion movement of direct-action advocates such as Joseph Scheidler, who outlined his methods in his 1985 book *Closed: 99 Ways to Stop Abortion.* The tactics practiced by Scheidler and others include various kinds of "sidewalk counseling" techniques, which anti-abortion activists use when approaching women entering abortion clinics to try to talk them out of having abortions. They also include the use of "truth teams," consisting of a woman and her partner who enter an abortion clinic by making an appointment for the woman and, once inside, begin to have "second thoughts" and discuss the "pro-life" point of view, sometimes with literature obtained from sidewalk counselors outside the clinic, with the goal of engaging legitimate clinic clients in conversation and dissuading them from having abortions. Among the many other direct-action techniques used with increasing frequency since the early 1980s are sit-ins and pickets at clinics and pickets of the homes of doctors who perform abortions.

All of these tactics were forerunners of the massive direct-action campaign known as "Operation Rescue" that began in 1988. Founded by evangelical Christian Randall Terry, Operation Rescue was designed to use the bodies of anti-abortion activists to stop the operation of abortion clinics. In this strategy, the target is kept secret prior to a "rescue" to prevent police and pro-choice activists from blocking the operation. Once at the clinic, the "rescuers" lie down in doorways to prevent access to the clinic and, borrowing a technique of the civil rights movement, go limp when arrested. "Sidewalk counselors" accost women arriving to use the clinic, and "prayer supporters" sing hymns and observe the police (see Dobie, 1989; Wills, 1989, for detailed descriptions of Operation Rescue procedures). After it began in 1988, Operation Rescue was carried out in numerous cities, and large numbers of demonstrators were arrested.

Operation Rescue and other direct-action tactics aimed at abortion clinics stimulated grass-roots response from pro-choice supporters. Throughout the country, pro-choice groups organized counter-demonstrations and clinic escorts for women entering abortion clinics, and activists and clinics filed lawsuits to win injunctions against certain forms of harassment (see Donovan, 1985a). When Operation Rescue began, it provoked a variety of responses from pro-choice activists. Taking exception to the "minority religious views" that were often shouted at the "rescues," the Religious Coalition for Abortion Rights attempted to promote a pro-choice religious perspective by launching "Operation Respect," a campaign to provide counseling and escorts for abortion clinic clients when requested by clinics (*Options,* Winter 1988). Other pro-choice activists staged large counter-demonstrations and offered clinic escorts in response to Operation Rescue. When Operation Rescue came to Los Angeles in March 1989, hundreds of pro-choice activists were on hand, using their cars to block the anti-abortionists' access to the clinic, escorting women into the clinic, and drowning out the countermovement's songs with their own pro-choice chants (see Dobie, 1989, for a firsthand account). The highly visible "rescue" tactic thus served not only to mobilize anti-abortion activists but also to reenergize pro-choice supporters. As one pro-choice observer commented:

> Operation Rescue's direct actions have forced almost everyone to take a side and to defend their position, and may turn out to be a disastrous strategy turn for the "right to life" movement. The specter of women at a very vulnerable moment being assaulted in the name of morality has provoked a widespread revulsion and the need to articulate a counter morality, one that values the lives of women. . . . The paradox of Operation Rescue is that it visually alerts a wide population to the reality that it is women who are under attack in the anti-abortion mobilization. (Erlien, 1988:15)

In Chicago, in answer to Operation Rescue, Women Organized for Reproductive Choice spawned a new group called the Emergency Clinic Defense Coalition (ECDC). Although WORC had previously responded to anti-abortion attacks on clinics, by 1988 the group's reproductive rights activities had fallen off because of a lack of tactical opportunities and a switch in concern among some activists to the issue of women and AIDS (see Appendix A). In fact, WORC was being "kept together artificially" by coordinator Cathy Christeller, who continued through the late 1980s to send out a newsletter for the organization. When Operation Rescue announced plans for a "National Day of Rescue," however, a new mobilization commenced. As Cathy Christeller recalled:

> I sent a letter out under WORC's name—there were some other people [involved] too who weren't in WORC—but there were people who wanted to discuss doing clinic defense. After there'd been this lull in activity, I felt we had to give people a chance to do something. There were people who wanted to do clinic defense, people who wanted to respond to Operation Rescue. . . . It was really amazing how people came out to work on clinic defense. There was one person from Jane who had never been involved in WORC but who was just really moved by the whole problem of women having access to the clinics. We got all kinds of calls and worked on getting people signed up to do clinic defense. So first it was Operation Rescue—they really mobilized our people—and then it was the *Webster* decision. There was this whole new constituency that could be mobilized into ECDC. (interview with Cathy Christeller, 1990)

Most important to this new constituency were young women, including both high school and college students, who were anxious to defend abortion rights in response to Operation Rescue and later the 1989 Supreme Court decision, *Webster* v. *Reproductive Health Services*. The Emergency Clinic Defense Coalition held a successful counter-demonstration when Operation Rescue came to Chicago in 1988 and set up a "response network" to guard against any future "rescues." Then in January 1989, ECDC built on the momentum generated by Operation Rescue to stage a large demonstration marking the anniversary of *Roe* v. *Wade;* some 750 people, including many college students, marched past two bogus clinics to the State of Illinois Building in downtown Chicago. In doing so, ECDC's goal was to focus attention on the legal threats to abortion posed by the upcoming *Webster* decision, anti-abortion harassment of clinics, and the cutoff of state funding for abortions (Gudenkanst, 1989).

The Emergency Clinic Defense Coalition was but one of many such groups across the country that rallied in reaction to Operation Rescue and other attacks on abortion clinics. Despite the successful mobilization, however, "clinic defense" was not a strategy that united the pro-choice movement. As ECDC activist Cathy Christeller observed:

> Clinic defense really emerged as a major split in the movement. . . . The problem with clinic defense—there really is a physical violence potential. We had very serious discussions about it, and we concluded that clinic defense is not purely a good thing to do. I mean, pickets and so forth are one thing, but the problem with clinic

defense is that it's scary to the very people we're trying to defend—the women trying to use the clinics. We had a lot of discussion around that, but people said, "We still have to do this" because if there is no response, they will shut down the clinics. (interview with Cathy Christeller, 1990)

Other organizations, such as NARAL of Illinois and Chicago NOW, working through the Illinois Pro-Choice Alliance, were concerned about participating in demonstrations that were difficult to control and that might further upset women using the clinics. But because there was so much interest in responding to Operation Rescue, they did become involved in the demonstrations. They concentrated, however, on providing "clinic escorts" for women rather than on more confrontational "clinic defense." As Illinois NARAL's executive director commented about her organization's differences with ECDC:

> Their tactics are very different; they are more confrontive. NARAL works hard to work within the system. Like if we are going to do something, I will call the Chicago police and tell them that the opposition might show up and ask if they [the police] will be there—we want the police to be there. And they've been great. But people in ECDC don't necessarily feel the same way about the police. (interview with Illinois NARAL director Pat Dougherty, 1990)

For their part, activists in ECDC felt that groups like Chicago NOW and Illinois NARAL were limited by a "control mania" manifested in actions like hiring a public relations person (dressed in a suit and heels) to be at a demonstration to speak to the press (interview with ECDC activist Cathy Christeller, 1990). Thus, clinic defense mobilized grass-roots constituents but it also created divisions over strategy within the pro-choice movement. This was because more formalized movement organizations like NARAL were less comfortable with the direct-action tactics than were informal organizations like ECDC.

Ongoing Political Battles

Abortion clinics were not the only fronts on which the abortion battle continued in the 1980s. Movement and countermovement forces continued to spar in the political arena, where groups like NARAL and NOW were quite comfortable. In the 1984 Presidential election, anti-abortion forces picketed the appearances of Democratic Vice-Presidential candidate Geraldine Ferraro for her pro-choice views, while pro-choice groups, particularly NOW chapters, demonstrated in support of Ferraro and opposed the reelection of Ronald Reagan. In 1988, NARAL and other pro-choice organizations endorsed pro-choice Democratic candidate Michael Dukakis, while anti-abortionists supported George Bush, who pledged to continue Ronald Reagan's anti-abortion stance. In the 1980s there were also referenda campaigns in a number of states over the issue of state funding of abortions (see *American Medical News,* 1988b; Donovan, 1985b, 1986) that kept both sides involved in the political arena as well as in direct-action battles over abortion services.

The Reagan–Bush War on Abortion

In the 1980s, countermovement initiatives were important to keeping alive the abortion conflict and the pro-choice movement. Nevertheless, there were limits to the countermovement's ability to continue the struggle indefinitely. Observers sympathetic to the anti-abortion cause have themselves noted serious splits within the countermovement and the problems it has had in maintaining grass-roots support (cf. Low, 1987; Wharton, 1986). Indeed, the founder of the Life Amendment Political Action Committee, which was in debt after the 1984 elections, commented in 1987 that "the pro-life movement has lost momentum" (*New York Times,* August 9, 1987). Moreover, tactics that once mobilized supporters and attracted public attention to the anti-abortion cause may lose their novelty and/ or be countered by the opposition (cf. McAdam, 1983). For example, Bernard Nathanson's sequel to *The Silent Scream,* a film called *Eclipse of Reason* that shows a late second-trimester abortion, was released in 1987 (*American Medical News,* 1988a) but received almost no media publicity, in contrast with the earlier film. Although Operation Rescue revitalized the countermovement when it began in 1988, the organization was scaling back its operation by 1990 because of severe financial difficulties stemming from pro-choice lawsuits and government fines.[12] Tactical innovations alone, it would seem, could not have sustained the abortion conflict indefinitely. Support for the anti-abortion movement from the Reagan and Bush Administrations was critical in keeping alive the abortion conflict and in bringing about the 1989 Supreme Court decision.

The Reagan Administration's war on abortion extended far beyond support for efforts to limit abortion through legislation. Countermovement sympathizers were appointed to lead a number of federal agencies, and the agencies' regulatory powers were used wherever possible to fight abortion. Most notably, the Reagan Administration attempted to change the regulations of Title X of the Public Health Service Act (even though it had never funded abortion services) to prevent Title X recipients such as Planned Parenthood from counseling clients about abortion or referring them to services and to require that recipient programs be completely separate from any privately funded abortion services (see Klitsch, 1988). The attack on abortion through Title X and other anti-abortion initiatives of the Reagan and Bush Administrations have served to arouse pro-choice opposition among professional organizations, such as the American Medical Association and the American Public Health Association, and to maintain the heavy involvement of organizations like Planned Parenthood in the pro-choice movement.

Significantly, the attack on Title X funding was held up by court injunction against the regulations. The Reagan Administration was stymied in its war on abortion by both Congress—which failed to pass a number of anti-abortion bills during the Reagan years—and the courts. The Administration's most potent weapon against abortion, therefore, was its ability to alter the composition of the courts, including both the lower federal courts and the Supreme Court, through judicial appointments. By the late 1980s, anti-abortion judges appointed by Ronald Reagan dominated the lower federal courts (see Walker, 1990:348).[13] In 1987, open warfare broke out over the abortion issue and the Supreme Court when Reagan nominated Judge Robert Bork to fill the vacancy left by the retirement of Justice Lewis Powell. Although Reagan had previously appointed two conservative Justices, Sandra Day O'Connor and Antonin Scalia,[14] and elevated *Roe* v. *Wade* foe William Rehnquist to Chief Justice, the nomination of Robert Bork sparked a vociferous conflict because Bork was not only a very conservative judge, but he was also on record as opposing *Roe* v. *Wade* as well as affirmative action and other liberal causes. Moreover, the nomination was a critical one because Powell had been a moderate swing vote who had voted with the Court's pro-choice majority, which had been narrowed to five to four in the 1986 abortion case, *Thornburgh* v. *American College of Obstetricians and Gynecologists* (see Rubin, 1987:145–49).

The result was an outpouring of pro-choice sentiment against Bork, which once again reinvigorated the pro-choice movement. NARAL, in particular, saw its organizational fortunes increase in response to the Bork nomination, after having suffered a decline in resources in the mid-1980s (see Appendix A). As NARAL director Kate Michelman described the problems that NARAL had in enlisting support and the impact of the Bork nomination:

It was difficult in 1986 [when she began as executive director]; it was very hard on a national scale to mobilize people around the threat to abortion rights. The frustrating thing was that we knew the anti-choice strategy. We knew that they were working through the courts and that they were working on legislation that would ultimately get to the courts and provide a challenge to *Roe*. They were working to reshape the lower judiciary, pushing judges who were anti-abortion. But the American public—their level of sophistication is naturally less because they're not in touch with the issue on a day-to-day basis—was not aware of all this. And the Court did continue to reaffirm *Roe*. In 1986, we won on the *Thornburgh* case, but it was a five to four decision. The public didn't necessarily understand the importance of that nuance, but we knew—we saw the assaults on the courts. But the public didn't necessarily believe there was a threat. There were moments when we could galvanize the pro-choice forces. For example, there were state ballot initiatives that we worked on where we had some successes . . . but those were threats that were close to home. We were not able to mobilize in a general way, on a national basis, around the right that was being taken away, because people didn't see the threat. . . . In 1986 we had the *Thornburgh* case, which was a five-to-four decision; then Reagan appointed Scalia and made Rehnquist Chief Justice. But the big turning point was the Bork nomination— NARAL's membership really shot up at that time. Before Bork, NARAL really did not have the public stature—the general public didn't really know about the organization. With Bork, we took a leadership role, and NARAL became better known. (interview with Kate Michelman, 1990)

NARAL and other single-issue pro-choice organizations joined with women's movement organizations, civil rights groups, and civil liberties organizations in an intense campaign to defeat Bork. The strength of the coalition produced a stunning defeat for the right-wing backers of Bork, which resulted in the eventual appointment by Ronald Reagan of Anthony Kennedy.[15] In the end, however, the appointment of Kennedy proved a victory for the countermovement, as he joined the anti-abortion majority in the 1989 Supreme Court ruling *Webster* v. *Reproductive Health Services,* which represented an important loss for the movement and another critical juncture in the abortion conflict.

Conclusion

The pattern of the abortion conflict in the years between 1983 and 1989 was in many ways similar to that of the 1973–76 period. The victories of 1973 and 1983 brought increased legitimacy to the pro-choice cause and some opportunities for proactive action. After both movement victories, countermovement initiatives helped maintain movement mobilization, but the movement was forced to do battle in arenas of the opposition's choosing. Whereas the countermovement fought in the institutionalized legislative arena following *Roe* v. *Wade,* the battle was taken back into the streets after 1983, thereby preventing pro-choices forces from settling into the status of an established interest group.

Contrary to many media accounts that refer to the "complacency" of the pro-choice movement since *Roe* v. *Wade,*[16] the pro-choice movement survived the 1980s as a relatively strong movement capable of acting simultaneously in several arenas. The movement's organizational structures were important in sustaining it in a period in which many constituents felt the battle had been won. Formalized movement organizations such as the National Abortion Rights Action League, together with established organizations like Planned Parenthood, kept the movement stable through the "cold" periods of the long abortion conflict. When the abortion conflict intensified, and when the countermovement provided tactical opportunities for the movement, grass-roots constituents could be rallied, by both informal movement organizations and formalized organizations such as NARAL, which proved itself capable of borrowing from the repertoire of the women's liberation movement to meet challenges like *The Silent Scream.* Thus, the movement was far from unprepared when the abortion conflict intensified again following the anti-abortion victory served up by the Supreme Court in the 1989 *Webster* ruling.

11

The *Webster* Ruling and Its Aftermath

In July 1989 a Supreme Court reconstituted with Reagan appointees upheld important provisions of a Missouri anti-abortion statute in *Webster* v. *Reproductive Health Services*. Although the Court did not overturn *Roe* v. *Wade*, it allowed the states significant leeway in limiting abortion rights and seemed to invite other challenges that might further dismantle the 1973 Court ruling.[1] The *Webster* decision was a critical event marking the beginning of a new round of intense conflict over abortion in which the state legislative and political arenas would become the primary battlefields.

Changes taking place in the pro-choice movement in the wake of the 1989 countermovement victory parallel many of the developments of the post-Hyde period of the abortion conflict. In both instances, the pro-choice movement remained mobilized during the relatively "slow" periods following the major victories of 1973 and 1983, so that movement organizations were prepared to respond when the conflict heated up after major countermovement victories. In 1989 the pro-choice movement was in a particularly strong position after having fought and won the battle over the nomination of Robert Bork to the Supreme Court in 1987. As movement supporters were alerted to the new threats to abortion rights posed by the *Webster* case, professionalized movement organizations quickly took advantage of constituent concerns to enlarge their resources by means such as direct mail. Grass-roots participation also increased, and new movement organizations formed, following the Court ruling. Coalition work was stepped up as a result of the new threats and the movement was faced with the problem of devising new strategies and tactics.

The Battle Intensifies

Webster v. *Reproductive Health Services* took on major significance in the abortion conflict when the Reagan Administration filed a friend-of-the-court brief shortly after the 1988 Presidential election which asked the Court to use the case as an opportunity to overturn *Roe* v. *Wade;* after George Bush took office in 1989, a similar request was again made by the Justice Department under Attorney General Richard Thornburgh (see *New York Times*, January 10, and March 26,

1989).[2] Although the state of Missouri had originally argued that the state abortion law under consideration in the case was consistent with *Roe* v. *Wade*, the state changed its tactics with this support from the Reagan and Bush Administrations and joined in asking the Court to overturn its 1973 decision. Because of its significance, *Webster* v. *Reproductive Health Services* led to even greater movement and countermovement activity both before and after the July 1989 decision.

Prior to the Court ruling, the National Organization for Women worked with other pro-choice groups to organize a massive abortion rights march in Washington, D.C., on April 9, 1989. The march, which was intended to send a signal to the Supreme Court, attracted some 300,000 abortion rights supporters, according to media reports, and received a great deal of publicity. The event provided an opportunity for several generations of abortion rights activists, together with women who were new to the movement, to share stories about the "bad old days" before *Roe* v. *Wade* and to experience a sense of solidarity and commitment to the pro-choice cause (see *New York Times* coverage of the march, April 10, 1989). Viewed by NOW as the kickoff for a new campaign to protect the right to abortion, the march was an important mobilizing event for the pro-choice movement, and, predictably, it also provoked counter-demonstrations by anti-abortionists.

Beyond the activities that took place around the abortion rights march, movement and countermovement organizations both sponsored letter-writing campaigns to the Supreme Court[3] and used political advertising campaigns to raise money and rally supporters. They also orchestrated the filing of a record seventy-eight *amicus curiae* briefs for the *Webster* case. On the pro-choice side, the briefs came from a wide variety of groups and organizations, including, in addition to the usual pro-choice organizations, 167 scientists and physicians,[4] the American Medical Association and other medical organizations, 281 historians who countered the Justice Department's argument that abortion had been condemned throughout U.S. history, the National Coalition of American Nuns, and 2,887 women who had had abortions (see Moore, 1989; *New York Times*, April 23, 1989).

All of this anticipation of the Court ruling was organizationally quite beneficial to both movement and countermovement, but particularly to the pro-choice side. NARAL had built up its resources following the Bork campaign of 1987 and was prepared to take advantage of the new opportunity for growth. Using both the mass media and direct mail, NARAL increased its membership to 200,000 before the July Court ruling and in May 1989 alone reported raising $1 million. Between 1989 and 1990, NARAL's membership doubled to 400,000 (interview with NARAL director Kate Michelman, 1990). NOW's membership also rose, from about 160,000 in January to about 200,000 in July 1989. And both Planned Parenthood and the ACLU reported large increases in contributions and membership in response to advertising and direct mail regarding the *Webster* case (see Kornhauser, 1989a; Matlack, 1989).

When the Court handed down its decision in the *Webster* case on July 3, 1989, it was immediately viewed by all concerned as a disaster for the pro-choice cause and a victory for anti-abortion forces. But unlike outcomes that spell the end of a battle and create the danger of demobilization for the victor, this one opened up new tactical opportunities for countermovement forces. Anti-abortion groups immediately began lobbying for new state laws that would curtail abortions and bring about further challenges to *Roe* v. *Wade* through the courts. In response, pro-choice organizations, including NARAL, NOW, and RCAR, announced their own campaigns to fight the legislative initiatives and to campaign against anti-abortion state legislators (see *National Journal,* 1989). Thus, the 1989 Court ruling energized both movement and countermovement.

As the new round of fire in the abortion battle began, a number of commentators observed that the anti-abortion forces were better prepared than the pro-choice forces to fight the upcoming state legislative and political battles (cf. Garb, 1989b; Kornhauser, 1989a). Although pro-choice leaders have conceded that the countermovement is better organized in some parts of the country, the history of the pro-choice movement in the post-Hyde period of the abortion conflict reveals that this is not the first round of intensified conflict. Organizations such as NARAL and NOW began the new phase of the abortion battle with experience in combining professional expertise at the national level with grass-roots organization in the states. This previous experience and the ongoing mobilization of pro-choice forces in the 1980s allowed the movement to expand rapidly in response to heightened concerns about abortion rights. Nevertheless, the movement was faced with a new political opportunity structure and new strategic choices in the aftermath of *Webster.*

Electoral Politics

State political races took on immediate significance for the pro-choice movement following the Court's decision to allow the states to place new restrictions on abortion. Both the National Abortion Rights Action League and the National Organization for Women pledged involvement on behalf of pro-choice candidates. Two gubernatorial races following the *Webster* decision in 1989 provided immediate opportunities: In New Jersey, pro-choice forces backed Democrat James Florio in his successful campaign for governor against the avowed anti-abortion Republican, Jim Courter. In Virginia, a pro-choice position became central to the campaign of Democrat Douglas Wilder, who defeated Republican J. Marshall Coleman to become the nation's first elected black governor.

Pro-choice movement organizations were centrally involved in these electoral contests, which were considered the first rounds in a new political battle. NARAL, in particular, gained prominence for its role in framing the issue as a matter of private choice versus government interference, a theme that came out of research with "focus groups" conducted for NARAL in anticipation of the *Webster* ruling. Making its first independent expenditures for political candidates, NARAL waged a highly professionalized media campaign on behalf of the pro-choice candidates in both states. In Virginia, candidate Wilder successfully used the abortion issue to gain the edge in the close race for governor by adopting NARAL's theme that the decision to have an abortion should be made by individuals rather than by the government. In New Jersey, where there was no NARAL affiliate at the time, NARAL used its resources to run a professionalized campaign on behalf of the pro-choice candidate. As NARAL director Kate Michelman described this effort:

> We began organizing in New Jersey in 1988—we went in there with a very sophis-
> ticated approach. We hired a consultant, did a voter identification campaign with
> 200,000 voters, and got 53,000 to pledge to vote only for a pro-choice candidate.
> We made abortion a cutting-edge issue in that campaign. Now we have a very
> active affiliate in that state. (interview with NARAL director Kate Michelman,
> 1990; see also Kornhauser, 1989b:14)

In Illinois, NARAL worked with its affiliate in the March 1990 primary elections on behalf of pro-choice candidates. The national organization paid for an
organizer and offered technical advice and financial support for direct mail, advertising, and literature, while the local affiliate contributed activists. In a campaign
against state Representative Penny Pullen, a leading sponsor of anti-abortion legislation in the Illinois legislature, NARAL placed some 450 local volunteers in the
campaign of pro-choice challenger Rosemary Mulligan, who won the primary by
thirty-one votes (interview with Illinois NARAL director Pat Dougherty, 1990).
According to NARAL's executive director, the effort in Illinois was "very typical"
of NARAL's strategy of providing financial resources and technical expertise to
its affiliates to promote grass-roots activism in state legislative campaigns following the *Webster* decision (interview with Kate Michelman, 1990).

Although there are sharp differences of opinion among analysts on the long-
term political significance of the abortion issue and its likely impact on the Democratic and Republican parties (cf. Ladd, 1989; Schneider, 1989a), the momentum appeared to be with the pro-choice movement following *Webster*. Polls taken
after the Supreme Court decision found an average of 36 percent of Americans
supporting the ruling, while 57 percent opposed it (Schneider, 1989b), leading to
a widespread perception that the pro-choice position was the most politically
advantageous.[5] Indeed, a number of politicians reacted to this news by moderating
their former anti-abortion positions. In Congress, twenty-seven members of the
House who had voted against abortion rights in 1988 switched to the pro-choice
side in October 1989 in voting to allow the federal funding of abortions (Cohen,
1989).[6] In the gubernatorial races in New Jersey and Virginia, and in the mayoral
election in New York in 1989, all the Republican candidates attempted to modify
their previously staunch anti-abortion stands when it became clear that their
opponents were benefiting from their pro-choice stances (Germond and Witcover,
1989). In California, a Catholic pro-choice candidate for the state senate won an
upset victory after the bishop of San Diego denied her the right to receive communion in the Church (see Conn, 1990). And, after reviewing the poll data, aides
to President Bush concluded that he should avoid the abortion issue as much as
possible (*Newsweek,* October 2, 1989).

A number of states did begin considering new anti-abortion laws after *Webster,* and in November 1989, Pennsylvania became the first to pass a new law that
was even more restrictive than the Missouri law upheld by the Court (*New York
Times,* November 19, 1989). In 1990, the U.S. territory of Guam passed a ban on

nearly all abortions, which, however, was blocked by the courts. The state legislature in Idaho passed a bill banning abortion "as a means of birth control" that also would have banned most abortions, but the governor vetoed the bill. In Louisiana, the governor vetoed two different versions of a tough anti-abortion bill intended to challenge *Roe* v. *Wade.* In all, by 1990, over one hundred restrictive abortion bills were pending in state legislatures (see *New York Times,* April 2, 1990).

Along with these threats, however, were some very favorable developments for the pro-choice movement. The Idaho bill helped to mobilize the pro-choice movement, which threatened an economic boycott of the state, to include Idaho potatoes, prior to the governor's veto. In Florida, a state legislature with a history of support for restrictive abortion laws, rejected six proposals to restrict abortion made by Governor Bob Martinez in the first legislative session called to address the issue since *Webster* (*New York Times,* October 15, 1989). Most importantly, in Illinois the American Civil Liberties Union won an out-of-court settlement of *Turnock* v. *Ragsdale,* one of three cases scheduled to be heard by the Supreme Court after *Webster.* The Illinois case involved regulations for abortion clinics that would have greatly increased the cost of abortions and, of the three cases, was seen as the most serious threat to *Roe* v. *Wade.* Illinois Attorney General Neil Hartigan had appealed the case to the Supreme Court but was also a Democratic candidate for governor in the 1990 Illinois elections and apparently sought the settlement in order to present himself as a pro-choice candidate (see *New York Times,* November 23, 1989). In addition to Hartigan, four other Democrats running for governor in 1990 shifted their positions on abortion to the pro-choice side (Barnes, 1990).

Clearly, the perception among many politicians following *Webster* was that the pro-choice position had become politically advantageous. This was evidenced in Congress as well as in state politics as pro-choice legislators took the initiative in sponsoring a Freedom of Choice Act that would legalize abortion legislatively. As NARAL's Kate Michelman explained about the origins and intent of the bill:

> [The Freedom of Choice Act] was initiated by our friends on the Hill and we were consulted about it. The goal of our friends on the Hill with this legislation was to pick up on the momentum created by *Webster* and to give members of Congress a chance to go on record on the issue. The bill is very simple; it simply puts *Roe* v. *Wade* into national legislation. . . . Then there are hearings, which provide a forum for the issue. (interview with Kate Michelman, 1990)

Although the bill was not expected to pass right away, it is significant that a number of members of Congress *wanted* an opportunity to go on record in support of legal abortion. The bill also became an important focus of pro-choice lobbying, which picked up momentum as a result of the Court decision. Numerous organizations that had previously been inactive or minimally involved in pro-choice lobbying became advocates of the Freedom of Choice Act and other abortion-related legislation. For example, Zero Population Growth, which had earlier scaled down its involvement in the movement, increased its attention to the abortion issue as a result of the new threats (interview with ZPG legislative representative Pam Lichtman, 1990).

Grass-Roots Mobilization and
Direct Action

At the same time that large organizations like NARAL and NOW were employing the tactics of political insiders, pro-choice groups were also stepping up direct-action tactics and grass-roots mobilization in response to *Webster*. NOW sponsored a range of activities beyond conventional political tactics, including a second abortion rights march in November 1989, which included rallies in various cities across the country as well as in Washington, D.C. In preparing for political activity in the states, NOW used a "Freedom Caravan for Women's Lives" that began traveling the states in August and September 1989, starting with New Jersey and Virginia, where gubernatorial elections were taking place, and Florida, where there was a special session of the legislature. The caravan held rallies, organized volunteers, and participated in defending abortion clinics against Operation Rescue. In 1990, NOW used its Freedom Caravan in connection with a search for candidates to challenge incumbent anti-abortion legislators in Pennsylvania and to support or oppose referenda and legislation in other states (see *National NOW Times,* July–August–September 1989; January–February 1990).

The *Webster* decision also helped rally high school and college students and other young women in support of abortion rights. The presence of young women was particularly conspicuous at the spring 1989 abortion rights march, and a "Feminist Futures" conference aimed at young women that was held on the weekend of the march was reportedly attended by five hundred women (Baker, 1990).[7] New student organizations were created in the wake of *Webster* and mainstream pro-choice organizations such as NARAL initiated campus-organizing efforts.

One of the new student organizations formed in 1989 was Students Organizing Students (SOS), a nationwide organization that by early 1990 claimed chapters on over one hundred campuses (see Illick, 1990). Early activities of SOS included a boycott of Domino's Pizza, whose founder and sole stockholder has contributed to a number of anti-abortion groups (see Eder, 1989; Vita, 1989), campus teach-ins on reproductive rights, and a voter registration project. Interestingly, SOS has drawn on the traditions of the student and women's liberation movements of the 1960s and has adopted the feminist reproductive rights perspective. Not only has SOS employed direct-action tactics, but the organizers also have professed their commitment to "participatory democracy." And, like earlier reproductive groups, SOS has adopted a multi-issue agenda:

> S.O.S. does not view abortion as a single issue, but as part of a broad agenda of health and reproductive rights issues. This agenda includes safe, legal, free abortion on demand, protection against sterilization and reproductive abuses, adequate and accessible pre- and post-natal care, AIDS education, treatment, and activism, minor's rights to abortion and birth control, adequate sex and sexuality education, and access to free and adequate childcare. (SOS pamphlet, n.d.)

By expressing concern for "choice" beyond legal abortion, SOS aimed to bring minority women and young mothers into the organization. As one SOS organizer explained, "What SOS means by prochoice is not just legal abortion. We mean that if a woman chooses to have the baby, she has the right to clothe, feed and house that baby" (quoted in Illick, 1990).

General interest in the reproductive rights perspective was revived first by the need to respond to Operation Rescue and later by the spring 1989 abortion rights march and the July 1989 *Webster* decision. As we saw in Chapter 10, local reproductive rights groups, such as Women Organized for Reproductive Choice and its offshoot the Emergency Clinic Defense Coalition, became active in direct action to defend abortion clinics. Following the *Webster* decision, there were further opportunities for mobilization by such groups. In Chicago, for example, ECDC sponsored a speak-out following the Court ruling to allow women to talk about their experiences with abortion. In all of their activities, such groups have tried to advance the multi-issue reproductive rights perspective that was promoted earlier by the Reproductive Rights National Network. This perspective also dominated a conference "In Defense of *Roe* v. *Wade*" that took place in Washington on the weekend of the spring abortion march, which deliberately included a majority of minority women (see Erlien, 1988).[8] For many reproductive rights activists, the climate following *Webster* seemed to present an unprecedented opportunity to create a multi-issue movement that would bring in poor and minority women as well as other grass-roots constituents (cf. Davis, 1989; Fried, 1989; Petchesky, 1989).

Coalition Work

One of the ways in which reproductive rights groups have always hoped to create such a movement is through coalition work with other pro-choice organizations as well as with minority groups. The *Webster* decision, like other countermovement victories, did present new opportunities for coalition work in the pro-choice movement. Although pro-choice groups had previously been working together in a Congressional lobbying coalition, active participation in coalition work expanded greatly following *Webster,* just as it did in the post-Hyde period. NARAL's executive director noted that "there were only about seven or eight organizations really involved [in pro-choice lobbying] before *Webster;* now there are about forty-five" (interview with NARAL director Kate Michelman, 1990). And beyond coalition work on Congressional lobbying, the large national pro-choice organizations—including NARAL, NOW, Planned Parenthood, and the ACLU—also worked to coordinate their strategies in other arenas (see Matlack, 1989).[9]

NARAL took the lead in promoting this work, chairing the expanded Washington, D.C., coalition and sharing its research with other organizations. As Kate Michelman described NARAL's contribution to the coalition:

> NARAL has really nurtured the coalition, especially with our message work. We have been sharing everything we learn with the coalition. For example, we just put out an issues manual which deals with ways to talk about various aspects of abortion. It's been really well received by Congressional staff, other organizations.

> Like the nurses' organization just said they wanted to send copies to all of their affiliates. So NARAL is hosting the coalition and we're disseminating our message to the other groups—we have a very coherent and consistent message that we're putting across. (interview with NARAL executive director Kate Michelman, 1990)

This leadership is likely to create stability in the pro-choice coalition, but it is not likely to allow for its expansion into the broader agendas of reproductive rights organizations such as SOS, nor is it likely to foster unconventional strategies.

That a coalition of major pro-choice organizations is likely to rein in groups with divergent strategies is evidenced by the reactions of other pro-choice groups to some of NOW's proposed activities. When NOW decided to sponsor a second abortion rights march in the fall of 1989 following the spring 1989 march, other pro-choice organizations expressed concern that the energy could better be used to organize in the states. As a compromise, NOW agreed to make the Washington march one of several rallies across the country (see *New York Times,* November 13, 1989). And when NOW delegates voted at the July 1989 NOW convention to explore the possibility of creating a third political party to advance women's interests, other pro-choice groups were alarmed that the strategy would make the movement look foolish and harm their attempts to exert political influence. However, differences between NOW and other pro-choice groups were at least partially resolved as the threats from *Webster* created strong incentives for unity (see Simpson, 1989a).

Just as they are likely to be cautious about strategic options that might damage the pro-choice cause, large pro-choice organizations like NARAL are likely to stick to a single-issue pro-choice message. Nevertheless, there have been some opportunities for joint work between reproductive rights activists and other organizations. Women of color groups such as the National Black Women's Health Project were visible participants in the spring 1989 abortion rights march, sponsoring a contingent of pro-choice women of color by offering funding for minority women to attend the march. The "In Defense of *Roe* v. *Wade*" conference at the spring abortion march brought together in a spirit of unity a number of minority reproductive rights groups, as well as representatives from the Religious Coalition of Abortion Rights and its Women of Color Partnership Project, NOW's Women of Color program, and state representatives of NARAL, Planned Parenthood, NOW, and other "mainstream" groups as well as reproductive rights groups (see Erlien, 1988). And Students Organizing Students has since worked with civil rights groups on a voter registration drive (interview with SOS staff member Lynn Veitzer, 1990).

Whether or not lasting cooperation on a multi-issue pro-choice agenda focusing on the needs of minority and poor women can be achieved is another question; the experience of the Reproductive Rights National Network in trying to build coalitions in the post-Hyde period suggests that there are significant obstacles to such a goal. Nevertheless, reproductive rights groups have been encouraged by the increased amount of organization and activity on reproductive rights among minority women, notably the Black Women's Health Project. In addition, there are indications that the multi-issue reproductive rights cause has been taken up by organizations that are more stable than R2N2 was. The Religious Coalition for Abortion Rights, for example, has become increasingly active in fostering this perspective since beginning its Women of Color Partnership Program in 1985. In 1990, Students Organizing Students, though small in comparison with NARAL or NOW, had a national office with a staff of four and a budget of $200,000 raised from foundations and other sources. Although the SOS chapters are independent, the national office provides some stability to the organization (interview with SOS staff member Lynn Veitzer, 1990).

Professionalization Versus Grass-Roots Action?

Professionalization is one of the trends in the pro-choice movement that is likely to accelerate even further in the 1990s. Increasingly, movement professionalization is coming to mean not only the professional leadership of movement organizations (cf. McCarthy and Zald, 1973; Staggenborg, 1988), but also the use of the latest political technologies employed by political parties. With the increased resources accumulated as a result of their constituents' response to the new threats to abortion rights, pro-choice groups have hired additional staff and have adopted techniques like polling, focus groups, and radio and television advertising. NARAL, in particular, began using paid political consultants for advice in running its new media and legislative campaigns following *Webster* (see Kornhauser, 1989a, 1989b; *New York Times,* July 21, 1989). Although this approach has drawn criticism from some in the movement, NARAL director Kate Michelman contends that "we are the political arm of the movement and part of being political is being sophisticated about our message as well as organizing at the grass-roots level" (interview with Kate Michelman, 1990).[10]

A critical issue for the pro-choice movement is the extent to which grass-roots action on behalf of abortion rights will be sacrificed to professionalization. In the period of intense mobilization following passage of the Hyde Amendment, we saw that professionalization actually facilitated grass-roots mobilization. Is this scenario likely to be repeated, or has professionalization entered a new stage in which grass-roots mobilization will be disdained in favor of other strategies?

There is certainly the potential for conflict between professionalization and grass-roots mobilization. One source of conflict is the way in which the issues are framed. Professionalized national organizations may be oriented toward reaching potential supporters in the "middle-of-the-road" public, whereas local organizations are concerned with maintaining the participation of committed activists, thereby necessitating a different type of appeal (cf. Oliver and Furman, 1989). This problem could manifest itself in the pro-choice movement as organizations like NARAL seek professional advice in framing the pro-choice position to appeal to a broad spectrum of Americans. As noted above, the advisers hired by NARAL concluded that the movement could benefit from playing up the theme of undesirable government interference in private lives, a concern felt by many people in "focus groups" who were otherwise uncertain about the abortion issue (see *New York Times,* July 21, 1989). Grass-roots activists, on the other hand, might be better mobilized by—and more inclined to want to use—more feminist rhetoric about women's right to control their bodies. Indeed, the SOS pamphlet quoted above employs the women's liberation call for "free abortion on demand."

Competition for resources between national and local organizations is another potential source of conflict that may be exacerbated by the increasing professionalization at the national level. Expensive media campaigns, for example, may preclude extensive grass-roots organizing efforts. However, the experience of the pro-choice movement in the post-Hyde period suggests that the movement can be greatly strengthened by the combination of national professional expertise and local activism in response to new threats to abortion rights. During that period, as we have seen, NARAL was able to use the resources that it mobilized nationally to implement a highly successful grass-roots organizing campaign. In fact, part of NARAL's "Impact '80" organizing program was actually developed by one of NARAL's affiliates, so that grass-roots activists were both influencing national strategy and receiving resources from the national organization.

In the post-*Webster* period, new forms of professionalization may make it more difficult for local activists to contribute strategic and tactical ideas to national organizations. That is, when sophisticated political technologies are employed, national organizations may rely less on input from local activists and more on professional advice. Nevertheless, there is evidence that resources and strategies generated at the national level are being used to promote grass-roots organizing. NARAL, in particular, has continued to pump resources into its affiliates, as shown in the case of political work in Illinois. If a national organization is taking in large amounts of resources, there need not be competition between national strategies, such as media campaigns, and local efforts; indeed, the national resources can further grass-roots organizing.

Conclusion

Like the passage of the Hyde Amendment and other threatening events in the late 1970s and early 1980s, the 1989 Supreme Court ruling resulted in an expansion of the pro-choice movement. National pro-choice organizations such as NARAL greatly increased their financial resources and consequently were able to adopt ever-more professional political tactics. The movement also swelled at the grass-roots level: Young women in particular flocked to the movement following *Webster,* as they did in the early 1980s, in response to what they perceived to be new threats to abortion rights. Indeed, as long as opposition to the movement persists, mobilization of the pro-choice movement is likely to continue (cf. Ferree and Hess, 1985; Taylor, 1989a).

The pro-choice movement enters the 1990s populated by a mix of grass-roots activists and professional leaders, feminists and single-issue activists. Although there is some potential for ideological and organizational conflict within the movement, its various organizations and constituents also lend different strengths to the cause. The abortion conflict is likely to heat up, and further losses for the pro-choice side can be expected as a result of the changed makeup of the Supreme Court[11] and opposition to abortion by the Bush Administration, but the pro-choice movement is in good shape to do battle, through both direct action and institutionalized means.

12

Conclusion

The pro-choice movement is a remarkable reform movement that succeeded first in legalizing abortion and later in remaining mobilized to become a significant force in American politics. I have argued that the staying power of the movement is due in large part to its development of formalized organizational structures and professional leadership. At the same time, and in part as a result of these structural changes, the movement managed to maintain a grass-roots presence. An equally important countermovement aroused by the pro-choice movement also aided the mobilization of pro-choice forces even while limiting their ability to bring about changes beyond the legalization of abortion. This chapter examines the implications of this account of the pro-choice movement for more general theories of social movements.

The Cycle of Protest

The cycle of protest of the 1960s and early 1970s was the most significant source of political opportunity for the abortion movement. Although the movement to legalize abortion began to form in the early 1960s, it did not attract a critical mass of supporters until the late 1960s when the protest cycle was well under way. As Tarrow (1989) notes, the activities of social movements that are "early risers" in a protest cycle and the responses that they provoke affect the opportunities of movements that are "late comers" in the cycle. For movements that originate a cycle of protest, like the American civil rights movement, political opportunity stems from large-scale changes—such as the electoral realignments of the 1930s and the migration of southern rural blacks to the cities—that influence organizational bases and resources and make elites vulnerable (see McAdam, 1982; Piven and Cloward, 1977). Once a cycle of protest is under way, existing social movements facilitate the emergence and maintenance of new movements by providing experienced activists, organizational and ideological bases, and tactical models (cf. McAdam, 1988).

In the case of the pro-choice movement, these requisites of protest were provided by the social movements of the 1960s and by the family-planning movement that had become institutionalized by the 1960s. The extraordinary influence that the civil rights movement had on many subsequent social movements was very much in evidence: Key constituents of the abortion rights movement, including students, women, and clergy, were activated by the civil rights struggle (cf. Evans, 1979; McAdam, 1988), and the movement provided models for both the direct-action and institutionalized tactics that were used in the struggle to legalize abortion. Both the women's liberation movement and the population movement, which contributed large numbers of participants to the early abortion rights movement, relied greatly on the student constituencies first rallied by the civil rights movement. Other participants were drawn into the movement through the network of Planned Parenthood clinics and organizations that brought together staff and volunteers sympathetic to abortion law reform. All of these constituents had both grievances and a tactic—abortion referrals—that helped mobilize them.

Just as the expanded social movement sector of the 1960s provided opportunities for mobilization, the decline of the cycle of protest also had significant consequences for the pro-choice movement. Although multi-issue movement organizations were present following the legalization of abortion and played an important role in keeping the movement alive, by the mid-1970s, much of the grass-roots activity of population and women's liberation movement groups had disappeared. The pro-choice movement continued because it was able to compensate for the contraction of the social movement sector.

Rupp and Taylor's (1987) account of the women's rights movement in the years before the "rebirth" of the women's movement in the 1960s shows that one way in which movements can survive "dry" periods is to develop exclusive, "elite sustained" structures such as that of the National Women's Party. The experience of the pro-choice movement suggests that there are also a number of other "abeyance" processes in social movements.[1] Organizational structures are clearly important in maintaining continuity in social movements over time, but this function might be served by different types of organizations, including alternative institutions created by movement organizations, established organizations, and formalized social movement organizations.

These abeyance processes maintained the pro-choice movement despite the decline of the protest cycle and despite some decrease in interest in the abortion issue among pro-choice constituents following legalization. When women's liberation groups like the Chicago Women's Liberation Union and population organizations such as Chicago-area ZPG dissolved, they left behind alternative institutions like the Health Evaluation and Referral Service and the Midwest Population Center, which could act as local movement centers to bring together pro-choice activists when the need arose. After *Roe* v. *Wade,* established organizations such as Planned Parenthood, the ACLU, and Protestant and Jewish religious denominations also helped maintain the movement by investing substantial resources in the defense of abortion rights. And movement organizations like NARAL began to develop the kinds of formalized organizational structures that could be sustained despite changes in the political climate.

The continuous mobilization that has been generated by the abortion issue is relevant to the problems of explaining the rise and decline of cycles of protest and defining their boundaries. Cycles of protest can be identified by the sheer volume of protest activity taking place over a period of time, but the individual movements that make up a protest cycle do not typically have clear endings: Movements that survive the decline of the protest cycle may serve an abeyance function for other social movements. Although there has been a well-noted decline in the cycle of protest that began with the civil rights movement, the movements that originated in the 1960s have not completely disappeared. As McAdam (1988:235) notes, even movements such as the New Left that seem to have vanished "do not so much die as survive on a smaller scale." In the case of the pro-choice movement, the movement not only survived but also increased in scale in the 1970s and 1980s, in large part because of threats from the anti-abortion countermovement. Although the 1970s and 1980s appear to have been dominated by a cycle of conservative movements, it is important to recognize that these movements have helped keep alive the movements of the 1960s. Cycles of protest are thus linked together, and the organizational structures of movements from previous cycles provide the seeds for new periods of intense mobilization (cf. Taylor, 1989b).

The abortion issue has played an important role in keeping organizations of the broader women's movement mobilized and in involving individual activists in many different types of organizations. Many veterans of the early abortion movement have continued to work on the issue, through both movement organizations like NARAL and established family-planning and civil liberties organizations. Veterans of the women's liberation movement have found homes in the women's health and reproductive rights components of the pro-choice movement. The National Organization for Women has recruited numerous members through its visibility in the pro-choice movement. And, importantly, the movement has continued to attract young, new participants as well as seasoned activists. Not only does this combination give movement organizations a powerful mix of skills and energy, but the ability of the pro-choice movement to mobilize new generations of women with feminist sympathies is likely to be one of its most enduring contributions to subsequent social movements.

Movement–Countermovement Dynamics

The presence of a countermovement is clearly critical to the ability of a movement to perpetuate a cycle of protest. The interaction between movement and countermovement influences mobilization as well as the strategic and tactical options of both sides. The nature of this interaction changes with the outcomes of collective action by both movement and countermovement; that is, victories and defeats for one side alter the organizational and tactical advantages of the other side in a protracted conflict. As Zald and Useem (1987:253) argue, an analysis of movement–countermovement interaction over time allows us to see how "events from one period limit the choices and responses of the next."[2]

After achieving a significant victory, movement actors may be in a position to make further demands or to adopt new goals. Success brings a certain legitimacy to a movement, which may increase support from established organizations and elites. When a movement spawns a countermovement, however, a major movement victory helps spur the opposition. If the countermovement succeeds in gaining significant support, the advantages of victory will be partially nullified, and the movement will be forced into a reactive stance. After the countermovement wins a victory, the movement's options become further constrained, despite the advantages of increased resources that can be mobilized in response to countermovement threats.

Before *Roe* v. *Wade,* the interaction between the movement to legalize abortion and its opponents was "loosely coupled" (Zald and Useem, 1987). In this period, the abortion rights movement took the offensive; although the anti-abortion countermovement organized in response, it lagged behind in critical areas, and the movement did not spend the majority of its time reacting to countermovement tactics. Organizations like NARAL and ICMCA took bold stances in favor of the radical goal of abortion law repeal, and women's liberation groups such as the CWLU's Jane collective experimented with new forms of health care delivery centered on women's needs, a cultural reform that had far-reaching effects (cf. Ruzek, 1986). The movement was able to take proactive action in this period as a result of the environment of support created by the social movements of the 1960s, the relatively underdeveloped state of the anti-abortion countermovement, and the organizational shape of the movement itself. The informal structures of movement organizations allowed leaders to make quick decisions to engage in direct actions and other tactics in response to political opportunities. In the case of the women's liberation movement, organizational structures were both informal and decentralized, promoting innovation and independent action by small groups such as Jane (cf. Staggenborg, 1989b).

The 1973 movement victory, ironically, gave the organizational advantage to the countermovement, which was able to mobilize outraged constituents in response to the Court ruling.[3] There were no longer the same immediately felt grievances to rally pro-choice constituents, but countermovement threats to the newly won right to abortion did keep the movement from demobilizing after 1973. There were some opportunities to use the skills and experiences gained before 1973 to press for further advantages in the wake of the victory, but as countermovement forces gained momentum, the battle over abortion became more closely joined and the opportunities for proactive action decreased. Although countermovement activities helped to sustain movement organizations and to involve established organizations like Planned Parenthood and the ACLU after 1973, the need to neutralize the opposition's tactics (cf. McAdam, 1983) limited the movement's ability to push its own initiatives. Organizational changes also lessened the movement's inclination toward proactive direct action after 1973: Grass-roots women's liberation organizations began to decline, removing from the movement an important source of innovative direct-action tactics. Other movement organizations gradually began to formalize their structures to engage in the institutionalized tactics employed by the countermovement. The greater involvement of established organizations, and the resources that they provided for legislative lobbying, furthered the trend toward mainly reactive, institutionalized actions.[4]

After the countermovement began to win major victories, beginning with passage of the Hyde Amendment in 1976, the movement's actions became more reactive and narrowly focused than ever before. At the same time, the organizational momentum shifted to the movement, which was able to take advantage of its constituents' alarm about intensified threats to abortion rights. Movement organizations like NARAL and NOW became more professionalized and formalized in order to engage in single-issue politics and other institutionalized tactics, but they also succeeded in recruiting large numbers of grass-roots supporters. Reproductive rights organizations advocated a multi-issue, proactive approach, but they were limited by their reliance on countermovement threats to provide tactical opportunities and by their own decentralized and informal structures, which made it difficult to maintain their organizations and develop programs for action.

After the 1983 pro-choice victories, the pattern was similar to that following *Roe* v. *Wade.* The movement lost some organizational momentum, but briefly enjoyed an offensive strategic position. As the countermovement responded by changing the arena of the conflict, the movement was forced to follow suit and respond to tactics like *The Silent Scream.* After the 1989 *Webster* ruling, the dynamics were similar to those following passage of the Hyde Amendment: The movement expanded its resources and consequently was able to wage an aggressive defense, but nevertheless had to react to countermovement threats.

This pattern of interaction between the pro-choice movement and the anti-abortion countermovement suggests that there is no end in sight for the abortion conflict. Analyses of long-term trends toward secularization and liberalism in public opinion suggest that the conflict will ultimately be settled in favor of legal abortion; as Davis (1980) argues, support for the anti-abortion movement might turn out to be "conservative weather in a liberalizing climate" (see also Rossi and Sitaraman, 1988).[5] For the foreseeable future, however, mobilization is likely to be continuous for both sides in a conflict in which the opponents each have sizable constituencies with enduring moral commitments. Victories for the movement lead to heightened countermovement mobilization, which in turn keeps the movement going by creating threats and tactical opportunities. Victories for the countermovement lead to even greater movement mobilization, which helps feed countermovement forces. Although they are no doubt necessary for ongoing mobilization, victories also have the unintended effect of aiding the opposition organizationally.[6]

The same factors that facilitate mobilization of a movement also limit the forms of collective action that can be employed. Not only do movement tactics affect countermovement tactics, as Mottl (1980) emphasizes, but countermovement activities that create an environment of threat strong enough to keep movement constituents alert—even after a major victory—also constrain a movement's strategic and tactical options. In response to countermovement threats, movement organizations are forced to engage in reactive tactics in arenas chosen by their opponents and, in some cases, to alter their organizational structures so as to engage in new tactics. In the 1970s and 1980s, the pro-choice movement successfully maintained itself, and even grew in strength, but its ability to bring about social change has been constricted since 1973 by the need to respond to countermovement activities and successes with largely reactive and single-issue goals and tactics.

Social Movements in the American Political System

Although the pro-choice movement was not able to maintain a proactive stance after the legalization of abortion, it did win a monumental victory in 1973 and has since become an important player in American politics. The history of how this was accomplished is relevant to theoretical questions regarding the relationship between social movements and the political power structure. Do social movements gain access to political power by securing the support of elites or by using mass protest tactics? Does collective action inevitably become more institutionalized over time? How do social movement organizations with professional leaders and formalized structures differ from established interest groups? How are movement organizations limited in their ability to bring about social change?

The experience of the pro-choice movement makes clear that models of social movements as either "insiders" or "outsiders" to the polity are too simple. As Tarrow (1989:18) contends, both spontaneous mass mobilization and institutionalized groups are important to social movements. Both elite support and indigenous resources are sources of protest. Rather than debating their relative importance, therefore, social movement theorists need to examine the different ways in which movements obtain access to power.

Movements do need to gain elite support, but there are a variety of ways in which this can be accomplished. In some movements, such as the civil rights movement, grass-roots activists *force* support from political and economic elites through disruptive direct-action tactics (see Morris, 1984:266). In the case of the pro-choice movement, the early movement combined the skills and energies of young constituents eager for direct action with those of activists seasoned in conventional methods of influence. The latter were not the representatives of established interest groups, but they were persons with connections to wealthy individuals, legislators, professionals, and other influential people and organizations. The social networks of movement leaders thus provide one avenue of access to elites.[7] In other cases, political "insiders" may directly advance a movement's cause. For example, women in positions of power in the government actively aided the growth of the women's rights movement (Duerst-Lahti, 1989).

The varying ways in which movements gain power need to be taken into account in models of the place of movements within the political system. As Rule (1988:193) argues, Tilly's (1978) "polity model" requires a sharp distinction between "members" of the polity, who enjoy routine access to power holders, and "challengers," who lack such access. In fact, the lines are much less clearly drawn and the composition of the "polity" is more complicated than allowed by such insider–outsider models. Different types of polity "members" with varying amounts of power, including established organizations and wealthy individuals, may become movement allies at different times. And, as Tarrow (1989:8) points out, protest increases both outside and within the polity during cycles of protest. The pro-choice movement was never a complete outsider, insofar as it always had some access to power holders through its influential supporters.[8] After the legalization of abortion, however, the means of access shifted from an individual to an organizational basis. The movement came to rely less on the social networks of individuals and more on its own organizational structures as well as on the participation of established organizations like Planned Parenthood and the ACLU, which after 1973 committed greater resources to the movement.

The fluidity of the boundaries between insiders and outsiders in the polity can also be seen in cases where established interest groups lose their influence and become "movement-like" as a result. Useem and Zald (1982) show how this occurred in the case of pro-nuclear interests as a result of the successes of the antinuclear power movement, leading to the creation of a pro-nuclear movement. In the abortion conflict, Planned Parenthood is a good example of an organization that has seen its insider status, including its funding from government sources, jeopardized as a result of its support of the pro-choice movement during the tenure of the anti-abortion Reagan and Bush Administrations.[9]

Just as there is no sharp line between the statuses of political outsider and political insider, there is no easy way to distinguish movements from other political phenomena on the basis of their tactics or organizational structures. McCarthy and Zald (1977:1218, n. 8) follow Lowi (1971) in suggesting that "movement organizations" can be considered "interest group organizations" when they become highly institutionalized and have routine ties to authorities. It is difficult, however, to specify the criteria for institutionalization; movement organizations may take on characteristics such as bureaucratic structures and professional leadership without losing other movement-like features. Tarrow (1989:16) defines the social movement sector as "individuals and groups willing to engage in disruptive direct action against others to achieve collective goals." However, many social movements engage in a mix of direct action (which may not be disruptive) and institutionalized forms of action. Social movements, it seems, differ from established interest groups in that they draw on some kind of grass-roots participation, engage in some direct action, and lack completely routine access to authorities.

Some theorists do see inevitable contradictions between the professionalization and formalization of social movements and the mobilization of grass-roots protest. Piven and Cloward (1977) argue that the creation of large bureaucratic organizations leads to the decline of disruptive collective action. Oliver and Furman (1989:156) attempt to go beyond debates about whether or not "organization" furthers or hinders protest by pointing out that there are different forms of organizational strength and that "the features which make for a strong national organization with a sound membership base are different from those which foster active mobilization of the membership." They identify problems that are created when organizations attempt to sustain both local organizing and a large national operation supported by "paper" members. According to this analysis, one of the disadvantages for local chapters of national organizations is that they are burdened with the organizational maintenance needs of the national organizations to which they belong.

The case of the pro-choice movement reveals that the professionalization of leadership and the formalization of movement organizations are not necessarily incompatible with grass-roots protest. Large national organizations may drain resources away from their local affiliates, but this is not always the case. Rather, there are a variety of possible relationships between national and local organizations, which evolve over time. In the 1970s, chapters of the National Organization for Women did feel that they were burdened by dues that they paid to the national organization without receiving services in return from the national office (see Freeman, 1975:88–90). These tensions were eased as NOW developed additional sources of funding such as direct mail and worked with its chapters on campaigns such as the ERA drive, although the chapters continued to share with the national organization the income from membership dues. NARAL, on the other hand, has given grants to its affiliates and used its professional staff and resources generated from paper members to aid grass-roots mobilization. In general, the development of large national organizations has not precluded local mobilization in the pro-choice movement. Grass-roots protest, such as that of the reproductive rights movement, has emerged in response to new developments in the abortion conflict, but formalized organizations have generally been more effective than informal organizations in sustaining movement activity during slow periods.

Nor have professionalization and formalization led to the complete institutionalization of tactics. Formal movement organizations with professional staffs do exhibit a preference for conventional pressure-group tactics such as legislative lobbying. But there has never been a simple progression in the movement from the use of direct-action tactics in the early years to institutionalized forms of action once the movement gained acceptability. From the start, the pro-choice movement employed a mix of direct action and institutionalized actions, and it has continued to do so. One reason for this is that the anti-abortion countermovement prevents the pro-choice movement from becoming completely "established." During times when the countermovement has lost momentum in institutionalized arenas, it has switched to direct-action tactics, and the movement has been forced to follow suit. The political environment, including countermovement activities, thus combines with the movement's internal structures to influence ongoing mobilization and collective action.

In terms of its accomplishments, the pro-choice movement certainly ranks among the important social movements originating in the 1960s. The legalization of abortion is a major change with far-reaching social implications, and it is unlikely that any future restrictions placed on access to legal abortion will be able to reverse all of the changes that have resulted. In addition, the movement has maintained itself for many years and has become, along with allies such as Planned Parenthood, a major political force. This mobilization will no doubt affect future cycles of protest. At the same time, the movement, like other movements of the 1960s, has aroused powerful opposition. The need to defend against countermovement attacks and to build organizations capable of sustained mobilization and institutionalized action limits the movement's goals and tactics. A new lobby representing the interests of feminist women has been created, but a number of forces operate to narrow its ability to bring about further social changes.

APPENDIX A

Structures and Resources of Pro-Choice Movement Organizations

This appendix provides brief histories of the changes that occurred in the organizational structures and resources of thirteen pro-choice movement organizations, including six national organizations and seven state and local organizations. All of these organizations were studied systematically through documentary and interview data (see Appendixes B and C) from their origins through 1983 (or the demise of the organization). Additional information for surviving organizations was obtained for the years after 1983 from newsletters and literature, interviews with organizational leaders and staff, and media reports.

National Organizations

*National Abortion Rights Action League
(NARAL); (until 1973 the National Association for
Repeal of Abortion Laws)*

One of the first internal conflicts in NARAL was over the organization's structure. On the last day of the "First National Conference on Abortion Laws" at which NARAL was launched in February 1969, the organizers of the conference presented a proposal for an organization consisting of local organizational and individual members, an advisory committee, a board of directors, and an executive committee. The proposal raised a number of concerns among conference participants, including feminists, about whether the structure allowed for democratic participation in NARAL. After much debate, hampered by time constraints, the participants finally agreed to appoint a twelve-person planning committee that would meet in New York to work out a structure for the organization. The conference also elected Lawrence Lader as chairman of the organization and appointed subcommittees to write a constitution, rent an office, and hire an executive director (transcript of final session of NARAL founding conference in NARAL of Illinois Records, University of Illinois at Chicago library).

According to a September 1969 report from NARAL's first executive director, Lee Gidding, the planning committee appointed at the conference 'performed a staggering amount of work, contributing expertise in many areas important to NARAL's development." The work of the planning committee included setting up an office and hiring an executive director and part-time secretary; raising money ($13,000 was raised between February and September 1969 "through the efforts of a few members of the Planning Committee"); creating a structure consisting of officers, a board of directors, an executive committee, and a nominating committee; and drawing up a set of policies and a program for the organization. Membership in NARAL was open to both individuals and organizations, but organizational memberships were initially emphasized (NARAL Executive Director's Report, September 27, 1969; NARAL of Illinois Records, University of Illinois at Chicago library).

Formally, this structure placed decision-making power in the hands of the board of directors, which was representative of state organizational members, but in practice the board's role in the organization was limited in the early years. In fact, efforts to make the organization democratic helped limit the board's involvement by making it an unwieldy size of, at first, sixty and, later, ninety representatives. As one NARAL leader I interviewed joked, "I think at one point almost everyone in the organization got on the board." As a result, meetings were held only once a year; NARAL could not afford to pay travel expenses for its board members; and a smaller executive committee of the board held the real decision-making power in the organization.

According to Lader (1973:95), the "activists" who wanted to go ahead with a national program rather than worry about formal organizational structure prevailed before 1973 over a minority of "go-slowers" who wanted to spend more time developing an organizational structure and holding elections. Decision making was informally and centrally controlled by a small number of activists on the executive committee who used means such as proxy votes and phone calls to other executive committee members to make major decisions. Organizational members were very loosely affiliated state-level groups that operated completely independently. A mailing list of five hundred to two thousand individual "members" was obtained more or less accidentally and was not systematically maintained. Funds were raised largely through the leaders' personal connections with wealthy contributors.

After the legalization of abortion in 1973, a somewhat more formalized structure began to take shape as practices such as the use of proxy votes were discontinued. Professional leaders began to be hired. State affiliates (as opposed to organizational members) began to be created in 1974, and direct mail began to be used to recruit a dues-paying membership. By the late 1970s, NARAL had a much more formalized structure that included an affiliated political action committee (PAC) and a foundation. The size of the board of directors was reduced, and the organization began to pay transportation costs so that regular board meetings could be held. State affiliates were actively recruited and given financial aid, strategic programs, and training for staff in return for carrying out NARAL programs. Professional leadership became more and more important as the staff expanded and the division of labor became more specialized (e.g., lobbyists, media specialists, etc. were hired).

With regard to resources, in 1969 NARAL had 130 individual members, 18 organizational members, a mailing list of about 1,000 names, and a budget of $30,000. In 1970 there were 23 organizational members and a budget of $75,000. In 1972, continued growth was reported, although no figures are available. These resources allowed NARAL to hire a full-time executive director and some paid secretarial help. For the most part, however, NARAL relied on the contributions of volunteer activists (documents in NARAL of Illinois Records, University of Illinois at Chicago library; interview with former NARAL director Lee Gidding, 1985).

In 1973, after the legalization of abortion, a report from the national organization admitted that contributions had fallen off "drastically" because supporters thought that the battle was over. At this point, in order to become a more effective lobbying force, NARAL decided to develop "as large a national individual membership as possible" and, as an initial step, asked local organizational members to send the names of its active members along with $5.00 per name in dues (minutes of NARAL Board of Directors' Meeting, October 21, 1973, in NARAL of Illinois Records, University of Illinois at Chicago library). In 1974, NARAL acquired a new executive director, Beatrice Blair, who had experience with direct-mail techniques. She began a modest direct-mail project for NARAL that brought in both members and financial resources. According to Blair's estimates (interview, 1984), there were about two thousand individual members before the direct-mail campaign and about ten thousand afterwards by 1975 or 1976. The direct mail brought in more money in the form of small membership fees, reducing the organization's reliance on large contributors. By 1975, the NARAL budget had reached about $200,000, allowing the organization to employ a full-time secretary in addition to the full-time director, two part-time lobbyists in Washington, and one part-time field organizer.

After the NARAL headquarters were moved to Washington in 1976 and after the passage of the Hyde Amendment banning federal funding of abortions in late 1976, NARAL grew even more rapidly. Because of a combination of external crises and professional direct-mail campaigns, the membership reached 26,000 by 1977, 40,000 by 1978, and 90,000 by 1980. The election of an avowed anti-abortion President, Ronald Reagan, produced a particularly sharp rise in membership and contributions for NARAL; by 1982 the membership had reached 140,000 and the organization had a budget of over $3 million. The huge increases in resources allowed NARAL to employ a staff of about 25 full-time persons. Membership reached a high of about 150,000 by 1983 and then fell to about 90,000 by the mid-1980s (figures from NARAL newsletters and interviews with NARAL leaders). Despite this decline in membership, however, NARAL was able to remain stable, until its membership gradually began to rise again in response to external events, including a narrow pro-choice victory in the Supreme Court in 1986 and Ronald Reagan's appointment of Antonin Scalia to the Court and his elevation of William Rehnquist to Chief Justice. NARAL's membership then rose sharply with the nomination of Judge Robert Bork (interview with NARAL executive director Kate Michelman, 1990). In advance of the *Webster* decision, it reached 200,000 by July 1989 and reached an all-time high of 400,000 by 1990. The NARAL budget (for its political, non-tax exempt 501c4 organization) reached $10 million (Kornhauser, 1989a; interview with Kate Michelman, 1990).

Along with the increase in individual memberships, NARAL raised the number of its state affiliates to forty in 1982 and dramatically increased the number of activists, as opposed to "paper members," working at the local levels. This was made possible by the increase in national resources, which permitted large financial investments in targeted state affiliates, smaller grants to other affiliates, and active help from the national organization in training the leaders of all the local affiliates. Paralleling the drop in membership, the number of affiliates then dropped to about thirty-five by the mid-1980s but rose to forty-eight in response to NARAL's organizing activities in the wake of *Webster* (interview with executive director Kate Michelman, 1990; *NARAL News,* Spring 1990).

Religious Coalition for Abortion Rights (RCAR)

The Religious Coalition for Abortion Rights (RCAR) was formed in 1973 as an organization of churches, synagogues, and religious organizations (e.g., the National Council of Jewish Women). Membership requirements for religious denominations and organizations were relatively loose. Organizational members were not required to make financial contributions to RCAR, although they were encouraged to do so. There were no formal guidelines for the level of activity expected from RCAR members, although it was assumed that denominations and organizations joining RCAR wished to be active on the abortion issue. The only firm requirement for membership was that denominations and organizations support the goals of RCAR and provide a statement of their support for public distribution by RCAR.

Perhaps because all of RCAR's members were established organizations with traditional structures, the creation of an organizational structure was not problematic. A board of directors was set up as the national decision-making body that includes a representative from each national denominational or organizational member, many of which are headquartered in Washington, D.C. The working body of the board is an executive committee that is elected once a year by the larger body. Paid staff members, including an executive director, are responsible for the organization's day-to-day administration. There also are individual "sponsors" who are well-known religious leaders and theologians who lend prestige to the organization. Other individuals can become "contributing members" or "supporters" of RCAR who donate money and/or volunteer time (typically money at the national level).

The state affiliates of RCAR began to form in 1974. Between 1974 and 1977, thirteen state RCARs were created. Although the national staff tried to establish affiliates at this time, many of the early affiliates were begun by local activists who had heard about the formation of the national coalition organization and wanted to form a local one. No guidelines for the formation of affiliates were set down when the first affiliates were formed (including Illinois RCAR), so that most were informally structured with boards of directors consisting of interested individuals rather than formal representatives of denominational and organizational members. In 1977, a field organizer was hired to develop additional affiliates, and, at that time, more formal criteria were established for the affiliates. As former RCAR field organizer and later executive director Fredrica Hodges recalled in a 1984 interview:

> When we built the last fourteen [affiliates added between 1977 and 1981] there were specific parameters: number of members, appointment of policy council representatives, willingness to accept purpose, to work within denominations—all kinds of things to gurantee that those affiliates were going to do what we set them up to do. . . . [After the new affiliates were organized] we went back and started rebuilding the original thirteen to fit the parameters that we had established. That took longer, because people had already been operating in a certain mode, and they weren't as quick to change their focus to do the kinds of things that we thought were necessary.

Gradually, then, RCAR, like NARAL, moved toward requiring greater accountability by its affiliates to the national organization. Affiliates had to create formal boards of directors or "policy councils" that were representative of their denominational and organizational members, and they had to make annual reports of their financial expenditures and activities to the national RCAR organization.

The national RCAR organization provides its affiliates with literature, information, training for its coordinators (begun in the late 1970s), and a small yearly grant (originally less than $2,000; by the 1980s, $4,800) to assist the affiliates in hiring coordinators. Besides the creation of more formalized guidelines for affiliates in the late 1970s, the other major structural change that has been made is the addition of local "area units" consisting of individuals working with the RCAR affiliates who are not necessarily official representatives of denominations or religious organizations. This structure is designed to increase grass-roots participation. By 1990, RCAR had twenty-three area units in addition to its state affiliates.

RCAR expanded both its affiliates and its organizational members in the 1970s and 1980s. About ten affiliates were organized in 1974, and three more were added by 1977. A field organizer was hired in 1977 to form additional affiliates, and fourteen more affiliates were added between 1977 and 1981. In 1984 there were a total of twenty-eight RCAR affiliates in twenty-six states (with two states, California and New York, having two RCAR affiliates each). The number of denominational and organizational members of the national RCAR rose from twenty-four by the end of 1974 to thirty-one in 1984 to thirty-four in 1990. In terms of financial resources, RCAR has always had a modest budget. It began at about $100,000 and grew to about $700,000 in 1984, enabling the organization to employ a staff of six. By 1990, RCAR had a budget of about $850,000 in its 501c4 organization and about $480,000 in its 501c3 organization, supporting a staff of nine.

Attempts to expand the number of RCAR affiliates have been limited by lack of funds to provide grants for state coordinators and other affiliate expenses. A small grant from the national organization is considered essential to establishing a viable state affiliate. In 1980, however, RCAR began to expand its influence in unaffiliated states by building a network of individual supporters or "sponsor-contacts" in those states. In 1981, the national office kept records of requests for publications and reported receiving requests from every state, including a large number from unaffiliated states. As RCAR's national newsletter reported:

> The distribution of publications in unaffiliated states is significant in that it indicates that RCAR is "spreading the word." Through clergy contacts, NARAL and Planned Parenthood chapters, and reproductive health clinics in the unaffiliated states, RCAR is becoming known in areas where there has been little effort to organize in the religious community. (*Options,* July–August 1981)

In 1981, RCAR also began to increase the number of its individual supporters through the use of direct mail.

Zero Population Growth (ZPG)

Zero Population Growth (ZPG) was founded by the biologist and environmentalist Paul Ehrlich who, along with several other individuals, incorporated the organization in the fall of 1968. ZPG was originally a campus-based organization, headquartered in Palo Alto, California—near Stanford University where Ehrlich was located—until January 1974 when the main office was moved to Washington, D.C. A lobbying office was opened in Washington in late 1969, employing several paid staff members. Because ZPG was originally established to allow political lobbying work, in 1971 a tax-exempt arm, initially called the ZPG Fund, was also set up in Washington. After the tax laws were changed to permit tax-exempt organizations to engage in some lobbying work, and after the main office was moved to Washington, ZPG was consolidated under one tax status (the 501c3 educational group status).

Individuals were recruited as ZPG members on a completely inclusive basis as soon as the organization was founded. According to informants, many of the first members joined by mailing in a coupon from the back of Ehrlich's 1968 book, *The Population Bomb.* By 1970, ZPG chapters had formed throughout the country. Many of the affiliates were on college campuses and tended to be very autonomous from the national organization. Although there were many discussions among ZPG board members concerning ways in which to increase coordination with the local affiliates, this was never accomplished, and the number of ZPG chapters began to drop quickly in the early 1970s. In the early 1980s, the national office began trying to support chapter activities by offering small grants to affiliates for specific projects. Grants were made for a wide range of projects (e.g., the Seattle chapter's contraceptive boutique called "The Rubber Tree"), and chapters were not compelled to adopt national ZPG priorities.

Besides work through affiliates, "active" members participate in ZPG through an "action alert network" by writing letters when called upon to do so by the national office. Members also receive a national newsletter and can attend an annual meeting that gives them an opportunity to attend workshops, hear speakers, and exchange ideas, but there is no other direct participation in the national organization by local activists. Policy decisions are made by the national board of directors which is not elected by the membership but, rather, is appointed by the board itself. There are no limitations on the number of years that a board member can serve, and some persons have been on the ZPG board for many years. There was some discussion in the early 1970s about how to open up the decision-making process at the national level to the general membership. But it was not considered desirable to have the membership vote on board positions, as local members would have no basis on which to make a decision other than information in the newsletter. At this time, however, ZPG did begin to solicit chapter and state recommendations for the board in an attempt to create closer ties to local affiliates.

In the early years, however, one of the reasons that greater input from local members into the national organization was not more strongly encouraged was that there were political differences between ZPG leaders and one element of the ZPG constituency. As former executive director Roy Morgan explained in a 1984 interview:

> There were some people in ZPG in the early years, at the local chapter level for sure . . . who hopped on the ZPG bandwagon because they were rather draconian about what they wanted to do to bring down the population. Some of them were racist—there's no doubt about it—some of them were restrictionist; they didn't want any more people in. A lot of them were environmentalists—some environmentalists really don't want a lot of people using the parks; they really don't want a proliferation of people in the parks, in the wilderness areas. Some are also restrictionists, so they're very hard-lined about population growth. There was a lot of that. It was mostly in the early years. [When he was executive director of ZPG from 1976 to 1981] they were still around, but we were trying to ignore them, trying to push them off to the side. It was primarily local people, individual members. They would occasionally come to meetings, and it would be kind of embarrassing. We tried to push them off to the side.

Because of the continued presence of such persons within the predominantly liberal ZPG constituency, the national organization took the step of issuing guidelines on the use of the ZPG name. According to a staff member interviewed in 1984, the political differences between the national office and local members were not considered a major problem, but some did exist. For example, some local affiliates working on the immigration issue have taken what the national office considers "crazy positions" like opposing all immigration. Consequently, the national ZPG guidelines require chapters or local activists to make clear that, in taking such positions, they are not speaking for the national organization.

In contrast with the local members, ZPG board members were very active in the organization, at least until the mid-1970s. In fact, there are a number of examples of staff persons who first served as board members before joining the staff. As the population movement declined, however, ZPG's staff came to play a greater role in the organization. By the 1980s, staff members tended not to come to ZPG from backgrounds as population movement activists but as professionals with backgrounds in various areas.

With regard to resources, in 1969 ZPG had about 100 individual members. By the end of 1970, there were 150 ZPG chapters throughout the country and

20,000 members. The organization's membership peaked in late 1971 with about 400 chapters and state organizations and 35,000 individual members. Beginning in 1972, however, the ZPG membership began to decline dramatically. By February 1973 it had dropped to 18,200 individual members and 190 affiliates. The membership continued to fall, so that by 1977 there were only 8,500 individual members and 60 affiliates. By 1979 the individual membership had reached a low of about 5,500, and the number of affiliates stood at about 40. But beginning in 1980, as a result of a direct-mail recruitment drive, ZPG began to increase its individual membership for the first time since 1972, although the number of affiliates continued to decline. By the end of 1980 there were about 9,500 individual members, and by 1981 there were about 11,000 members. The membership continued to rise, reaching about 12,000 by 1984 and 20,000 by 1988. Like other organizations, ZPG then took advantage of the *Webster* decision to increase its membership by direct mail to 30,000 by 1990. The number of affiliates dropped from about 38 in 1980 to 20 in 1984, although, according to a national staff member interviewed, about half of these chapters consisted of only one or two persons at that time. By 1990, these inactive chaptes had disappeared, leaving the organization with nine active chapters. Since 1980, ZPG has also maintained a list of between 2,000 and 2,500 members who participate in its alert network by writing letters to legislators and other targets when asked to do so (figures from ZPG reports and interviews with ZPG staff).

The drop in ZPG's membership in the 1970s was no doubt due in part to public perception that the goal of "zero population growth" had been achieved in the United States. And as Roy Morgan, the executive director who succeeded in turning around the decline in membership, explained:

> I'll tell you what I found in digging through the records. . . . I found that there was very sloppy follow-up on members. Most of those members in the first two years were students, and you could tell from the record keeping that they simply lost track of them. They moved away, and there was no way to follow up or find them, and many members did not renew because they could not keep track of them. So many of them were students; it was obvious from the records that were sent from Palo Alto. The office was in Palo Alto; it was there next to Stanford so they could be next to Ehrlich. It was a student-based, campus-based organization largely. . . . Plus they consciously got out of direct mail in the early 1970s; they had been doing a lot of solicitation, and when I got there there was no real direct-mail campaign. (interview with former ZPG executive director Roy Morgan, 1984)

This executive director had a difficult time convincing ZPG's board of directors to resume direct-mail recruitment in the late 1970s because the board was not convinced that direct mail worked. But after the ZPG membership hit its low point in 1979, the board approved a direct-mail program, and the trend of membership loss was reversed.

The organization's financial resources did not decline in the same way that the membership did because the organization found alternative sources of support. In the early years, ZPG did rely on membership dues fairly heavily, and there were financial problems when the membership began to decline. But the organization made up for this loss of revenue from dues by soliciting more gifts from large donors and foundations and, before about 1976, received a small amount of money from the federal government. ZPG never had a very large budget, but by 1976 it had risen to around $350,000 and by 1980 to about $500,000. In 1984, the ZPG budget was about $650,000, and by 1988 its annual income totaled just over $900,000 (ZPG Annual Report, 1988; interviews with ZPG staff members, 1984 and 1990). The budget has enabled ZPG to maintain a staff to keep the organization going and also to provide limited financial support to its affiliates, but this has not been sufficient to keep most of the affiliates viable.

National Organization for Women (NOW)

The initial structure of the National Organization for Women consisted of a national board of directors and officers, all volunteer leaders elected at an annual membership conference. In the early years when the membership was small, major decisions were made by members at a national conference. Chapters spread rapidly throughout the country in the early 1970s, and three national offices were opened in 1973 with several paid staff each, including an administrative office in Chicago, a legislative office in Washington, and a public information office in New York. As Freeman (1975:83) notes "this wide geographic distribution of functions made NOW very decentralized and often chaotic." Communication with the chapters was very poor. Regional directors and national task forces were created to coordinate activities, but they lacked adequate funds and means of communication with the chapters. As the organization grew, it became clear that its decision-making structure needed revamping. Although it was feasible to give each individual attending the conference one vote when the membership of NOW was small, it was clearly impractical to make decisions in this manner when several thousand individuals began attending membership conferences and when the chapters consisted of many more members who were effectively disenfranchised by their inability to travel to the membership conferences.

The result of these growing pains was a period of internal conflict for NOW as the organization struggled to create a viable, and democratic, organizational structure. In 1972, pre-convention discussion materials were distributed to chapters in an effort to get more business done at the convention, and a delegate system for the convention was proposed but rejected. In the absence of an adequate organizational structure, communication problems and divisions within NOW multiplied, coming to a head in 1974 at a divisive and bitter national convention. In that year, for the first time, there was a real contest in the elections of national officers. A number of persons from the Chicago chapter, one of the largest and best organized in the country, which prided itself on its leadership skills and contributions to the national organization, ran as a slate. This caused resentment, and the emergence of another faction consisting of individuals concerned that the organization was getting too hierarchical and that more decision-making power and resources needed to be concentrated at the local levels. The result was the election of a president (Karen DeCrow) from the latter faction and a majority of other officers and board members from the former faction and a lot of hard feelings.

After the 1974 convention, two factions developed within the national board, one consisting of NOW's president and a minority of board members and the other consisting of the majority of board members. The split in the national organization became so serious that members of the former faction, calling themselves the "Majority Caucus," walked out of a December 1974 board meeting. The remaining board members passed resolutions without them, including a call for a mail ballot to get a membership vote on whether or not to establish a delegate system for the national convention, a move opposed by the Majority Caucus as undemocratic. The result was a lawsuit by the Majority Caucus against NOW for illegally undertaking the mail ballot. The lawsuit was won on a technicality (a violation of Washington, D.C.'s incorporation laws forbidding mail ballots) and cost NOW $13,000 in legal fees.

Needless to say, this did nothing to solve NOW's organizational problems. There was another divisive membership convention in 1975 at which members of the Majority Caucus called for taking NOW "out of the mainstream, into the revolution." Members of the Majority Caucus were successful in winning the presidency and a majority on the board, a result that led other national activists to announce the formation of an opposing "network" called "Womansurge" which planned to reorient NOW to "mainstream" issues.

Although the conflict was framed in terms of strategic and programmatic differences, observers of the organizational conflict at the time contend that there were in fact few disagreements on issues and goals (cf. Freeman, 1975; *The Spokeswoman*, 1975). (One of the goals of the "revolutionary" Majority Caucus was participation by NOW in electoral politics.) Rather, much of the conflict was due to the lack of communication and the failure to develop a workable organizational structure. This interpretation appears to be correct, because persons from the different factions later worked together quite cooperatively in the national leadership. In 1976, the convention was once again somewhat divisive, but a few national leaders made efforts to bridge the factions, and the merits of a delegate system were again debated. This time, NOW decided to have a "constitutional convention" to work out a delegate system, with the result that a workable system was put into place after the national convention in 1976.

By the late 1970s, many of NOW's internal difficulties were resolved as the organization established a single office in Washington, developed a delegate system of voting, began paying salaries to its elected officers, and hired more professional staff as its resources expanded. Although the elected leaders of NOW differ from other professionals in that they tend to work their way up through NOW rather than coming in from other movement organizations, they nevertheless tend to become career activists. Once a formalized structure was established, NOW was able to increase both its resources and its coordination among chapters through the use of direct mail and professional staff.

When NOW was organized in 1966, there were three hundred charter members and no budget or office. Within a year there were about 1,200 members, fourteen chapters, and a small budget of about $7,000. Between 1967 and 1974, the organization experienced a large spurt of growth, reaching a membership of about 40,000 individuals and seven hundred chapters in 1974. The budget rose more modestly, to about $500,000 in 1974. After this point, the membership continued to rise sharply, particularly in the late 1970s, reaching 100,000 in 1979. Financially, however, the organization was not doing well enough to meet its needs because of internal difficulties in the 1974–76 period. In 1975, the national board declared financial problems to be its main concern, and the Legislative Office in Washington declared a "budgetary crisis" that necessitated a cutback in mailings to chapters. In 1976, a national task force coordinator's report indicated that expectations of the national task forces were too high, given their lack of resources, and that, owing to a lack of money, their only means of communicating with the chapters was through the national newsletter. Once the organizational problems began to be resolved, however, NOW's financial fortunes picked up, particularly with the sharp rise in membership in the late 1970s. By 1980, the organization had a budget of about $3.5 million and was paying its officers salaries of between $35,000 and $40,000. By 1983, the membership had risen to about 250,000 and the budget to about $6.5 million (figures from NOW newsletters and documents in National Organization for Women Chicago Chapter Records, University of Illinois at Chicago library). In part because of the failure of the ERA campaign, NOW's membership fell to about 150,000 in the mid-1980s, and its income was reduced to about $5.5 million by 1988 (NOW financial statement, 1988). As the abortion conflict intensified with the 1989 Supreme Court ruling *Webster* v. *Reproductive Health Services,* however, NOW's membership rose to 270,000 by 1990, with financial contributions of $10.6 million (*New York Times,* July 1, 1990).

In addition to the sheer numbers, NOW has always had an abundance of dedicated volunteers, both nationally and locally, who got the organization through the lean years (cf. Freeman, 1975). The organization also has a skilled and committed staff, many of whom began as volunteers in the organization. Rather than hiring an executive director, NOW has elected—and paid—officers who have typically worked their way up through the organization, beginning at the chapter level. In the view of one informant, this makes them more accountable to the organization's membership. In any case, there is no doubt that NOW has established itself as a stable organization with a formalized structure.

National Women's Health Network (NWHN)

The National Women's Health Network was begun informally in 1975 by five volunteer women's health movement leaders who decided that the movement needed a voice in Washington. The organization was officially incorporated in 1976 after the founders brought together representatives of some fifty local women's health organizations throughout the nation. The organization's bylaws called for a twelve-member board of directors, which was initially recruited through the personal networks of the NWHN's founders. Members included both organizations and individuals. After a few years, there was an attempt to create a more formal means of recruitment to the board, and board members began to be elected through mail ballots sent to members. One of the founding members was hired as the executive director, and other staff members were added in the late 1970s. Attempts were made to strengthen ties to local groups and, in the early 1980s, the NWHN began to organize a few state affiliates (as opposed to organizational members).

The NWHN has always had a core of highly skilled women working at the national level, some of whom are nationally known figures. This is evidenced by the high quality of the literature put out by the national office, by the kinds of expert testimony provided by NWHN activists at Congressional hearings, and by the organization's ability to bring in substantial amounts of grant money. By 1977, the NWHN had raised enough money to hire its first paid director. By the 1980s, the Network's budget supported a growing staff (ten in 1983) and allowed the organization to pay its board members' travel expenses in order to expand their participation in the NWHN. In 1978, the budget was $22,000; in 1979, $80,000; in 1980, $189,000; in 1981, $369,000; and in 1982, $435,000 (National Women's Health Network Annual Report, 1983). In 1983, the budget reached about $500,000 (interview with board member Sybil Shainwald, 1985), although by the end of the decade it had fallen to $400,000 (interview with staff member Cindy Pearson, 1990).

Once an executive director was hired, the NWHN began to experience considerable growth in its membership. Organizational membership rose from 47 in 1978 to 118 in 1980, and individual membership reportedly quadrupled during the same period, reaching 3,000 in 1980. In 1980, the Network began exchanging its mailing list with other women's groups as part of an active membership campaign "to reach out to the women's movement" (*NWHN News,* January–February 1980). In 1981 a direct-mail membership drive was begun, and in 1982 the membership had increased from 7,000 to 10,000 individuals and from 240 to 300 organizations within a year (*NWHN News,* September–October, 1982). In 1983, the membership consisted of 13,000 individuals and 300 organizations. Increases in the individual membership allowed the Network to become less dependent for support on grants from foundations. In 1982, membership dues accounted for 55 percent of the NWHN budget (National Women's Health Network Annual Report, 1983). Direct mail was not used consistently, however, and by the mid-1980s, the membership dropped to about 7,000 or 8,000. With a later increase in direct mail, the individual membership then rose to 10,000 while the organizational membership stood at about 400 in 1990 (interview with NWHN staff member Cindy Pearson, 1990).

Reproductive Rights National Network
(known as R2N2)

The Reproductive Rights National Network was a decentralized organization consisting of affiliated groups such as Women Organized for Reproductive Choice. At first, decisions were made at two national conferences attended by representatives of member organizations. Later, a steering committee was created through the regional election of representatives, and membership conventions were held once a year. The steering committee provided leadership, aided by a single staff member in a New York office. The quality of leadership varied, depending on whether or not individuals on the steering committee took the initiative to provide direction to R2N2. Because turnover on the steering committee was high, the organization often found itself with a leadership void. Many of the organizational "members" of R2N2 were not very involved in the organization. Issue committees were created by vote of the membership at conferences, but R2N2's organizational structure was informal, and many of the committees failed to become active.

In terms of financial resources, R2N2 had some success in raising money from foundations, primarily small ones located in New York City. Through this source of revenue, the organization was able to hire a full-time staff coordinator and occasional office help, with a budget ranging from about $20,000 in the early years to a high of about $80,000, with $50,000 being the most typical budget. According to former staff coordinator Margie Fine (interview, 1984), however, R2N2 was "too dependent" on foundation money. This source of money began to dry up by 1983 as the foundations turned their attention to other causes such as the peace movement, creating severe financial strains for R2N2. R2N2's decentralized organizational structure made it difficult for the organization to mobilize the skills that might have enabled it to raise money through other means, and in 1984 the organization dissolved because of a lack of money and national leadership.

State and Local Organizations

National Abortion Rights Action League
of Illinois (NARAL of Illinois); until 1975
called Illinois Citizens for the Medical
Control of Abortion (ICMCA) and from
1975 to 1978 called Abortion Rights
Association of Illinois (ARA)

Like the national NARAL organization, Illinois Citizens for the Medical control of Abortion looked formalized on paper in its early years, with an advisory board, elected officers, board of directors, and advisory committees. In practice, however, the organization was informally run by a small group of dedicated activists, including Lonny Myers, a volunteer who served as the first director and provided most of the energy for ICMCA in its first few years. Later, most of the responsibilities were transferred to Helen Smith, a highly competent woman who had begun as a volunteer in ICMCA in 1970 and who was hired as a part-time paid director in 1971. As Smith recalled in a 1983 interview about the organization's decision-making structure, "I don't remember any real votes, it was not that formal; things were done more by consensus. . . . I had pretty much of a free hand, because they [the board] could see that I was pretty effective." Under Smith, who served until 1976, there was no formal division of labor; she simply recruited volunteers for various organizational tasks as needed and put in a large number of volunteer hours herself. Many of the same persons served on the board for many years, as there was no formal procedure for selecting board members. A more formal structure was not put in place until 1980, when a director who was a movement "professional" took charge and insisted that formal procedures for board selection be instituted so that new active volunteers could serve on the board with board terms being systematically rotated. The position of executive director was made a full-time one and additional staff were hired, resulting in the development of a more formal division of labor in the organization.

In terms of financial resources, the organization has had its ups and downs. There have always been some substantial contributions from wealthy supporters, including persons known to the early organizers as longtime contributors to Planned Parenthood. Early on, the Playboy Foundation began to contribute various resources, including grants, printing of the newsletter and use of the Playboy Mansion in Chicago for fund-raisers. The Midwest Population Center, a nonprofit birth control and abortion clinic founded by some of the same activists who began ICMCA, provided office space to the organization (free of charge until the early 1980s when NARAL of Illinois began to pick up part of the tab for the office space shared with the Midwest Population Center). Before 1976, the Midwest Population Center also gave financial support to the organization.

Throughout most of its history, ICMCA/ARA just got by financially. As executive director, Smith was paid a small salary for part-time work, but she also put in a lot of volunteer time and was not always paid on time when money was short. Although there was sometimes enough money to hire secretarial help, ICMCA/ARA relied primarily on volunteers. By 1975, however, the organization was in debt and making an urgent plea to supporters for money. In 1976, when Smith resigned, she was owed $500 in unpaid salary. The situation deteriorated even further in 1977 when it was reported that there was not enough money to send a newsletter. Board members were asked to contribute $100 each, which most did, to help alleviate the financial crisis. In 1978, the newly hired director, Cindy Little, reported that there were only sixty persons on the mailing list who were still sending money.

Little cultivated new sources of income, which included contributions from abortion clinics, and put a great deal of effort into rebuilding the membership. Between 1978 and 1980, Little estimated that the budget of NARAL of Illinois ranged from only about $12,000 in the first year to a high of about $40,000, not counting in-kind contributions (interview with Cindy Little, 1984). After Jan Ryan was hired as executive director in 1980, she began to build up the "house meeting" program that was part of the national NARAL organizing strategy, and the local affiliate's financial fortunes took a sharp upward turn. Money was raised through individual contributions at "house meetings" and, after establishing a tax-exempt arm, NARAL of Illinois began to be successful in convincing foundations to provide grants. As Jan Ryan explained in a 1984 interview, "If you can say you're raising $20,000 from individual contributions, then they think, heh, they really do have a solid base and are worth funding." As a result of the successful use of the house meeting organizing tool to capitalize on the interest in the issue generated by visible anti-abortion successes and the election of Ronald Reagan during the post-Hyde period, Illinois NARAL experienced rapid financial growth in a short period of time. The director, who was initially hired on a part-time basis, began to work full time; later an office worker and two organizers were hired. The budget grew to a high of about $80,000. But in 1982, because of a decline in interest in the abortion issue after a period when the issue was very "hot," the NARAL affiliate experienced something of a drop in resources. NARAL organizers hired to run programs were laid off, and the budget was reduced. This decline was later reversed in the period of the 1989 *Webster* ruling as the budget for NARAL's 501c4 organization reached about $150,000, supporting a staff of four.

The size of the organization's "membership" in its early years is somewhat difficult to gauge, given changes in its definition of membership together with incomplete records. No formal membership dues were required until the late 1970s, but contributions were solicited from persons on the mailing list who can be considered paper members of the organization. A substantial statewide mailing list of about ten thousand names was compiled in the early years. The number of contributing members was no doubt considerably lower; in 1971, a steering committee report refers to a list of seven hundred "active" members—which must have meant persons contributing money as there certainly were not that many persons participating in organizational activities (document in NARAL of Illinois Records, University of Illinois at Chicago library). In 1978, there were only sixty contributing members as a result of organizational failures, but this number was greatly increased in subsequent years. A 1980 newsletter reports four thousand members, but, according to Cindy Little (interview, 1984), it is likely that this figure was inflated by the inclusion of national NARAL members living in Illinois who were not actually local members as well. (In NARAL, members of a local affiliate are not compelled to join the national organization, and vice versa.) By the end of 1983, however, membership in the local affiliate had actually risen to four thousand (interview with former director Jan Ryan, 1984). In 1990, after the *Webster* decision, the dues-paying membership reached six thousand (interview with executive director Patricia Dougherty, 1990).

Illinois Religious Coalition for Abortion Rights (IRCAR)

As a chapter of the national Religious Coalition for Abortion Rights, Illinois RCAR has always been part of a federated organizational structure, receiving information, advice, and some financial aid from the national office. Like all RCAR affiliates, IRCAR has its own decision-making body, called the Policy Council, which is supposed to consist of one elected representative from each member denomination or organization. At the start of the organization's existence, the Policy Council did not have formally elected representatives but, rather, individuals who belonged to different denominations, some of them clergy and some laypersons, not all of whom were closely tied to their denominations. In later years, after the national organization tightened its requirements for affiliates, IRCAR changed the composition of the Policy Council to include "official" representatives from its member denominations and organizations.

Because Illinois is a large state geographically, however, there has been some difficulty in getting representatives from non-Chicago member organizations to participate in the Policy Council. There have been attempts to hold meetings in locations outside Chicago, where IRCAR has been strongest, to increase the involvement of non-Chicago RCAR members. The Policy Council meets once or twice a year to make major decisions, but this is rarely a formal process, and most decisions are made by consensus rather than vote. In the 1980s, IRCAR successfully developed "area units" in Chicago and Springfield in order to bring more religious activists into the organization to carry out local programs.

IRCAR has always had a part-time coordinator, the organization's sole staff member. The coordinator sends a newsletter and administers the organization's programs. Originally, the coordinators worked from their homes, until an office was opened in Chicago, then moved to Springfield in 1983. The move to Springfield was part of an attempt to strengthen the religious coalition in parts of Illinois outside Chicago. By the late 1980s, however, the office was once again located in Chicago.

Illinois RCAR was for many years a very low-budget operation. In its first year, the budget was about $2,500, of which $1,200 was provided by the national RCAR organization, and the rest was raised from contributions by member groups and individuals. The money was mainly spent for the coordinator's salary and the newsletter. By the early 1980s, the budget had increased, but not by a great deal; in 1983, the organization received $4,800 from national RCAR, supplemented by contributions, for a total budget of less than $10,000. By 1990, however, the RCAR budget had increased to $40,000 (figures from interviews with IRCAR coordinators).

Until the late 1980s, raising money was not a high priority for IRCAR. As the organization's coordinator in the mid-1970s observed, "Money was not the critical piece. It was trying to get religious people together, to say here we are, a nonprofit group, who believe that abortion can be an ethical choice" (interview with Carol Mullins, 1984). There were no membership dues, but member organizations were encouraged to donate money, and individual "sponsors" were sought out to make individual financial contributions to IRCAR. In the late 1980s, however, IRCAR increased its budget by securing grants from foundations in order to expand its program in a period of renewed concern about abortion rights.

IRCAR also grew in terms of its mailing list of individuals who donated money. When the organization began in 1975, a mailing list was compiled using some lists provided by Planned Parenthood members who were working with RCAR, as well as some church lists provided by other activists. After that time, RCAR compiled its own list of supporters that, as a consequence of the efforts of the RCAR coordinator, increased from 600 to 1,500 in the early 1980s (IRCAR newsletter, Summer 1984). By 1990, the mailing list reached 4,000, and, in addition, IRCAR had a list of about 150 "friends" who could be called upon to participate in activities such as legislative lobbying (interview with IRCAR coordinator Pat Camp, 1990).

Chicago-area Zero Population Growth
(Chicago-area ZPG)

Documentation of the existence and activities of the local ZPG affiliates is scant, but in 1970 there were a number of active chapters in the Chicago area, possibly as many as eleven (based on names on a letterhead), many of which were based on college campuses in the area. Beginning in late 1970, representatives from the chapters began to work together to try to open a central ZPG office in the Chicago area. In June 1971 a Chicago-area ZPG office was opened at the Midwest Population Center, a nonprofit clinic that was begun by Dr. Lonny Myers and other persons active in the population movement, some of whom had served on the national ZPG board (interviews with Chicago ZPG activists and documents in NARAL of Illinois Records, University of Illinois at Chicago library).

With the formation of the Chicago-area ZPG organization, there were attempts to coordinate the activities of the local chapters, but there was never any centralized control over the activities of the chapters. The Chicago-area ZPG organization did have a board of directors and a director for a short period of time, but it did not develop a structure in which local chapters were represented. For the most part, the local affiliate was very informally organized, with a few activists providing the impetus for activities such as speaking engagements.

In the early 1970s Chicago-area ZPG experienced a drop in membership as dramatic as that on the national level. No figures on individual membership are available, but the number of area chapters fell from about eleven in 1970 to perhaps three in 1973. At that point, Chicago-area ZPG consisted of a small number of activists, most of whom were also active in ICMCA, which shared office space at the Midwest Population Center, so that ZPG scarcely had an identity independent of that of the larger ICMCA organization. The ZPG affiliate did have an active director in 1973, Shelagh Covington, who kept the group going with programs such as a speaker's bureau. But most of the people who had helped organize the Chicago ZPG office turned their attention to work on the abortion issue. As Shelagh Covington commented in a 1983 interview, "If the truth be told, we didn't organize ZPG well enough.... You know, you talk about the theoretical issues [population], but you tend to get involved with the practical solutions [abortion]."

In 1974, after ZPG lost its director, the Chicago-area office was officially closed, although the director of ICMCA, Helen Smith, kept up a minimal presence for the organization by sending out literature in response to requests for information. After 1974, a few individuals did some public speaking on the population issue in the name of ZPG, but the organization was, for all practical purposes, defunct until 1977 when it experienced a brief revival. This came about because one individual, who had not been active in the earlier period, was interested in reestablishing the chapter. He made contact with former ZPG activists in the Chicago area whose names were provided by the national office. At the time, the national ZPG office was trying to organize a day of press conferences by affiliates on the immigration issue, a project that provided a concrete task around which to open a new chapter in the Chicago area. The person attempting to organize the group did have some success in getting formerly active ZPG members to set up the chapter and to give a press conference. The organization continued this minimal existence, sponsoring a few speakers and sending some mailings to members in the Chicago area, but as the coordinator of the group admitted in an interview:

> We were really just a public relations arm of ZPG rather than an active chapter. We did have some very talented people who worked with the group, but we were never able to motivate people on the membership list to become active. After about two and a half or three years we just gave up and sent the money we had to the national organization.

The individuals who became active in Chicago ZPG at this point were persons who had skills in public relations work and public speaking but who did not have enough contacts or organizing experience to motivate new people, such as college students, to join. And many of the older members who were asked to become reinvolved had lost interest in the population issue. As one such person told me, "ZPG had fulfilled its purpose at that point; the birthrate was falling; ZPG could die happy. . . . My interest had really died."

Chicago Chapter of the National Organization for Women (Chicago NOW)

Like all NOW chapters, Chicago NOW has always had on paper a formal structure consisting of a board of directors, elected officers, standing committees, and a parliamentary procedure. But in practice the structure was very informal in the early years. The board at first consisted of virtually all of the activists in the chapter, and standing committees were formed whenever anyone took the initiative to organize them. Beginning in the early 1970s, however, a few leaders were influential in moving the organization toward a more formal structure. In 1973 a new policy of voting on chapter "priorities" was adopted so that committees were no longer allowed to form simply because enough members were interested; rather, the chapter began to vote on three or four priority issues per year, with the intention of concentrating its resources on feasible programs. Proposals for chapter projects were submitted to the board for screening prior to a vote by the chapter membership based on criteria that included whether or not the actions would help build NOW's membership (documents in National Organization for Women Chicago Chapter Records, University of Illinois at Chicago library). Chicago NOW leaders made an explicit decision to focus on raising money and conserving resources so that staff could be hired, beginning with the first paid staff in 1973. As the Chicago NOW staff grew in the 1970s, so did the functional division of labor. Gradually, the chapter began to focus on fewer and fewer issues (working almost exclusively on the Equal Rights Amendment campaign by the mid-1970s) and to organize committees according to skills (e.g., public relations, fund-raising) rather than issues.

Chicago NOW's record on mobilizing resources is an impressive one for a local movement organization. Because of the influence of key leaders in the chapter, Chicago NOW began at an early date to pay a good deal of attention to organizational maintenance. The organization developed highly successful fund-raising techniques, enabling it to employ staff since 1973. The chapter has also steadily increased its membership. By the mid-1970s, to prevent the dilution of resources by too many programs, all activities began to be weighed in terms of their effect on the organization's growth and maintenance. As a result of the effort put into fund-raising, the budget of Chicago NOW expanded from about $10,000 in 1973, when the first full-time staff person was hired, to $175,000 in 1984, to $205,000 in 1990. Since the early 1980s, the Chicago NOW budget has supported five full-time staff members (figures from interviews with Chicago NOW directors Karen Wellisch, 1984, and Sue Purrington, 1990).

Full-time staff members are an important reason for Chicago NOW's organizational stability, growth in membership, and visibility. Staff members, including an executive director, have done much of the organizational maintenance work and have also kept the chapter before the public eye by maintaining ongoing contact with the local media. Through careful attention to recruitment by the Chicago NOW leadership the chapter membership has grown steadily over the years, from about five hundred in 1974 to about one thousand in 1980 to three thousand in 1984 to five thousand in 1990. The tremendous growth in membership in the 1980s was due in part to external events (the impending defeat of the ERA, the election of Reagan, and the *Webster* decision in 1989) and in part to the chapter's greater sophistication in attracting members through means that have included phone solicitation. And this ability to attract members has been one payoff of years of attention to the chapter's public image and visibility by an increasingly formalized organization.

Chicago Women's Liberation Union (CWLU)

A number of small women's liberation groups were already in existence at the time that the Chicago Women's Liberation Union was organized, and the initial structure was set up to preserve the autonomy of the small groups. Existing groups, and new small groups that formed after the Union was founded, were incorporated either as "chapters" based on geographic location or as "work groups" based on function. A steering committee was set up with representatives from each chapter or work group, but it was often difficult to get subunits to participate on the steering committee. Membership was ill-defined and included anyone who participated in a chapter or work group, as well as members "at large." Voluntary contributions, rather than dues, were intially requested; later, dues were required but never systematically collected. The CWLU's structure was continually modified to deal with problems such as a lack of communication among subunits, the integration of new members, decision making, and fund-raising. An office was rented, and two part-time staff were hired from the ranks of the membership. They were paid $50 per week but often went without salary when the organization was short of money, which was frequently. The CWLU's structure remained decentralized and informal, in the sense that a formalized division of labor was never developed. As a result, tasks such as fund-raising were difficult and leadership was sporadic.

Despite lengthy discussions and many experiments with different structural arrangements, the CWLU did not solve many of its organizational problems, including the problem of infiltration by left-sectarian groups. The CWLU was left open to such attacks because its membership requirements were initially limited to agreement with the statement of principles and because its structure was so decentralized that anyone who wanted to take an active role in the organization could do so. In 1970, the group faced a takeover attempt by members of the Socialist Workers Party and its youth organization, the Young Socialist Alliance, who began coming to city-wide meetings as "members" of the CWLU and trying to influence the organization despite their lack of participation in work groups or chapters. Ultimately the problem was solved by adopting a new requirement that voting "members" of the CWLU must participate in a chapter or work group or, for members at large, in the speaker's bureau, office work, or work on the newsletter and that every member must pay one dollar per month in membership dues unless financially unable to do so.

Problems with infiltration by sectarian leftist groups recurred, however. Between 1974 and 1975, members of the Revolutionary Union succeeded in getting themselves elected to the steering committee (one member as co-chair of the CWLU) and to the planning committee. In 1975, a sectarian group called the October League infiltrated one of the Union's major work groups. By late 1975, sectarian groups had formed two chapters within the CWLU and began causing tremendous conflict in the organization by attacking its basic political tenets (including feminism itself). The end result was that the Union became riddled with internal conflict and eventually dissolved in 1977.

With regard to financial resources, the CWLU never had a very large budget; my estimate is that $15,000 would have been about the most the organization raised and spent in a year. Money was raised through speaking engagements, the sale of literature and buttons, benefit concerts and other fund-raisers, such as an occasional rummage sale, and dues and contributions from members. The organization had a difficult time staying ahead financially because dues were not systematically collected and speaking engagements fell off during the summer.

Although the Union was perpetually short of financial resources, the organization did have a committed, enthusiastic, and active core of members. During the early 1970s, when the Union was at its peak, there were perhaps fifty women who formed a core of very active members (cf. Rothstein and Weisstein, 1972). In addition, some two hundred women participated in about twenty work groups and chapters, and another one hundred at-large members were active in some way. There was also a mailing list that reached nine hundred by the end of 1970 (and probably continued to grow for several years). Moreover, the CWLU's work groups tended to be highly inclusive, attracting participants who were not necessarily members of the Union. Although there were many problems associated with the CWLU's decentralized organizational structure, it did produce some innovative work groups and chapters that created a "woman's culture" in Chicago in addition to more issue-oriented projects (see Staggenborg, 1989b, for a more detailed description and a comparison with Chicago NOW).

Chicago Women's Health Task Force (CWHTF)

After the breakup of the Chicago Women's Liberation Union, the Chicago Women's Health Task Force was formed by some former CWLU members who had worked on women's health issues and some participants in the University of Illinois's Urban Preceptorship Program who were connected to the CWLU women through an instructor in the program, Jenny Knauss, who was a longtime CWLU member and women's health movement activist. The original idea was to have a group that was balanced between community health workers and more academic types. Trying to maintain such a balance, the Task Force was initially an exclusive study group.

In June 1977, in response to a threatened cutoff of state Medicaid funds for abortions, the CWHTF decided to open itself to new members and become politically active. Even at this point, however, there was no strong attempt to recruit persons outside a preexisting network of independent socialist feminists, although there were attempts to make connections with other groups concerned about health care. In part, this relative exclusiveness of the group was due to the experiences of CWLU women with sectarian takeovers within the Union. Because of the CWHTF's small size, no formal organizational structure developed; as activist Arden Handler explained in a 1983 interview, "It was not so big that we needed that. We met as a collective, about twelve to fifteen members, I would say." When Task Force members did decide it was time to expand and create a more formal organization, the CWHTF disbanded and a new group called Women Organized for Reproductive Choice was formed.

Thus, the CWHTF remained a relatively exclusive group with about fifteen members and no financial resources to speak of during its two-year lifetime. But the group did have highly committed members who were willing to put in long hours to do the nitty-gritty work of organizing demonstrations, putting out leaflets, and so forth. They were women who had years of experience with direct-action approaches to issues like abortion. Moreover, CWHTF members had connections to a fairly large number of former CWLU members and other women's health movement activists and to students in the Urban Preceptorship Program at the University of Illinois. Consequently, the CWHTF was able to mobilize a much larger number of people outside its membership for demonstrations and other activities.

Women Organized for Reproductive Choice (WORC)

Like the CWLU, Women Organized for Reproductive Choice experimented with a variety of structures. At different times, depending on its size, WORC had a steering committee, an outreach committee, a coalition committee, and various issues-oriented committees such as teen pregnancy and infant mortality committees. After a period of great constituent concern about abortion, brought about by the advent of the New Right and the Reagan Administration, WORC shrank to a base of about ten members who worked together very informally.

WORC inherited some of the longtime activists who had been involved with the CWLU and the CWHTF, and it attracted additional women from various leftist groups. The size of WORC's core of activists varied from a peak of about twenty-five or thirty active members during the 1979–80 period of the New Right threat to a low of seven to ten really committed members in the early 1980s. In addition to this core of active members, WORC had between 100 and 150 dues-paying members. According to activist Arden Handler, these members were mostly "old-time women's movement types who've been around for years" plus some people who came in touch with WORC through the group's "outreach" activities such as street-corner leafletting. Although the contribution of these members to WORC consisted, for the most part, of paying dues (on a sliding scale of $10 to $20 per year in the early 1980s), the larger membership could be persuaded to turn out for fund-raising benefits or other "events" such as an International Women's Day program. In addition to the "members," WORC also had a larger mailing list of names that were collected from petition drives and sign-up sheets at programs held by WORC.

WORC was able to survive for a number of years by retaining a small number of experienced and highly committed women who kept the organization alive and enabled the group to take part in the local pro-choice movement. When the abortion issue got "hot," or some other issue came along to galvanize members, WORC was able to expand. With funding from a couple of local Chicago foundations committed to supporting "activist" organizations, WORC was able to maintain a part-time paid coordinator for a number of years. The coordinator, Cathy Christeller, was an activist from the ranks of the organization who was paid for about ten hours per week of work but who also volunteered much of her time. Her leadership ensured some organizational stability until the late 1980s when WORC gradually ceased to exist as a real organization. However, spinoffs from the original group took its place.

By the mid-1980s, WORC had become an amorphous organizational entity; at that time there were "small numbers of people, organizing activities around different reproductive rights issues," according to Cathy Christeller (interview, 1990). One of the activities spawned by WORC was the Chicago Abortion Fund, which raised money to pay for abortions for women who could not afford them in the absence of state and federal funding; this project involved a number of local pro-choice organizations and in 1986 became independent of WORC. WORC continued to engage in other activities at this time through its Abortion Access

Committee, but it had a difficult time making progress on "access" issues such as government funding. By 1987, a number of women in WORC became interested in the issue of women and AIDS (Acquired Immune Deficiency Syndrome). As Cathy Christeller recalled:

> There was a proposal in WORC that that's where we should be working, on women and AIDS, that there were many feminist issues that weren't being touched on by anyone. Our perspective focused on who was suffering and raised issues about the lack of access to health care for poor and minority women. As with any shift, there were some people who were not interested in working on this at all. So we had more discussion, and then it was really a new core of people who wanted to work on women and AIDS. (interview with former WORC coordinator Cathy Christeller, 1990)

Grant money for the kind of reproductive rights activities in which WORC had previously engaged had become scarce, but there was money available for women and AIDS projects, and WORC received a $5,000 grant from the Ms. Foundation to launch the Chicago Women's AIDS Project. Other grants followed, and the project eventually evolved from an advocacy group into a social service agency for women that was independent of WORC.

WORC itself was kept alive in name by Cathy Christeller, who continued to send out a WORC newsletter until 1989, although by that time she was employed by the Women's AIDS Project rather than WORC. WORC activists also continued to get together for various projects, and Christeller was active in the Illinois Pro-Choice Alliance as a representative of WORC. In the fall of 1988, WORC activists helped create the Emergency Clinic Defense Coalition (ECDC), which formed in response to anti-abortion threats to abortion clinics. ECDC survived as a reproductive rights group, while WORC gradually disappeared as an organization (interview with former WORC coordinator Cathy Christeller, 1990).

APPENDIX B

Organizational Newsletters and Documents

Newsletters were used as a primary source of the historical data for most of the thirteen movement organizations that I studied through 1983. There were no newsletters, however, for two small local organizations—Chicago-area ZPG and the Chicago Women's Health Task Force—and Women Organized for Reproductive Choice did not begin producing a newsletter until 1984. I recorded information from these newsletters using a simple coding sheet with five categories: (1) issues and goals, (2) strategies and tactics, (3) resources, (4) organizational structure, and (5) coalition work and interorganizational relations. When they were available, I used other documents to supplement the newsletters to obtain this and other information. The following are annotated lists of the newsletters and manuscript collections that I used. Any documents cited in the text without reference to one of the following collections are materials provided by organizations and individuals.

Newsletters of National Organizations

NARAL News *or* NARAL Newsletter

The newsletter of the National Association for Repeal of Abortion Laws, later the National Abortion Rights Action League, was first published in the summer of 1969 as the *NARAL News* and was later called the *NARAL Newsletter*. Its publication was sporadic up until 1976 when the newsletter began to be published more regularly. From that point, the newsletter provides a good record of organizational activities. The most complete collection of the newsletter is located at the Schlesinger Library at Radcliffe College; a good, although incomplete, collection can also be found at the Northwestern University library's Special Collections Department.

Options

Options is the newsletter of the Religious Coalition for Abortion Rights. The newsletter began publication in May 1974 and continues regularly, reporting on

RCAR activities as well as developments in Congress and the like. A near-complete collection is located at the Northwestern University library's Special Collections Department. I was able to obtain from the organization the several issues missing from this collection.

ZPG National Reporter *or* ZPG Reporter

Publication of the ZPG newsletter apparently began in 1969, but I could not find any issues published before 1970. The newsletter consists mostly of articles on issues of interest to ZGP members, including articles on abortion rights. There are reports on ZPG activities, but they do not appear regularly. There also are some useful reports on organizational membership and the results of various membership surveys done by the organization. Newsletters published between 1970 and 1974 are in the Special Collections department of the Northwestern University library. The most complete collection that I found is in the ZPG office in Washington; I was able to obtain a near-complete set by visiting the office and photocopying newsletters for which duplicates were not available.

NOW Acts, Do It NOW, National NOW Times

The newsletter of the National Organization for Women was first published as *NOW Acts* in the fall of 1968; *Do It NOW* began to be published in 1971, although *NOW Acts* was also published up until 1973, reflecting the organization's decentralized state. *Do It NOW* survived as the primary organizational newsletter until December 1977, when the newsletter was changed to the *National NOW Times* and a newspaper-type format was adopted. From a researcher's point of view, *Do It NOW* is a much better newsletter than is the *National NOW Times* because the former was really used to provide information to members in the absence of other means of communication, whereas the latter is primarily a public relations tool. The newsletter does continue to report on many NOW activities, however, and supplies information on the NOW budget. The most complete collection of NOW newsletters is at the Schlesinger Library at Radcliffe College, but the Northwestern University library's Special Collections Department also has many of the newsletters.

Network News

The newsletter of the National Women's Health Network was first published in October 1976 and has continued to appear regularly. The newsletter tends to provide articles and reports on issues of interest to its members rather than on organizational activities per se, although some activities are reported. A board member that I interviewed told me that more recently the newsletter has attempted to chronicle the Network's actions, but that in the past it did not do this consistently. The newsletter does provide other information such as membership figures. A fairly complete collection of the newsletters can be found at the Northwestern University library's Special Collections Department. I was able to obtain from the organization all of the newsletters missing from that collection.

Reproductive Rights Newsletter

The newsletter of the Reproductive Rights National Network was first published in February 1978 and has been published two to three times per year since then. I obtained all but two issues, published in 1978 and 1979, from the organization and from activists in Chicago, where the newsletter was produced until 1984. The newsletter has been used as a "outreach" tool by R2N2 and consists of articles and debates on reproductive rights issues, as well as discussions of strategy and reports on organizational growth and activities, including those of the affiliates.

Newsletters of Local Organizations

ICMCA Newsletter, *Abortion Rights Association of Illinois* Newsletter, Illinois Pro-Choice Voice

The name of the Illinois NARAL affiliate's newsletter changed (as did that of the organization)—from Illinois Citizens for the Medical Control of Abortion (1966–75) to the Abortion Rights Association of Illinois (1975–78) to NARAL of Illinois (1978 to date)—but the format has remained fairly consistent. The newsletter features many reports on legislative developments and offers a good history of the organization's activities, along with some membership figures and other useful information. Many of the early newsletters, together with more recent newsletters, can be found in the NARAL of Illinois Records at the University of Illinois at Chicago library; many more recent newsletters are located in the Special Collections Department of the Northwestern University library. Other early ICMCA and ARA newsletters were provided to me by informants.

Illinois RCAR Newsletter

The Illinois RCAR newsletter has varied widely in format, depending on the coordinator writing it. It was first published in August 1975 and was typically produced several times per year, using names that varied from the Illinois RCAR *Newsletter* to the *Illinois Voice for Choice* to *The Choice.* I obtained copies of all newsletters that were available from the organization and cannot be certain how many, if any, are missing from the collection, but I have no newsletters from 1981 or 1982. The newsletters available provide some history of organizational activities along with other information.

Act NOW

The newsletter of the Chicago NOW chapter was first published in February 1969 and has since appeared regularly. *Act NOW* is a good source of information on chapter activities, resources, and connections with the national NOW organization. A near-complete set of the newsletters can be found in the Special Collections Department of the Northwestern University library, and I was able to obtain from the organization the several issues missing from this collection.

CWLU News, Womankind

The regular newsletter of the Chicago Women's Liberation Union, *CWLU News,* was first published in December 1969 and continued until March 1977, when the final issue was published. The newsletter is an incredible source of data because it contains detailed reports on CWLU strategies and tactics, evaluations of these activities, and numerous discussions about organizational structure, ideology, and so forth. The newsletter is exceptionally informative because the CWLU was deliberately using it to try to bring as many members as possible into the organization's decision-making process. Because *CWLU News* was used for this purpose, a second newsletter, *Womankind,* began to be published in 1971 to serve as an outreach tool intended for women not yet initiated into the organization. *Womankind* was published through 1973 and contains information on CWLU activities as well as articles about various issues. The most complete collection of CWLU newsletters is at the Special Collections Department of the Northwestern University library; however, additional newsletters can be found in the CWLU papers at the Chicago Historical Society.

WORC Newsletter

Women Organized for Reproductive Choice did not begin to produce a newsletter until 1984. I obtained from the organization those published from 1984 to 1989.

Manuscript Collections

Women's Collection of the Northwestern University Library, Special Collections Department

The Women's Collection at the Northwestern University library contains good collections of many newsletters of feminist and abortion rights organizations. In addition, there are folders containing documents relevant to the abortion issue from national and local organizations including NARAL, RCAR, ZPG, CWLU, ICMCA/ARA/NARAL of Illinois, and the coalition organizations WONAAC, TRIAL, and the Ad Hoc Committee for Abortion Rights.

National Abortion Rights Action League of Illinois Records, Special Collections Department, The University Library, The University of Illinois at Chicago

The NARAL of Illinois papers are an invaluable collection that contains all kinds of organizational documents, including early newsletters. In addition to documents of the local organization, there are minutes from national NARAL board and executive committee meetings from the years when ICMCA leaders like Lonny Myers and Helen Smith served on the NARAL board of directors. There also are communications between the national and local NARAL organizations, as well as some documents, probably the only surviving ones, from the Chicago-area ZPG organization, which once shared office space with ICMCA.

Lonny Myers Papers, Special
Collections Department, The University
Library, The University of Illinois at
Chicago

The papers of ICMCA founder Lonny Myers contain additional letters and information on the early abortion movement.

National Organization for Women,
Chicago Chapter Records, Special
Collections Department, The University
Library, The University of Illinois at
Chicago

The Chicago NOW papers are another valuable collection that contains all kinds of organizational documents, including communications with the national NOW organization.

Chicago Women's Liberation Union
Papers, Chicago Historical Society,
Manuscripts Department

All of the Chicago Women's Liberation Union papers were deposited at the Chicago Historical Society when the organization dissolved in 1977. Not only are the papers extensive, but they are sorted by year and by issue, making the collection a pleasure to use.

NARAL Papers, Schlesinger Library,
Radcliffe College

All of the NARAL papers have been deposited at the Schlesinger Library. A complete collection of newsletters and all publications are available to researchers, but at the time of my research the organization had closed much of the collection to researchers other than past or present NARAL board members until twenty or more years from the date of deposit.

NOW Papers, Schlesinger Library, Radcliffe College

The National Organization for Women also uses the Schlesinger Library as an archive and, like NARAL, at the time of my research had limited access by researchers to newsletters and other publications.

Lawrence Lader Papers, Rare Book and Manuscript Division, The Astor, Lenox and Tilden Foundations, New York Public Library

The Lawrence Lader papers contain materials that Lader collected when researching his books, *Abortion* (1966) and *Abortion II* (1973). They contain information about the early abortion movement in general and NARAL in particular, although at the time of my research many of the papers dealing with NARAL were restricted in accordance with the Schlesinger Library guidelines.

Private Papers

In addition to the preceding collections, several individuals and organizations gave me literature, newsletters, and other documents. Two persons, Jean Robinson and Jennifer Knauss, gave me access to a large number of private papers; documents from these papers are cited with the written permission of their owners. Jean Robinson was active in ICMCA/ARA, Planned Parenthood, the Midwest Population Center, the Ad Hoc Committee on Abortion Rights, and Chicago-area ZPG and served on the national ZPG board of directors in the early 1970s. Her papers contain documents from all of these organizations. Jenny Knauss was active in the Chicago Women's Liberation Union, the Chicago Women's Health Task Force, and the Ad Hoc Committee for Abortion Rights and served on the board of the National Women's Health Network from 1977 to 1980. Her papers contain documents from all of these organizations and also include what I have cited as the "CWLU working papers." The latter is a history of women's health care projects undertaken by CWLU-connected groups in Chicago until 1975. It was compiled by Jenny Knauss and others interested in writing a history of the local women's health movement and consists of descriptions written by participants in the projects.

APPENDIX C

Interviews with Pro-Choice Activists

The main interviews for this study were conducted between October 1983 and May 1985. During that period, I talked to a total of fifty different people, and I interviewed several more than once. Of these fifty persons, I talked to twenty-eight about their involvement in local pro-choice organizations, nineteen about their involvement in national organizations, and three about their involvement in both national and local organizations. Of the national informants, seven were active in NARAL, three in RCAR, six in ZPG, three in NOW (two of whom were also active in NARAL), two in NWHN, and three in R2N2. Of the local informants, many of whom were involved in multiple organizations, eleven were active in ICMCA/ARA/NARAL of Illinois, five in Chicago-area ZPG, two in Chicago NOW, four in the CWLU, five in the CWHTF, and four in WORC. I also interviewed five past coordinators of the Illinois Pro-Choice Alliance and several persons in other organizations, including Planned Parenthood, the ACLU, the Clergy Consultation Services, and Personal PAC.

In selecting these informants, I used two main criteria: (1) period of involvement, to cover all periods for all organizations, and (2) position in the organization, to get a mix of staff and volunteer activists. For multi-issue organizations, I chose informants involved in abortion-related activities. To find these people, I began with names obtained from newsletters and other documents, which was a good way to determine an individual's position and level of involvement in an organization. Many of the informants whose names I found in documents I located through the phone book. Once I began interviewing persons located in this manner, I received from them referrals and information on current addresses and phone numbers. I was able to cover all periods for every organization except the National Organization for Women, for which I could locate no informant for the years between 1973 and 1976, despite a number of phone calls to disconnected numbers and letters to wrong addresses. In this case, I had, from documents, the names of persons I wanted to interview, but no current addresses, and the organization declined to give me information about their whereabouts.

In addition to interviewing these fifty persons for the 1983–85 period, I talked to nine persons by phone in March and April 1990. These individuals included the current executive directors of national NARAL, NARAL of Illinois, Illinois RCAR, and Chicago NOW; staff members from ZPG, RCAR, the NWHN, and

Students Organizing Students; and the former coordinator of WORC, whom I had also interviewed for the previous period.

Most of the original interviews were done in person in Chicago, New York, and Washington, D.C., but some were done by phone in cases of persons in scattered locations across the country. All of the 1990 interviews were conducted by phone. Most of the interviews were not tape recorded (although some were), so that all quotations may not be exact, as they were written down from notes and memory immediately following the interviews. In addition to honoring explicit requests for anonymity, I have used my own discretion about identifying informants by name when quoted. Many informants talked frankly with me about sensitive topics such as internal organizational conflicts and interorganizational relations. A few persons asked that their names not be used. Consequently, I have used the names of some, but not all, of my informants in the text. I made some quotations anonymous when I thought that the person quoted would prefer that I do so, even if he or she did not request anonymity. (In some places, quotations are not attributed to individuals for stylistic reasons.)

Notes

Chapter 1

1. The best history of the U.S. abortion conflict before the twentieth century is James Mohr's (1978) *Abortion in America,* which is the source for the information in this paragraph.

2. The term "pro-choice" was not used until after the legalization of abortion in 1973, in response to the "pro-life" rhetoric of the anti-abortion movement. Before 1973, the single-issue component of the movement was referred to by participants as the "abortion movement." In the interest of historical accuracy, I do not use the term pro-choice in specific references to the pre-1973 period, although I do use the term in more general references to the movement as a whole.

One informant who was active before 1973 did register a strong objection to the term pro-choice on the grounds that it is a euphemistic and reactive response to the anti-abortion term pro-life. She urged me to use the term "abortion rights movement" instead of "pro-choice movement" because early activists had worked hard to bring the term "abortion" out in the open.

After hearing this objection, I asked two other pre-1973 activists how they felt about the term pro-choice. One said she liked it because it allowed people to express a preference for legal abortion without implying that they considered abortion other than a measure of last resort. The other informant said she understood the objection to the term pro-choice because "it was important before 1973 to avoid euphemisms in talking about abortion, but added, "I think the day for the shock value of the word 'abortion' is over; once you've gotten it out in the open it's probably not necessary to keep away from euphemisms. I use the term 'pro-choice' myself. I think, if it's useful, why not? Of course, it is a reaction to the 'pro-life' term, but the trick is to get things accomplished. Whatever works is what should be used." I decided to use the term pro-choice because the reality is that this is the term most commonly used to describe the movement. Moreover, the term pro-choice is somewhat more inclusive than abortion rights, so that reproductive rights groups, women's health groups, and other multi-issue groups are included with the term pro-choice.

On the other hand, I use the term "anti-abortion" rather than "right-to-life" or "pro-life" to refer to the opposing movement, in part because the term anti-abortion is widely used (cf. Kelly, 1989) and in part because this is the story of the pro-choice movement; from the perspective of the pro-choice movement, the opposition is an anti-abortion movement. I also refer to the anti-abortion movement as a "countermovement," a term used by social movement theorists to refer to a social movement that forms in order to oppose another social movement (cf. McCarthy and Zald, 1977).

3. "Direct-action" tactics, such as demonstrations or quasi-legal abortion referral services, are forms of collective action that bypass established channels of actions. "Institutionalized" tactics, such as legislative lobbying, employ conventional, institutional procedures for influencing authorities or other targets. Although this distinction is somewhat problematic—as direct actions such as demonstrations can certainly be highly routinized—it does capture the difference between tactics that attempt to bring about change from "outside" the system and those aimed at influencing authorities from "within" the system.

4. McCarthy and Zald (1977) define the "social movement sector" as consisting of all "social movement industries" in a society. A social movement industry, in their terminology, includes all social movement organizations oriented toward the same general goal(s). Tarrow (1989:16) defines the concept of a social movement sector somewhat more narrowly as "the configuration of individuals and groups willing to engage in disruptive direct action against others to achieve collective goals." I follow McCarthy and Zald's usage on the grounds that it is unworkable to separate "disruptive" actions from other forms of movement activity.

5. Seminal works in the perspective known as "resource mobilization theory," which has come to dominate the study of social movements in American sociology, include Gamson, 1975; McCarthy and Zald, 1973, 1977; Oberschall, 1973; and Tilly, 1978. Rule (1988, chap. 3) provides a useful discussion of earlier "collective behavior" theories, including the "irrationalist" treatment of collective action by European theorists such as LeBon and changes and continuities in this tradition in the hands of American theorists associated with the Chicago school of sociology.

6. Tilly (1978) uses the term "polity" to refer to the actions of the government and those "member" groups in the population that enjoy routine access to government resources.

7. McCarthy and Zald (1973, 1977) link this trend to an increase in government and private funding to support movement careers; as elite support becomes available, professional organizers act as "entrepreneurs" in creating social movements.

8. This phrase is used by Leites and Wolf (1970) and cited by McCarthy and Zald (1973) to distinguish their approach from previous emphases on individual states of consciousness in the mobilization of social movements.

9. A number of factors have been identified as aspects of the "political opportunity structure." See Tarrow (1988) for a summary of the important work in political opportunity theory.

Chapter 2

1. These words were used to describe the early movement by Lana Clarke Phelan, who began her work in the movement with the California Society for Humane Abortion, which was founded in 1961 (interview with Lana Clarke Phelan, 1984).

2. The ALI recommended that abortion be allowed in cases of danger to the physical or mental health of the mother, physical or mental defect in the fetus, and pregnancy resulting from rape, incest, or felonious intercourse (Tatalovich and Daynes, 1981:24–25).

3. In the early years of the abortion movement, there were divisions between advocates of "reform" of the abortion laws who desired changes in the law to allow abortion under certain circumstances (e.g., danger to the mother, damage to the fetus, rape, or incest) and advocates of "repeal" who wanted complete repeal of the abortion laws from the criminal codes.

4. The four states were Hawaii, Alaska, Washington, and New York. New York was the most important insofar as it provided a place for many women who could afford to travel to go for legal abortions.

5. Lawrence Lader, an early movement activist, makes this point about the limited nature of established organizational and professional support in a June 3, 1984, letter to the *New York Times Book Review* in response to a review of Kristin Luker's *Abortion and the Politics of Motherhood.* He argues:

> The first board of the [National Association for Repeal of Abortion Laws], a coalition of nationwide abortion groups formed in 1969, had only eight doctors among its 62 members. Only one could be considered from the medical "Establishment." The sole medical organization represented was the liberal Physicians Forum. The American Public Health Association (including all categories of health professionals) joined us in a year. Planned Parenthood's medical committee entered the abortion rights movement in 1969, after approval by the membership. The American Medical Association's House of Delegates voted to approve abortions in accredited hospitals with the consent of two consulting physicians only after the passage of New York State's landmark law in 1970.
>
> For Miss Luker to credit the medical profession rather than women's organizations for playing a "central role" in abortion rights in the 1960's is fallacious. The first board of the National Association for Repeal of Abortion Laws had 34 women among its 62 members, representing grass-roots organizations in California, Massachusetts, Wisconsin, Illinois and other states. It was women (and men), not the medical profession, who produced years of campaigning to win the New York law, a political phenomenon of this century.

6. New York Civil Liberties Union members Aryeh Neier and Harriet Pilpel were quite active in New York, and Pilpel introduced the issue to the national organization at a 1964 conference. At that time, however, *Griswold* v. *Connecticut,* the landmark contraceptive case that established a legal "right to privacy," had not yet been won, and the ACLU was reluctant to take up the issue (see Walker, 1990:301–2).

7. Freeman (1975) uses the term "older branch" for organizations such as NOW that were formed by comparatively older, professional women several years before the formation of what she calls "younger branch" women's movement organizations by younger women who typically had experience in student New Left groups. Freeman contends that the two branches are distinguished largely by structure rather than ideology, with the older branch organizations adopting more traditional organizational forms. Others, such as Hole and Levine (1971), use the terms "women's rights" and "women's liberation," which emphasize ideological differences, to refer to the older and the younger branches of the movement, respectively. I use both sets of terms, as I think the branches are distinguished by both structure and ideology.

8. The name "Jane" was used in the telephone recording for the service: When women called to arrange an abortion, the voice of a woman, identifying herself as Jane, gave them instructions.

9. There was a conscious effort to keep the referral work of CCS separate from the political work of ICMCA for the benefit of the latter, according to Rev. Parsons (interview, 1984). In 1968, Parsons resigned the presidency of ICMCA to found the Chicago Clergy Consultation Services, but he remained active in ICMCA behind the scenes.

10. Documents on the role of the SWP in WONAAC can be found in the Women's Collection of the Special Collections Department at the Northwestern University library. Several informants also confirmed this information.

11. The Abortion Rights Act was a bill supported by Representative Bella Abzug in an attempt to legalize abortion legislatively.

12. According to a CWLU report, the meeting was attended by representatives from

ICMCA, CCS, Chicago NOW, CWLU's Abortion Counseling Service, Planned Parenthood, a new organization called Freedom to Choose (to which I have seen no other references), and the American Friends Service Committee. At this meeting, "it was generally felt that broad areas of responsibility should be allocated to different groups" in order to coordinate actions and share resources, although ICMCA "agreed to act as the overall coordinator and clearinghouse" (*CWLU News,* June 1970).

13. Initial participants in TRIAL included the CWLU, ICMCA, Chicago NOW, Chicago Planned Parenthood, Chicago-area ZPG, SWP, and several other local organizations, mostly women's liberation groups.

14. As Killian (1984) emphasizes, the "organization" that produces a social movement can take the form of social networks among grass-roots activists rather than formal organizational structures.

Chapter 3

1. Gerlach and Hine's (1970) characterization of movements as decentralized, segmentary, and reticulate provides a good description of the pre-1973 movement to legalize abortion. Although some *movement organizations,* such as NARAL, were centralized in their internal decision-making structures, decision making in the *movement* was decentralized. The movement was segmentary in that it consisted of a number of independent local groups, and it was reticulate in that personal networks and overlapping memberships in movement organizations tied the movement together.

2. Data on public opinion from Gallup polls, the National Fertility Study, and the National Opinion Research Center all show an increase in public support for legal abortion from 1965 to 1973 (cf. Blake, 1971; Granberg and Granberg, 1980; Jones and Westhoff, 1973). The greatest increase in support occurred between 1965 and 1970 and was more pronounced for the "hard" reasons for having an abortion (danger to maternal health, rape, incest, and fetal deformity) than for the "soft" reasons (economic, unmarried woman, and personal choice).

3. One early abortion movement organization that does not fit this profile of nonconfrontational activism is the California-based Society for Humane Abortion. Founder Patricia Maginnis and her associates deliberately engaged in confrontational tactics such as offering classes on self-abortion to attract media publicity to their cause. The difference in strategy may be explained in part because Maginnis worked in more liberal places such as San Francisco (Lader, 1973:32) and in part because she and close associate Lana Clarke Phelan were moved to activism by their own experiences with illegal abortion, rather than being drawn into the movement via voluntary careers, as were many other activists in the single-issue abortion movement. Based on accounts of other abortion organizations in Hawaii (Steinhoff and Diamond, 1977), Iowa (Mohr, 1989), and Texas (Faux, 1988) and my research on Illinois, the California group is unusual for the single-issue branch of the movement.

4. An ICMCA activist that I interviewed explained that ICMCA was actually asking for less than the Supreme Court delivered in 1973 and showed me an ICMCA pamphlet that argued for legal abortion in the first trimester of pregnancy only. The Supreme Court ruling legalized abortion in the second trimester of pregnancy as well.

5. Helen Smith served as the executive director of ICMCA from 1971 to 1976 after beginning as a volunteer in 1970. She was paid a small salary for part-time work, but put in many more volunteer hours.

6. The affiliations of early NARAL board members included the National Organization for Women, Zero Population Growth, the Association for Voluntary Sterilization, the

American Public Health Association, Planned Parenthood, the New York Civil Liberties Union, the American Humanist Association, the American Baptist Convention, the National YWCA, and the Unitarian Universalist Women's Federation (NARAL letterhead, 1969, in NARAL papers; Schlesinger Library, Radcliffe College).

7. Although many women's movement organizations have refused to accept Playboy money, NARAL and its affiliates took from the start a pragmatic attitude toward accepting support from the Playboy Foundation.

8. The CWLU's decentralized organizational structure (see Appendix A) made the resolution of such strategic questions particularly difficult because subunits of the organization acted independently and there was little coordination of strategy.

9. Although the California bill was intended to be a moderate reform, implementation turned out to be quite liberal, with 99 percent of requests for abortions being granted by 1970 (Luker, 1984:94).

10. There is no doubt that the institutionalized Catholic Church played a role in the creation of an anti-abortion movement before the legalization of abortion in 1973. Not only were individual Catholics heavily involved in state and local anti-abortion organizations, but the National Right to Life Committee worked "in cooperation with the Family Life Division of the United States Catholic Conference" until the national organization was restructured in 1973 (*National Right to Life News,* November 1973, quoted in Hanna, 1979:152). In 1969, the Catholic bishops included a policy statement opposing abortion in a pastoral letter, and in 1972 "Respect Life" programs were initiated to activate Catholics on the issue at the parish level and a Committee for Pro-Life Activities was established by the Catholic bishops (cf. Hanna, 1979; Jaffe et al., 1981).

11. The two lawyers who filed *Roe* v. *Wade* followed the lead of civil rights lawyers in bringing the case to a three-judge court in Texas. Civil rights lawyers had discovered that these courts, which were little used until the 1960s, were particularly useful in striking down discriminatory legislation as they provided direct access to the Supreme Court (Faux, 1988:82).

12. The California Supreme Court struck down the old California abortion statute in the case of Dr. Leon Belous (who was arrested in 1967 for making an abortion referral before the passage of the California reform law) on the basis of a woman's "fundamental right" to choose whether or not to have children (Rubin, 1987:44–45). In Washington, D.C., in 1969, Dr. Milan Vuitch was arrested for performing abortions, and a District Court judge dismissed the charges on the grounds that the D.C. abortion law, which allowed abortions only when a woman's "health" was in danger, was "unconstitutionally vague." The case was appealed to the Supreme Court which ruled in 1971 in *United States* v. *Vuitch* that the abortion law was not too vague but that the government was required to prove that the abortion was *not* necessary to the woman's health rather than the physician being required to prove that it *was* necessary. The case was thus returned to the District Court (Rubin, 1987:46) and was considered a victory by abortion activists.

13. See Faux (1988) for an account of the conflict surrounding Lucas's involvement in the abortion movement.

14. Some of these lawyers no doubt hoped to make names for themselves, as had civil rights lawyers before them. However, the lawyers who initiated abortion cases also included women who were influenced by the women's movement and active in the abortion cause.

15. Rubin (1987:47) notes that the filing of *amicus curiae,* or "friend-of-the-court," briefs "is a subtle form of lobbying, a method by which organizations can indicate their support of a certain policy perspective."

16. This appears to be an instance of a negative, rather than a positive, "radical flank effect" (see Haines, 1988). That is, the presence of more radical groups creates difficulties

for more moderate groups instead of helping them by making their positions seem more reasonable. In this case, both feminists and single-issue abortion movement groups were advocating the same goal (repeal of the abortion laws), but they framed their demands very differently. Moderate groups had to compete with the more radical presentation of the issue in their attempts at persuasion.

Chapter 4

1. The Liberation School offered courses ranging from socialist–feminist theory to auto mechanics, in some years enrolling as many as two hundred women in twenty courses. The "Women and Their Bodies" course was first taught in 1970 after a woman from the New York Women's Abortion Project came to spend the summer with her friend in the CWLU and helped set up the course. One CWLU activist that I interviewed pointed out that the Liberation School was a natural activity for Union activists, given that many of them were students. It was also very much in the tradition of the Freedom Schools of the civil rights and student movements (see McAdam, 1988).

2. Echols (1989) credits the New York radical feminist group Redstockings with the invention of the speak-out. "Counter-hearings" were held by the group in 1969 to allow women to speak out as the "real experts" on abortion in response to state legislative hearings controlled by men. These hearings were apparently the first of this type of event, a tactic that was quickly adopted by feminist groups across the country.

3. In addition to the more institutionalized media tactics described in Chapter 2, ICMCA created its own forum by undertaking an advertising campaign in local newspapers in Illinois in order to bring the word "abortion" to a mass readership as a "respectable" idea (ICMCA newsletter, Fall 1968). The ads included mail-in coupons that brought a large response and helped ICMCA build its mailing list to a high of about ten thousand names.

4. In September 1969, NARAL held its first national press conference to announce its policy of full support for abortion referral services, including financial and legal help for persons arrested. In December 1969, a controversial announcement was again made at a press conference at which NARAL demanded free clinics for the poor in Washington, D.C., following a court ruling that the poor must have equal access to abortions. According to Lader, this press conference, at which NARAL threatened to open its own clinic if necessary, "produced the largest turnout of reporters and television cameras since the start of the abortion campaign" (Lader, 1973:112). After the 1970 repeal bill was passed in New York, NARAL issued a press release calling for outpatient clinics in place of standard hospital care for first-trimester abortions. When restrictive guidelines were issued by state and city health commissions, NARAL made headlines in the *New York Times* by publicly urging doctors to defy the restrictions. On July 1, 1970, NARAL held a well-publicized training session, conducted by NARAL's medical committee, to teach abortion techniques to doctors. In 1971, NARAL issued a position paper to the press opposing commercial referral services in New York, which were eventually banned.

5. In 1970, for example, NARAL coordinated "Lysistrata Day" demonstrations intended to attract local women's movement groups to draw media attention to the repeal victories of that year (see Nathanson, 1979:65). The Lysistrata Day demonstrations were inspired by the Aristophanes play in which women stayed away from men in order to stop war; the idea was to attract women's liberation groups and college students with the tactic of having women proclaim a day of sexual abstinence in protest of illegal abortion.

6. Other organizations and individuals provided abortion referral services without confrontational public relations strategies to accompany them. On the national level, Zero Population Growth operated a computerized Abortion Information Data Bank to provide

women seeking abortions with the names of doctors doing legal abortions in states with reformed laws.

7. Some activists in the Chicago Clergy Consultation Service were also involved in ICMCA, so that there was a keen awareness among ICMCA members of the need for abortion services for women who could not afford travel to New York or elsewhere for a legal abortion. In 1971, ICMCA tried to help alleviate the problem by sending small groups of people to hospitals to request their cooperation in accepting more women for legal "therapeutic" abortions—again, a nonconfrontational strategy that reflected the orientation of ICMCA leaders. However, it did not solve the problem, and in 1972 ICMCA, in cooperation with Chicago-area ZPG, organized a statewide drive to send people to Michigan to work on a referendum campaign to repeal the Michigan abortion law. This strategy was adopted in the hope of providing a nearby place for Illinois women to have abortions, as there was little hope for a repeal victory in the Illinois legislature and a referendum campaign was not feasible under Illinois law.

8. Taking their inspiration from the Yippies (Echols, 1989:76), the original WITCH (Women's International Terrorist Conspiracy From Hell) came out of New York Radical Women in 1968; a group of women dressed as witches performed street theater, including "hexes" of targets such as the New York Stock Exchange. WITCH "covens" soon began to appear in different parts of the country (see Hole and Levine, 1971:126–30). In Chicago, the WITCH group was separate from the CWLU but overlapped in membership.

9. Feminists saw themselves as more than just "troops" for the abortion movement and did in fact have an important impact on the single-issue movement, which adopted the "women's rights" frame for the issue.

10. One ZPG informant stressed to me in an interview that population activists shunned the term "population control" as too coercive.

Chapter 5

1. After January 1973, the National Right to Life Committee was restructured as a membership organization, soon becoming the largest and most visible countermovement organization. A number of new national organizations were also formed in response to the Court ruling. These include American Citizens Concerned for Life, founded in 1973 as American Citizens for Life; March for Life, founded in 1974 when the first mass demonstration was held on the anniversary of the Supreme Court ruling in Washington; the National Committee for a Human Life Amendment, founded by the Catholic bishops in 1974; and For Life, an organization formed in 1974 to help provide and distribute anti-abortion literature and other educational materials (see Encyclopedia of Associations, 1978). On the local level as well, new organizations were formed and many more individuals were recruited as a result of the sudden legalization of abortion (cf. Luker, 1984).

2. Because of the difficulties involved in passing any constitutional amendment, none of the proposed "Human Life Amendments" met with any success. Also unsuccessful were the proposed "states rights" amendments that would make abortion a matter for state regulation through a constitutional amendment (cf. Davidson, 1983; Potts et al., 1977; Sarat, 1982). Efforts to cut off funding of abortions were more successful. In 1973, an amendment to the Foreign Service Act was passed, preventing the use of federal funds to promote abortions outside the United States (Potts et al., 1977:365–66). A "right of conscience" amendment was also attached to a federal health bill in 1973 to protect recipients of federal funds from being forced to provide abortions and to prevent employment discrimination against staff persons refusing to cooperate with the performance of abortions (Davidson, 1983:38). In the area of fetal research, legislation was passed in 1973 to prohibit the use of federal

funds for research on aborted fetuses (Sarat, 1982:137). In 1974, the National Research Act prohibited the Department of Health, Education and Welfare (HEW) from supporting any fetal research (Hart, 1975:72). And beginning in 1974, there were attempts to prohibit the use of Medicaid funds for abortions through amendments to the annual Labor–HEW appropriations bill. These were unsuccessful until 1976 when an amendment to the 1977 appropriations bill sponsored by Representative Henry Hyde, which became known as the Hyde Amendment, was passed by Congress.

3. In 1973 alone, close to two hundred bills were introduced into the state legislatures; within two years, sixty-two laws restricting abortions had been passed by thirty-two state legislatures (Rubin, 1987:127). Rubin (1987:127–30) identifies seven types of restrictive laws passed after legalization by the Supreme Court: (1) performance regulations, specifying the conditions under which abortions can be performed; (2) consent requirements, including parental consent for minors and spousal consent for married women; (3) reporting requirements, requiring doctors and hospitals to keep records of abortions (some of which did not violate the patient's right to confidentiality); (4) advertising prohibitions; (5) public-funding restrictions, which began to be passed before the federal Hyde Amendment; (6) conscience clauses, to allow individual doctors and institutions to refuse to provide abortions; and (7) fetal protection laws to forbid fetal research and to save any fetus aborted live.

4. See Chapter 3, note 6 on the distinction between "hard" and "soft" reasons.

5. The Catholic Church reacted immediately to the Supreme Court ruling with a policy statement by the bishops condemning the decision. In 1973, abortion became the single most important issue for the United States Catholic Conference's Family Life Division (Hanna, 1979:151). The institutional Church became heavily involved in lobbying efforts for a Human Life Amendment, and in 1974 four Catholic cardinals were among those testifying at the first hearings on the anti-abortion amendments held by the Senate Constitutional Amendments Subcommittee (Doerr, 1976). Indeed, the Catholic Church was so deeply involved in anti-abortion lobbying that the Women's Lobby filed suit against the Church for failing to register as a lobby. The lawsuit was dismissed, but the Church subsequently set up a secular lobbying arm, the National Committee for a Human Life Amendment (NCHLA). Although separate from the Catholic Church, the NCHLA maintained close ties to the Catholic bishops (cf. Hanna, 1979; Jaffe et al., 1981:74; Tatalovich and Daynes, 1981:155).

Official Catholic opposition to abortion intensified in 1975 when the National Conference of Catholic Bishops issued its "Pastoral Plan for Pro-Life Activities." This document called for extensive educational and political activities by the Church aimed at restricting, and eventually outlawing, abortion. On the local level, the Pastoral Plan called for the establishment of "pro-life units" in every Congressional district in the country (cf. Hanna, 1979:151, Jaffe et al., 1981:74–75).

6. There was an organizational forum in which Washington-based religious groups could discuss social issues, called the Washington Inter-religious Staff Council (WISC). But because there were several Catholic groups in WISC, an agreement had been made that the abortion issue would not be discussed. The fact that this established forum could not be used to coordinate religious pro-choice activities was one impetus for the formation of RCAR (interview with Jessma Blockwick, 1984).

7. This was done to eliminate the red tape involved in setting up a separate organization and because RCAR organizers initially had no idea that the battle for abortion rights would continue for so many years. Although in practice RCAR always operated as an autonomous organization, the arrangement with the United Methodist Church did create a few problems. One difficulty for the church was that RCAR expenditures in its budget made it look as if the United Methodist Church was spending a disproportionate amount of its resources

on pro-choice activities over other social causes (interview with Jessma Blockwick, 1984). Another problem was the loss of one RCAR member, the Lutheran Church of America, because the Lutheran Church decided it was not appropriate to belong to a project over which the United Methodist Church had legal veto power. (The United Methodists never used their veto power, but according to its bylaws the church did have the authority to counteract any RCAR decisions) (interview with former RCAR director Fredrica Hodges, 1984). Because of these problems and because it had long been clear that the abortion conflict was a long-term one, RCAR was finally incorporated in 1981 as an organization legally separate from the United Methodist Church.

8. See Staggenborg (1989a) for a more detailed account of the decisions of ZPG, NOW, and other multi-issue movement organizations to enter and exit the pro-choice movement at different points in time.

9. Abortion became even less of a priority for Chicago NOW after legalization than it had been previously, for several reasons. First, the individual who had initiated virtually all of the chapter's activities on the issue before 1973, and who also participated in CWLU work groups dealing with abortion, was, after 1973, no longer the chair of NOW's committee dealing with abortion. Chicago NOW did continue to maintain a committee on "Reproduction and Its Control" for a while after 1973, but abortion was not a chapter priority. In contrast with the CWLU, Chicago NOW did not have a long-term ideological vision to motivate continued abortion-related activities. Second, the chapter was attempting by this time to control the number of projects it undertook, in order not to spread its resources too thinly (see Appendix A). Third, the national NOW organization was urging its chapters in those states that had not ratified the Equal Rights Amendment (including Illinois) to refrain from lobbying on abortion, so as not to mix the two issues (*Do It NOW,* September 1973).

10. Unfortunately, there is a lack of research on other local movements during this period, so it is difficult to judge how typical this decline was. In the late 1970s, however, national NARAL was attempting to reestablish contact with a number of state organizations, suggesting that this kind of decline had occurred elsewhere.

11. Chicago NOW was one local organization that also began to professionalize after 1973, but, as I have noted, the organization was not heavily involved in the pro-choice movement at this point.

12. In an interview, Helen Smith estimated that during her tenure there were thirty to thirty-five people whom she could call on who were very active. There were, as well, other persons (approximately fifty) who could be relied on to do certain things such as lend their homes for fund-raisers. In addition to the active members, ICMCA accumulated a statewide mailing list of about ten thousand names, in large part as a result of a newspaper campaign undertaken by Lonny Myers. Although there were no membership dues in the early years, the mailing list was used to solicit contributions and cooperation in actions such as letter writing. Through Smith's efforts, a number of chapters of ICMCA were also organized throughout the state of Illinois. After Smith left ARA, all of these resources declined and when a new director was hired to replace Smith's successor in 1978, she reported that only sixty contributing members were left.

13. In Tilly's (1978) terminology, "members" of the polity are those groups in the population that have routine access to government power holders.

Chapter 6

1. Tilly (1978:145–47) distinguishes between "*reactive* collective actions," which "consist of group efforts to reassert established claims when someone else challenges or violates

them," and "*proactive* collective actions," which "assert group claims which have not previously been exercised." Although Tilly focuses on the large-scale historical forces that have tipped the balance in favor of proactive actions over reactive ones, the distinction is also useful in looking at changes over the course of a social movement, particularly in movement–countermovement interactions.

2. ZPG also assisted NARAL in this strategy by asking its affiliates to investigate local services so as to help locate hospitals that were not providing abortions (ZPG *National Reporter,* June 1973).

3. Dr. Bernard Nathanson, who has since become known for his defection to the anti-abortion movement, was a member of the NARAL medical committee who also ran an abortion clinic in New York after abortion was legalized there in 1970.

4. Regarding the investigation of the Michican Avenue clinic, ICMCA executive director Helen Smith commented, "We tried to do that, but it was very hard. We tried to send someone in, but really we just were not trained for that. Now, Pam Zekman of the *Sun-Times* [a reporter who did a 1978 investigative report on Chicago abortion clinics], she knew how to do that, but we didn't." As for the Chicago Abortion Services Council, Smith recalled "that didn't quite catch either. We tried to get the clinics to agree to keep certain standards; some didn't want to. They wanted abortion legal, but they didn't want to be monitored" (interview with Helen Smith, 1983). In comparison with ICMCA/ARA, the Health Evaluation and Referral Service was better prepared to monitor service providers and to pressure them, by withholding referrals, into meeting its demands.

5. The anti-abortion movement has also engaged in some proactive activities in response to its opposition. Ginsburg (1989:97) reports that anti-abortionists became more involved in providing support to pregnant women in response to the pro-choice criticism that they had no concern for women seeking abortions. The "seamless garment" anti-abortion position formulated by Catholic Church leader Joseph Cardinal Bernardin also appears to be an example of a proactive response to opposition. It is likely that this comprehensive "pro-life" position—which links opposition to abortion to anti-nuclear, anti-poverty, and other "pro-life" efforts—was created in response to the common criticism of anti-abortionists as being opposed to abortion but unconcerned about the lives of people once they are born.

6. Evidence of this can be found in a number of NARAL memos sent to supporters in 1973 (documents in NARAL of Illinois Records, University of Illinois at Chicago library; and NARAL papers, Schlesinger Library, Radcliffe College) and in reports contained in the 1973 issues of the ZPG *National Reporter.*

7. Costain (1988) describes the development of a broader "woman's lobby" in Washington in the 1970s, which included pro-choice efforts. She emphasizes the role of traditional women's organizations such as the National Federation of Business and Professional Women, the American Association of University Women, and the League of Women Voters in assisting the development of a women's lobby.

8. This was one countermovement tactic that executive director Helen Smith viewed as "foolish" and "never considered" copying, but as long as anti-abortion groups provided the convenience, she called their hot lines daily (interview with Helen Smith, 1983).

9. There is some evidence (see Jenkins and Eckert, 1986; Morris, 1984) that direct-action tactics are more likely to be used by organizations with informal structures because these arrangements allow groups to act quickly when opportunities for action arise, whereas institutionalized tactics are more likely to be adopted by organizations with more formal or bureaucratic structures because they can be planned in advance and are suited to the schedules of the professional leaders who frequently head formalized organizations (see Staggenborg, 1988, for a more complete development of this argument).

10. Service projects like HERS were always the most successful types of projects for the CWLU because they were compatible with the Union's small-group structure (cf. Freeman, 1979). When the CWLU participated in institutionalized actions, which required different types of resources, members found that they could not always control the results. For example, the CWLU was asked by the attorney of a doctor at an abortion clinic to become a plaintiff in a lawsuit against the Chicago Board of Health to strike down restrictive abortion guidelines. The ATF agreed to do so because little time was required. However, the result of the lawsuit, according to an evaluation by ATF participants, was the "quashing of all regulations including those dealing with sanitation standards which was not the effect which the Task Force had intended" (CWLU working papers in Jennifer Knauss private papers).

11. Costain (1988:28) notes that effective lobbying work requires more centralized organizations, but that this conflicts with the value that many feminist groups place on non-hierarchical organization. As a result, there are pressures to avoid lobbying work. In the case of the pro-choice movement, however, countermovement threats created incentives for both feminist and single-issue organizations to engage in lobbying.

12. ICMCA executive director Helen Smith, a "conscience constituent" herself, had little faith in this attempt to persuade the direct beneficiaries of legal abortion to assist the movement. As she explained in an interview, "We got some letters that way, but not a lot. You know, women who are having abortions are not necessarily that concerned to fight for abortion. That tends to be done by, you know, people with a different kind of consciousness—it's usually not the people who benefit from a cause who fight for it." The clinic letter-writing project in Illinois gradually fizzled out.

13. Using the skills of national NARAL activists and staff, the organization also sponsored four regional strategy conferences in 1974 and wrote a strategy manual for state organizing entitled "Organizing for Action." Although there was no direct control over local strategy by the national NARAL organization during this period, NARAL did take a step toward greater nationwide coordination by regularly sending "Action Alerts" and strategy suggestions to state coordinators (some of whom were leaders of real local organizations like ICMCA, and some of whom were really just individuals trying to generate action as best they could).

14. After the National Conference of Catholic Bishops unveiled its Pastoral Plan for Pro-Life Activities in December 1975, RCAR announced at a press conference that the organization intended to expand its state affiliates and legislative lobbying work as a result of the bishops' strategy plan (*Options,* February 1976).

15. Beginning in 1973, the national coordinator of the Task Force on Reproduction and Its Control and the Legislative Office published a steady stream of information on current attacks on abortion in Congress, along with requests that individual NOW members write letters to their Congresspersons asking specific questions about their positions on abortion. At a time when many legislators did not feel compelled to answer a questionnaire from the National Organization for Women on their abortion position, NOW members were also asked to send copies of the responses they received from their Congresspersons to the Legislative Office to augment information collected by national leaders. In 1973, the national task force coordinator began to coordinate efforts by national and local task forces by requesting chapters to send her the names of their local coordinators so she could send them information (*Do It NOW,* April–May 1973). In the same year, the newsletter detailed a plan for chapters to lobby their legislators in their home offices (*Do It NOW,* September 1973).

16. As ICMCA's experience reveals, strong leaders can cope with the problems of ongoing mobilization, but a more formalized structure makes stability and continuity of activity easier to achieve (see Part III on the post-1976 experiences of ARA/NARAL of Illinois).

17. For nationally targeted lobbying activities, the mobilization problem was simplified

because Illinois RCAR could simply urge its members to tie into the national RCAR legislative alert system. The national RCAR organization was more formally organized in the post-1973 period.

Chapter 7

1. The Hyde Amendment passed in 1976 was a rider to the 1977 Health, Education and Welfare appropriations bill sponsored by Representative Henry Hyde. Since 1976, similar riders have been passed each year (see Rubin, 1987:164). I have treated this first important countermovement victory as a critical juncture for the pro-choice movement, although the movement did not feel the full impact of the loss until June 1977 when the Supreme Court cleared the way for state bans on Medicaid funding of abortion. Until that point, pro-choice groups were prepared to rely on the courts to strike down the Hyde Amendment. Although the Supreme Court did not actually rule on the Hyde Amendment until 1980, the 1977 ruling on state-level funding sent shockwaves through the movement.

2. Not only did the Republican Party take an anti-abortion position in 1976, but a single-issue anti-abortion Presidential candidate, Ellen McCormack, entered the Democratic Party primaries and qualified for $100,000 in federal funds, winning twenty-two delegates and much publicity for the countermovement (Tatalovich and Daynes, 1981:200).

3. In 1977, two single-issue political action committees, the National Pro-Life Political Action Committee and the Life Amendment Political Action Committee, were formed. Additional countermovement organizations were formed in the late 1970s and early 1980s either as a result of intra-movement schisms or to mobilize new constituents. The American Life Lobby was formed in 1979 by former National Right to Life Committee activist Judy Brown after she came into conflict with other NRLC leaders (Paige, 1983:150). Pro-Lifers for Survival was formed in 1979 by political liberals in the anti-abortion movement who wished to link opposition to abortion to opposition to nuclear arms (Encyclopedia of Associations, 1984:1224). The countermovement also expanded through the involvement of multi-issue New Right organizations like the Moral Majority, formed in 1979 (see Conover and Gray, 1983; Crawford, 1980; Petchesky, 1984).

4. In 1976, the Supreme Court ruled on one of these cases, *Planned Parenthood of Central Missouri* v. *Danforth,* a case challenging a 1974 Missouri law with parental and spousal consent requirements and a prohibition of saline abortions, among other restrictions. The Supreme Court decision in this case was largely favorable to the pro-choice movement, invalidating the consent provisions and most other restrictions (see Rubin, 1987:131–33).

5. In two cases dealing with Medicaid funding, *Beal* v. *Doe* and *Maher* v. *Roe,* the Court ruled that the states need not fund "nontherapeutic" abortions. In a third case dealing with the provision of abortions by public hospitals, *Poelker* v. *Doe,* the Court ruled that public hospitals can refuse to provide elective abortions (see Hayler, 1979:309–10; Rubin, 1987:165–69).

6. Note that these Supreme Court decisions on Medicaid funding preceded attempts by the Reagan Administration to make the Court hostile to *Roe* v. *Wade* by appointing anti-abortion justices (see Chapter 10). Rubin (1987:174) argues that the Court was influenced by the political controversy over abortion and that on the matter of funding the Court has always been unwilling to force Congress to fund politically controversial programs.

7. While expressing support for efforts to outlaw abortion through a constitutional amendment, the Republican plank conceded that there was sincere disagreement on the subject of abortion. Moreover, candidate Ford, whose wife Betty Ford was an outspoken advocate of legal abortion, continued to express a preference for an amendment giving states the right to regulate abortion (cf. Tatalovich and Daynes, 1981:198).

8. In late 1981, Senator Orrin Hatch introduced a constitutional amendment that declared that the right to abortion was not protected by the Constitution and that both Congress and the states had the right to regulate abortion. In 1982, Senator Helms countered this strategy with a new version of his Human Life Bill, creating more division within the anti-abortion camp in Congress.

9. In 1977, twenty-five organizations were members of the Exchange, and by 1983 over fifty groups were participating.

10. In the case of the environmental movement, Mitchell (1979) also finds that threats or "public bads" play a powerful role in mobilizing constituents.

11. According to Roy Morgan, a Friends of Family Planning (FFP) board member that I interviewed, FFP was the idea of philanthropist Stewart Mott, an early NARAL constituent (cf. Lader, 1973; Nathanson, 1979) and a longtime supporter of family-planning programs. Mott brought together representatives from various pro-choice organizations (to many of which he had donated money), including ZPG, NARAL, Planned Parenthood, and others, to discuss the idea of an independent PAC. Everyone expressed approval of the move, and the executive directors of most of the major pro-choice groups sat on the board of FFP when it was formed in the late 1970s. Meanwhile—and reflecting the origins of the pro-choice movement in the family-planning and population movements and in the women's movement—Voters for Choice (VC) was founded around the same time by some well-known feminists, including Gloria Steinem. According to Roy Morgan, neither FFP nor VC did terribly well on its own, and the two single-issue PACs decided to merge in 1984 to form Voters for Choice/Friends of Family Planning in order to pool their resources for the election year. The board of the combined PACs consisted of representatives from a wide variety of pro-choice groups based in Washington, including NARAL.

12. ZPG remained supportive of the pro-choice movement but turned its attention (and resources) to other issues in the mid-1970s, in large part because single-issue pro-choice organizations, together with established organizations like Planned Parenthood, had by that time taken leadership roles in the movement and the help of ZPG was less essential than it had been immediately following the legalization of abortion. NOW became preoccupied with the battle for passage of the Equal Rights Amendment but turned its attention back to the abortion issue in the early 1980s after the ERA campaign failed (see Staggenborg, 1989a, for a more complete discussion of variations over time in the participation of multi-issue movement organizations).

13. Although CARASA was based in New York, some branches were formed elsewhere, and the organization became nationally known among activists. R2N2 had affiliates throughout the country.

14. Movement-connected service organizations such as feminist health centers can play an important role in ongoing mobilization. Because they exist to provide a service such as health care and typically support themselves through fees, they are often more stable than are movement organizations, and they can serve as meeting places that keep activists in contact with one another. Bookstores, coffee houses, or other movement-associated organizations can also serve this function. For example, E. P. Thompson notes that an overlooked contribution of the New Left to the British Campaign for Nuclear Disarmament "was the provision of a meeting-point and organising centre for Youth CND in the Partisan Coffee House" (Thompson, 1989:30).

15. A group of about twenty-five women calling themselves the Chicago Women's Health Network was active in 1976 as a loosely connected work group of the Chicago Women's Liberation Union that included activists from the CWLU, HERS, the Chicago Women's Health Center, and other groups. Participants in this group formed the Chicago Women's Health Task Force in 1977 (documents in Jennifer Knauss private papers).

16. Although the NOW chapter was still preoccupied with the ERA campaign at that point, its leaders recognized that they needed to have another issue for members to work on in order to maintain and expand the chapter's membership. Given the political climate of threat to legal abortion, and NOW's perception that other pro-choice groups were not very strong at the time, abortion was selected as that issue (interview with former Chicago NOW director Karen Wellisch, 1984).

17. NARAL later did form an affiliated PAC in Illinois, but for the purpose of facilitating campaign work rather than raising money for contributions to candidates.

18. Other more professionalized pro-choice organizations, including NOW, ZPG, the NWHN, and RCAR, have, like NARAL, successfully implemented direct-mail projects.

19. Tensions came to a head in the early 1980s when NARAL was taking in large amounts of money and had to make a lot of decisions about how to distribute the funds. Some board members began to feel that the executive director was making decisions independently of the board. The executive director felt that the board members did not fully understand the consequences of their own policies; when states were "targeted" for financial aid, board members from affiliates receiving less money in "untargeted" states began to question the handling of funds. In any case, the situation eventually led to the forced resignation of NARAL's longtime executive director and to the hiring of a new director expected to carry out the board's policies as a paid professional.

20. Although both Smith and her successor were paid for part-time work, neither was a "professional" movement leader in the sense of being a career movement activist.

21. The name change was made at this time because ARA had lost its corporate status owing to its failure to file for renewal, and, given the need to reincorporate, it seemed like a good idea to change the name and capitalize on the visibility of the national organization.

22. The income from clinic contributions was supplemented by financial aid from national NARAL as well as in-kind contributions from the Concord clinic and other local organizations (see Appendix A). In fact, Cindy Little became involved in some national-level NARAL committee work and was soon put in charge of a region that included Illinois. As a result of her work in the national organization, she helped convince NARAL to offer financial resources as well as other benefits to local affiliates. Consequently, the Illinois affiliate, along with other NARAL affiliates, became eligible to apply for small grants for special activities that were initially provided by the national organization. Later the national organization decided to target Illinois as a key state for development, and additional financial resources were allotted to the affiliate.

23. Some of the longtime board members were quite relieved by this arrangement, happy to turn over the responsibility to younger and newer activists. A few others were alarmed that the new director was trying to put "her people" on the board and so left the board with hurt feelings.

Chapter 8

1. Immediately following passage of the Hyde Amendment, NARAL filed one of three class-action suits against the amendment which resulted in a temporary restraining order to prevent implementation of the funding ban nationwide (*NARAL Newsletter,* November 1976).

2. In 1983, the Supreme Court returned to the pro-choice camp with a ruling—in *City of Akron* v. *Akron Center for Reproductive Health* and *Planned Parenthood, Kansas City* v. *Ashcroft*—striking down most state and local restrictions on abortions. On Medicaid funding, however, pro-choice groups were forced to look to other arenas.

3. The Catholic Bishop's Pastoral Plan for Pro-life Activities called for extensive edu-

cational and political activities by the Church aimed at restricting, and eventually outlaw-ing, abortion. On the local level, the Pastoral Plan called for the establishment of "pro-life units" in every Congressional district in the country (cf. Hanna, 1979:151; Jaffe et al., 1981:74–75).

4. In 1975, NOW obtained a ruling from the Internal Revenue Service that the organi-zation could endorse political candidates without losing its tax-exempt status as long as political activities were not the major component of the NOW program. In 1976, NOW gave its first political endorsement to Bella Abzug, a strong supporter of pro-choice efforts as well as other women's rights issues in Congress. The organization also made a major effort at lobbying the Democratic Party to ensure the adoption of both pro-abortion and pro-ERA planks in the 1976 party platform.

Greater involvement in the political arena was postponed, however, as a result of inter-nal conflict in NOW, which included debate over whether NOW should get involved in campaign politics (see Appendix A). Consequently, NOW's full-fledged entry into the polit-ical arena was delayed until the late 1970s, when NOW had solved its major organizational problems and when external events had made political tactics more feasible.

5. Examining trends in public opinion between 1965 and 1980, Blake and Del Pinal (1981) argue that, although there is public support for legal abortion, there is not public support for the entire pro-choice platform, including the rights to Medicaid funding, abor-tion without parental or spousal consent, and second-trimester abortion. Moreover, they show that respondents to opinion polls on abortion who "equivocate" (i.e., approve of abor-tion for some reasons but not others) share more background characteristics and attitudes with outright opponents of abortion than they do with outright pro-choice supporters.

6. See Wilcox (1989) for a study of pro-choice and pro-life movement PACs. In the 1980, 1982, and 1984 election cycles, Wilcox found that pro-life PACs were more numerous and raised more money but that the contribution strategies of the opposing single-issue PACs were similar.

7. The major tactics of the Impact '80 program included (1) "house meetings" for edu-cating sympathizers about the threats to legal abortion, raising money for affiliates, and recruiting local activists; (2) political skills training workshops to prepare campaign workers and encourage active participation in the state and local campaigns of pro-choice candi-dates; and (3) postcards bearing the NARAL logo and the new Impact '80 slogan, "I'm Pro-Choice . . . and I Vote," to be sent to legislators. (Bumperstickers and buttons with similar messages were also widely distributed.)

8. A house meeting is held by a NARAL member or other interested person who agrees to host a meeting in her home. She invites friends, or the chapter invites persons who have expressed interest in abortion rights (e.g., when signing a NARAL postcard at a shopping center), to attend the meeting. Follow-up calls are made to remind invited persons to attend. At the meeting, a knowledgeable NARAL representative gives a presentation on the current threats to legal abortion, using a nationally produced NARAL slide show. (NARAL of Illi-nois later developed its own local slide show for this purpose.) Participants at the meeting introduce themselves and explain why they are there. Persons attending the meeting are asked for donations and for their active involvement in the NARAL affiliate. They are also asked to name pro-choice friends who might be interested in attending a future house meet-ing. In this way, the affiliate raises money, recruits activists, and obtains a continuing source of names for further use of the tactic. The house meeting tactic relies, of course, on the ability to attract new people to the meetings who provide "bridges" to new sources of poten-tial activists. It also seems to work best in periods when the abortion issue is "hot" (e.g., after the 1980 Presidential election) and pro-choice adherents are upset about threats to abortion rights.

9. Because the strategy of selecting states for targeting financial resources produced some resentment from NARAL activists and board members from untargeted states, the policy was adjusted to increase somewhat the financial aid to affiliates in untargeted states.

10. An election day phone bank to get NARAL members out to vote was also organized in 1982, but this proved unnecessary, as 100 percent of those contacted were already planning to vote!

11. The NARAL originators of this tactic did not intend it to be used to solicit funds from politically experienced individuals.

12. These tactics tended not to be financially expensive but, rather, ones that used RCAR's assets—the prestige of its clergy sponsors, the expertise of its staff, and the time of local activists—including the distribution of RCAR literature, an RCAR postcard campaign (similar to that of NARAL), a sponsor drive to collect names of national and local clergy who support the right to abortion, state fair booths, and press conferences with clergy members. Although the organization did not have enough funds to support affiliates in all fifty states, RCAR managed to distribute its literature through organizations like Planned Parenthood and NARAL as well as through individual clergy contacts and RCAR affiliates.

13. The NWHN board of directors also wrote various letters on behalf of the organization (e.g., to protest the Hyde Amendment cutoff of abortion funding). And after its membership began to climb again in 1980, ZPG composed a list of about two thousand "active" members who agreed to write letters to Congress when sent special "alerts" by ZPG. According to a staff member interviewed, about two alerts per year dealing with the abortion issue were sent in the early 1980s after this list of active members was drawn up.

14. During 1977, the Abortion Rights Association also managed to generate some letters to national figures in response to the Medicaid funding crisis, including letters to President Jimmy Carter, HEW Secretary Joseph Califano, and Illinois Congresspersons.

15. The NARAL of Illinois activists that I interviewed noted several indicators of the success of campaign work. First, they received direct feedback from politicians; in one case a state legislator who was narrowly reelected after NARAL workers supported his opponent told NARAL leaders that the close race had really scared him and that he would change his voting pattern on the abortion issue because he knew the NARAL campaign workers had made a difference in the vote. He did change his voting pattern, as did other legislators after NARAL instituted its political strategy. NARAL leaders also reported being treated more politely when lobbying Illinois legislators. And, finally, they reported that when their questionnaires were sent to legislators, they were quickly returned by those willing to vote in favor of abortion rights, whereas before the political activity, such questionnaires were often ignored.

16. Both NARAL of Illinois and Chicago NOW formed affiliated PACs to enable them to make endorsements and place workers in campaigns rather than to make financial contributions. Illinois NARAL did not try to raise money for financial contributions for candidates both because another local PAC, Personal PAC, had been formed for this purpose and because NARAL did not have the resources needed for such a tactic.

Chapter 9

1. The New American Movement later merged with the Democratic Socialist Organizing Committee to form the Democratic Socialists of America.

2. As Gamson (1975:44) points out, the distinction between multiple and single-issue demands is problematic: "It is not difficult to formulate any group's demands as either single or multiple. If a group has several issues, the level of generality can be raised so that they are seen as aspects of a single, larger issue, or any larger issue can be subdivided into

different aspects." In the case of the pro-choice movement, it is fairly easy to identify single-issue organizations as concerned solely with the abortion issue. But there is a finer distinction to be made between the approaches of organizations such as NOW, which are certainly multiple issue in the sense of being concerned about more than one issue, and the approaches of organizations like the NWHN or R2N2, which are more likely to insist that demands be linked to one another in their presentation.

3. The NWHN board of directors consisted of a diverse group of feminists, including both "younger" and "older" branch types. The statement, which was written by Jenny Knauss, a socialist–feminist member of the NWHN board of directors, was passed with the support of socialist and radical feminists on the board (interview with Jenny Knauss, 1984).

4. The National Women's Health Network did become more professionalized in the late 1970s (see Appendix A), but it did not yet have the resources or formalized structure necessary for the kind of grass-roots organizing campaign conducted by NARAL.

5. Minority women have organized in groups such as the National Black Women's Health Project, but historically both the women's movement and the pro-choice movement have had a difficult time recruiting large numbers of minority participants.

6. Through most of its history, R2N2 had one staff member, supported by money obtained through grants from New York foundations, but there was occasionally additional part-time help.

7. Colwell (1989) comes to a similar conclusion regarding the problems of informal organizations in the American peace movement. She finds that the peace movement is largely composed of small, inadequately funded organizations with few or no staff and little internal development; consequently "by their own evaluation, they are not very successful at mobilizing people for action or gaining widespread public support" (Colwell, 1989:40).

Chapter 10

1. The Court ruled on *City of Akron* v. *Akron Center for Reproductive Health* along with two companion cases, *Planned Parenthood, Kansas City, Missouri* v. *Ashcroft* and *Simopoulos* v. *Virginia,* in 1983. In *Ashcroft,* the Court let stand a requirement that two physicians be present at second-trimester abortions in case the fetus was aborted alive, a requirement that fetal tissue be sent to a pathologist, and a parental consent requirement that provided a judicial procedure for "mature" minors to gain access to abortion without parental consent (see Rubin, 1987:140–43).

2. This dilemma was also noted in the case of the peace movement following the early years of the Reagan Administration: "Whereas Reaganism seemed both invincible and terrifying in its early days, it is now wounded and faltering—a situation which creates new openings for peace work while also making it more difficult to mobilize people through immediate anxiety" (Trinkl, 1988:51).

3. The Reproductive Health Equity Act, which was sponsored by fifty-one House members, was first introduced into Congress on May 30, 1984 (see Cohodas, 1984:1323) but never made it out of the committees to which it was then referred. Since 1984, NARAL and other pro-choice organizations have continued to lobby for the legislation out of the conviction that "it's important that the funding issue get raised in this way every year" (interview with NARAL executive director Kate Michelman, 1990).

4. Such declines are not always evident in official "membership" figures, particularly for organizations that use direct mail to solicit contributions. NARAL continued to use the figure of 150,000 in public reports of its membership in 1984, which it calculated by combining the numbers of individuals contributing in the past two years with that of persons currently contributing. However, NARAL's executive director at the time told me in an

interview that the number of direct-mail contributions did fall somewhat after the 1983 victories, resulting in some budget cutbacks in 1983 and 1984 (interview with former NARAL director Nanette Falkenberg, 1984). By around 1985, NARAL's membership had dropped to about 90,000 (interview with NARAL director Kate Michelman, 1990). In the case of NOW, there was a well-publicized drop in membership from a high of about 250,000 after Ronald Reagan's election to about 150,000 a few years later. Although the defeat of the ERA campaign in 1982 had much to do with this drop in membership, the decrease in visible threats to abortion rights may have added to it.

5. Numerous medical specialists have called the arguments of the film inaccurate and its camera techniques misleading (see Levine, 1985:21).

6. NARAL and other pro-choice organizations later used the letters in an *amicus curiae* brief filed in 1985 (*New York Times,* September 1, 1985) for the abortion cases decided by the Supreme Court in 1986 (see Rubin, 1987:145–49), and NARAL published a collection of the letters, *Voices of Women,* in 1989 (Messing, 1989).

7. These efforts to respond to *The Silent Scream* and to present a feminist point of view continued throughout the 1980s. In 1989, Eleanor Smeal's Fund for a Feminist Majority released a video response, *Abortion: For Survival,* and the Federation of Feminist Health Centers in Los Angeles released the film *No Going Back,* which demonstrates the technique of menstrual extraction (Simpson, 1989b). The menstrual extraction technique, which was developed by a women's self-help group in Los Angeles in 1971, is a method, used at the onset of menstruation, of emptying the contents of the uterus by means of suction (see Rothman and Punnett, 1978). The film on its use might be interpreted as an attempt by feminists to reassert control over reproductive technologies to counter uses of technology such as that employed in *The Silent Scream.*

8. Mottl (1980) argues that countermovements turn to direct-action tactics when institutionalized means of change are blocked.

9. These include the Pearson Foundation, which was founded in 1969 and planned to increase its 130 clinics to 1,000 in the 1980s; Jerry Falwell's "Save-A-Baby" program, which began in 1984 with the goal of creating 1,000 centers; and the Christian Action Council, which was founded in 1980 and had 155 centers, with plans for 700 more in 1985 (Ridgeway, 1985). See also Ginsburg, 1989:100, 272, n. 1.

10. Many medical experts have contended that there is no evidence that this "syndrome" exists. A study of the physical and emotional effects of abortion conducted at the request of the Reagan Administration also failed to confirm the existence of such a syndrome, although Surgeon General C. Everett Koop claimed that the evidence was "inconclusive" and called for further study (see Holden, 1989). After Koop made this claim, the American Psychological Association commissioned a study that concluded that legal abortion in the first trimester rarely caused emotional problems for women (*New York Times,* April 6, 1990).

11. Like the women's health movement, groups like the American Rights Coalition are trying to alter the relationship between women and doctors. The difference is that the women's health movement has sought to make women active participants in their own health care, whereas the anti-abortionists are "attempting to reframe the relationship between a woman and her doctor [by] encouraging the woman to view herself as a pawn of the medical system" (Garb, 1989a:3).

12. In 1990, Operation Rescue closed its office in Binghamton, New York, owing to debts incurred in part as a result of successful lawsuits by the National Organization for Women, Planned Parenthood, and abortion clinics. In New York, a Federal District judge fined individual participants and organizations involved in Operation Rescue a total of $450,000 on the grounds that earlier fines had been ignored (see *New York Times,* February

1, 1990; February 28, 1990). The Supreme Court also ruled against Operation Rescue in 1990 by allowing state injunctions banning the organization from blocking the entrances of abortion clinics.

13. In the important case of *Hodgson* v. *Minnesota,* the eighth circuit court upheld a law requiring minors to notify both parents before obtaining an abortion; six of the seven judges voting in the majority were Reagan appointees (Walker, 1990:348).

14. Ironically, Reagan's first appointee, Sandra Day O'Connor, was actually opposed by anti-abortion forces on the basis of votes she had cast as an Arizona state senator, whereas liberals were generally pleased at the appointment of a woman to the Court (Rubin, 1987:180). However, both she and Scalia took the anti-abortion side in several decisions, including the 1989 *Webster* ruling.

15. Kennedy was actually Ronald Reagan's third choice for the position; second-choice nominee Douglas Ginsburg was forced to withdraw after admitting to smoking marijuana in the past.

16. See, for example, the July 17, 1989, coverage of the abortion conflict by *Time,* which argues that "pro-choice groups, confident that the *Roe* ruling had established an unassailable constitutional right, grew smug and complacent."

Chapter 11

1. The *Webster* ruling allowed the state of Missouri to ban the use of public funds, medical personnel, and facilities for the purposes of counseling women about abortion and performing abortions. The Court also agreed to hear three other cases involving further restrictions on abortion: *Hodgson* v. *Minnesota, Ohio* v. *Akron Center for Reproductive Health,* and *Turnock* v. *Ragsdale.* However, the last case, from Illinois, was subsequently settled out of court. In a June 25, 1990, ruling on the remaining two cases, the Supreme Court upheld parental notification requirements for teenagers.

2. Lawyers in the Justice Department reacted to Thornburgh's action by signing an unusual petition protesting the department's request that the Supreme Court overturn *Roe* v. *Wade* (see *New York Times,* March 26, 1989).

3. There were concerns expressed on both sides about the tactical wisdom of directly lobbying the Court in this manner, and some organizations selected alternative targets. The ACLU, for example, organized a letter-writing campaign to the Solicitor General to protest the friend-of-the-court brief filed by the Justice Department asking the Court to overturn *Roe* v. *Wade* (Moore, 1989).

4. This brief was written to address Sandra Day O'Connor's dissenting opinion in the 1983 *Akron* case in which she argued that *Roe* v. *Wade* was "on a collision course with itself" because scientific advances were pushing back the point of fetal viability, thereby invalidating the trimester framework of the 1973 ruling. The scientists' brief argued that the point at which a fetus could survive outside the womb "has remained virtually unchanged at approximately 24 weeks" (see *Newsweek,* May 1, 1989).

5. Public opinion on abortion remained remarkably stable between 1973 and 1987 (see Rossi and Sitaraman, 1988), and it is doubtful that *Webster* will alter long-term trends of support for legal abortion. However, polls taken after the Court decision did indicate an increase in public concern about government intervention in abortion decisions and political candidates' positions on abortion. They also showed majority support for parental notification requirements for minors and tests for fetal viability (see Witwer, 1989).

6. This vote represented the first time in eight years that the House voted to fund abortions in cases of rape and incest (*New York Times,* October 15, 1989). However, the appro-

priations bill was passed by Congress with language favored by President Bush, allowing Medicaid funding of abortions only in cases in which the mother's life was endangered.

7. The conference was organized by the Women's Caucus of the Progressive Student Network, a student activist group with chapters on about ten campuses that was founded in 1980 (Baker, 1990).

8. The conference was sponsored by the American Civil Liberties Union and the Religious Coalition for Abortion Rights' Women of Color Partnership Program.

9. A joint effort by the ACLU, NARAL, NOW, Planned Parenthood, and other pro-choice organizations to raise money for the November 12, 1989, abortion rights rallies held across the country was so successful that the coalition found itself with a surplus of $500,000 (see Kornhauser, 1990b).

10. Interestingly, the Catholic bishops had a much more difficult time defending their decision to use similar tactics. After hiring a public relations firm to help them convey their anti-abortion message, the bishops' Committee for Pro-Life Activities met with strong criticism, particularly from those who argued that the Church instead ought to be spending its money helping the poor (see *Newsweek,* April 23, 1990; *New York Times,* April 6, 1990).

11. With the resignation in July, 1990, of Justice William Brennan, a staunch supporter of *Roe* v. *Wade,* the leaders of abortion rights groups attempted to force George Bush's nominee to the Court, Judge David Souter, to make public his views on abortion. They were unable to do so, however, and because Souter appeared to be a nonideological, mainstream nominee, his appointment was approved by the Senate despite the opposition of pro-choice groups.

Chapter 12

1. Taylor (1989b:761) uses the term "abeyance" to describe the "holding process by which movements sustain themselves in nonreceptive political environments and provide continuity from one stage of mobilization to another."

2. Regardless of whether or not a countermovement becomes active, a longitudinal approach to the study of social movements avoids the pitfalls of a "single-outcome-as-goal" model of social movements (see Snyder and Kelly, 1979). Because movements typically maintain themselves through a series of outcomes, including both victories and defeats, we need to understand how such outcomes affect ongoing collective action.

3. Zald and Useem (1987:254) argue that movement success is likely to lead to the emergence of a countermovement, but that this is unlikely "if the movement wins a huge, crushing victory. Under these circumstances, the countermovement will become paralyzed as supporters see little chance of success." The 1973 *Roe* v. *Wade* decision was, however, a huge victory for the pro-choice movement, and it did lead to an increase in countermovement mobilization. In this case, countermovement constituents appear to have been motivated more by moral outrage than by any rational calculation of their chances for success.

4. Tarrow (1989:19) argues that the participation of established interest groups in social movements creates competition that will lead to the adoption of different strategies and tactics by movement organizations than by established organizations. He suggests that established groups may "monopolize conventional mass forms of action, producing incentives for others to use more disruptive forms of mass action to outflank them." In the case of the pro-choice movement, however, the presence of the anti-abortion countermovement led to a great deal of cooperation, rather than competition, between established organizations and movement organizations. Under conditions of external threat, greater cooperation, and less differentiation in terms of tactics, can be expected.

5. Analyses associating large-scale social trends such as the entry of women into the labor force with pro-choice attitudes and activism (e.g., Luker, 1984) also suggest that, if such trends continue, social consensus will eventually be reached on the abortion issue.

6. This argument contrasts with the model suggested by Zald and Useem (1987), in which a movement demobilizes following victory, a countermovement mobilizes, and a new "counter-countermovement" later emerges to oppose the countermovement.

7. Schmitt (1989) proposes that social movement leaders be considered a type of "elite challenger" and provides evidence in the case of the West German peace movement that movement leaders or "elites" are well connected to traditional elites through their participation in churches, the Social Democratic Party, unions, and other organizations.

8. Himmelstein (1990:64) finds that the conservative movement, similarly, shared characteristics of both polity members and challengers "or more precisely, that it combined many of the resources of a member with the capacity to talk like a challenger. Even as it railed against a political and cultural establishment, it drew on significant established sources of power."

9. Even an organization as established as the American Bar Association (ABA) may be subject to a certain amount of pressure. After adopting a policy supporting the constitutional right to abortion (which it later retracted), the ABA found that its role in rating judicial nominees was being questioned by the Justice Department under the Bush Administration (see Kornhauser, 1990a).

References

The following are references to academic and journalistic works and court cases cited in the text. Organizational newsletters and other documentary sources cited in the text are listed in Appendix B.

Addelson, Katherine Pyne. 1988. "Moral Revolution." *Radical America* 22(5):36–43.

Against the Current. 1989. "The Right's Phony Clinic Racket," May–June, pp. 6–7.

American Medical News. 1988a. "Conflict of Rights Central to Debate over Abortion," January 1, p. 14.

———. 1988b. "Medicaid Abortion Question Before Voters in 3 States," October 28, p. 10.

Baker, Karin. 1990. "Students Organize for Reproductive Rights." *Against the Current* 4(6):9–10.

Balides, Constance, Barbara Danzger, and Deborah Spitz. 1973. "The Abortion Issue: Major Groups, Organizations, and Funding Sources." Pp. 496–529 in *The Abortion Experience,* ed. H. J. Osofsky and J. D. Osofsky. Hagerstown, MD: Harper & Row.

Barnes, James A. 1990. "Flip-Flopping." *National Journal,* February 17, p. 418.

Bart, Pauline. 1987. "Seizing the Means of Reproduction: An Illegal Feminist Abortion Collective—How and Why It Worked." *Qualitative Sociology* 10(4):339–57.

Blake, Judith. 1971. "Abortion and Public Opinion: The 1960–1970 Decade." *Science* 171:540–49.

Blake, Judith and Jorge H. Del Pinal. 1981. "Negativism, Equivocation, and Wobbly Assent: Public "Support" for the ProChoice Platform on Abortion." *Demography* 18(3):309–20.

Carmen, Arlene and Howard Moody. 1973. *Abortion Counseling and Social Change.* Valley Forge, PA: Judson Press.

Chicago Sun Times. 1971. "Just the 2 of Them Try to Change Minds About Abortion," January 24.

Chicago Tribune. 1985. "More Antiabortion Violence Feared," January 11.

Clarke, Adele and Alice Wolfson. 1985. "Socialist-Feminism and Reproductive Rights: Movement Work and Its Contradictions." *Socialist Review* (no.78):110–20.

Cohen, Richard E. 1989. "Changing Their Mind About Abortion." *National Journal,* October 21, p. 2592.

Cohodas, Nadine. 1984. "House Campaign Launched to Restore Abortion Funding." *Congressional Quarterly Weekly Report* 42(22):1323.

Colwell, Mary Anna. 1989. "Organizational and Management Characteristics of Peace Groups." Working Paper No. 8, Institute for Nonprofit Organization Management, University of San Francisco.

Conn, Joseph L. 1990. "Out of Communion." *Church and State* 43(1):6–9.

Conover, Pamela J. and Virginia Gray. 1983. *Feminism and the New Right: Conflict over the American Family.* New York: Praeger.

Costain, Anne N. 1988. "Representing Women: The Transition from Social Movement to Interest Group." Pp. 26–47 in *Women, Power and Policy: Toward the Year 2000,* ed. Ellen Boneparth and Emily Stoper. New York: Pergamon.

Crawford, Alan. 1980. *Thunder on the Right: The "New Right" and the Politics of Resentment.* New York: Pantheon.

Daniels, Arlene K. 1988. *Invisible Careers: Women Civic Leaders from the Volunteer World.* Chicago: University of Chicago Press.

Davidson, Roger H. 1983. "Procedures and Politics in Congress." Pp. 30–46 in *The Abortion Dispute and the American System,* ed. Gilbert Y. Steiner. Washington, DC: Brookings Institution.

Davis, James A. 1980. "Conservative Weather in a Liberalizing Climate: Change in Selected NORC General Social Survey Items, 1972–1978." *Social Forces* 58(4)1129–56.

Davis, Susan E. 1989. "Pro-Choice: A New Militancy." *Hastings Center Report* 19(6):32–33.

Dobie, Kathy. 1989. "With God on Their Side: Operation Rescue Hits L.A." *Village Voice,* April 11, pp. 29–36.

Doerr, E. 1976. "Abortion and Politics." *Humanist* 36:42.

Donovan, Patricia. 1985a. "The Holy War." *Family Planning Perspectives* 17(1):5–9.

———. 1985b. "The People Vote on Abortion Funding: Colorado and Washington." *Family Planning Perspectives* 17(4):155–59.

———. 1986. "Letting the People Decide: How the Anti-abortion Referenda Fared." *Family Planning Perspectives* 18(3):127, 128, 144.

Duerst-Lahti, Georgia. 1989. "The Government's Role in Building the Women's Movement." *Political Science Quarterly* 104(2):249–68.

Echols, Alice. 1989. Daring to Be Bad: Radical Feminism in America 1967–1975. Minneapolis: University of Minnesota Press.

Eder, Bruce. 1989. "Dominoes Doesn't Deliver: Pizza Chain Sparks Boycott with Anti-choice Activities." *Village Voice,* November 7.

Encyclopedia of Associations. 1976 to date. *National Organizations of the U.S.* Detroit: Gale Research.

Erlien, Marla. 1988 [published 1989]. "Beyond *Roe* v. *Wade*: Redefining the Prochoice Agenda." *Radical America* 22(2–3):14–24.

Evans, Sara. 1979. *Personal Politics: The Roots of Women's Liberation in the Civil Rights Movement and the New Left.* New York: Vintage Books.

Faux, Marian. 1988. *Roe* v. *Wade: The Untold Story of the Landmark Supreme Court Decision That Made Abortion Legal.* New York. Macmillan.

Ferree, Myra Marx and Beth B. Hess. 1985. *Controversy and Coalition: The New Feminist Movement.* Boston: Twayne.

Forrest, Jacqueline Darroch and Stanley K. Henshaw. 1987. "The Harassment of U.S. Abortion Providers." *Family Planning Perspectives* 19(1):9–13.

Francome, Colin. 1984. *Abortion Freedom—A Worldwide Movement.* Winchester, MA: Allen & Unwin.

Freeman, Jo. 1975. *The Politics of Women's Liberation.* New York: McKay.

———. 1979. "Resource Mobilization and Strategy: A Model for Analyzing Social Movement Organization Actions." Pp. 167–89 in *The Dynamics of Social Movements: Resource Mobilization, Social Control, and Tactics,* ed. Mayer N. Zald and John D. McCarthy. Cambridge, MA: Winthrop.

Fried, Marlene. 1989. "Pro-Choice Agendas After Webster." *Against the Current* 4(5):18–20.

Gamson, William A. 1975. *The Strategy of Social Protest.* Homewood, IL: Dorsey.

Garb, Maggie. 1989a. "Abortion Foes Give Birth to a 'Syndrome.'" *In These Times,* February 22–March 1, pp. 3, 22.

———. 1989b. "Pro-Choice Advocates Girding for the Big One." *In These Times,* July 19–August 1, pp. 6, 11.

Gerlach, Luther and Virginia Hine. 1970. *People, Power, Change: Movements of Social Transformation.* Indianapolis: Bobbs-Merrill.

Germond, Jack W. and Jules Witcover. 1989. "Elections Show Importance of Abortion Issue." *National Journal,* November 11, p. 2776

Ginsburg, Faye D. 1989. *Contested Lives: The Abortion Debate in an American Community.* Berkeley: University of California Press.

Granberg, Donald and Beth Wellman Granberg. 1980. "Abortion Attitudes: Trends and Determinants." *Family Planning Perspectives* 12(5):250–61.

Gudenkanst, Norine. 1989. "Defending the Right to Choose." *Against the Current* 4(1):7–8.

Haines, Herbert H. 1988. *Black Radicals and the Civil Rights Mainstream, 1954–1970.* Knoxville: University of Tennessee Press.

Hanna, Mary T. 1979. *Catholics and American Politics.* Cambridge, MA: Harvard University Press.

Hart, Diana S. 1975. "Fetal Research and Antiabortion Politics: Holding Science Hostage." *Family Planning Perspectives* 7(2):72–82.

Hayler, Barbara. 1979. "Abortion." *Signs* 5(2):307–23.

Hershey, Marjorie Randon. 1986. "Direct Action and the Abortion Issue: The Political Participation of Single-Issue Groups." Pp. 27–45 in *Interest Group Politics,* 2nd ed., ed. Allan J. Cigler and Burdett A. Loomis. Washington, DC: Congressional Quarterly Press.

Himmelstein, Jerome. 1990. *To the Right: The Transformation of American Conservatism.* Berkeley: University of California Press.

Holden, Constance. 1989. "Koop Finds Abortion Evidence 'Inconclusive.'" *Science* 243:730–31.

Hole, Judith and Ellen Levine. 1971. *Rebirth of Feminism.* New York: Quadrangle.

Hopper, Rex D. 1950. "The Revolutionary Process: A Frame of Reference for the Study of Revolutionary Movements." *Social Forces* 28(3):270–79.

Illick, Hilary. 1990. "Calling All Students: S.O.S. Organizes Prochoice Actions." *New Directions for Women* 19:4.

Jaffe F. S., B. L. Lindheim, and P. R. Lee. 1981. *Abortion Politics: Private Morality and Public Policy.* New York: McGraw-Hill.

Jenkins, J. Craig. 1983. "Resource Mobilization Theory and the Study of Social Movements." *Annual Review of Sociology* 9:527–53.

———. 1985. *The Politics of Insurgency: The Farm Worker Movement in the 1960s.* New York: Columbia University Press.

———. 1987. "Interpreting the Stormy 1960s: Three Theories in Search of a Political Age." *Research in Political Sociology* 3:269–303.

Jenkins, J. Craig and Craig M. Eckert. 1986. "Channeling Black Insurgency: Elite Patronage and Professional Social Movement Organization in the Development of the Black Movement." *American Sociological Review* 51:812–29.

Jenkins, J. Craig and Charles Perrow. 1977. "Insurgency of the Powerless: Farm Workers Movements, 1946–1972." *American Sociological Review* 42(2):249–68.

Jones, E. F. and C. F. Westoff. 1973. "Changes in Attitudes Toward Abortion: With Emphasis on the National Fertility Study Data." Pp. 468–81 in *The Abortion Experience: Psychological and Medical Impact,* ed. H. J. Osofsky and J. D. Osofsky. Hagerstown, MD: Harper & Row.

Kalter, Joanmarie. 1985. "Abortion Bias: How Network Coverage Has Tilted to the Pro-Lifers." *TV Guide* 33(45):6–17.

Kelly, James R. 1989. "Winning *Webster* v. *Reproductive Health Services:* The Crisis of the Pro-Life Movement." *America* 16(4):79–83.

Killian, Lewis M. 1984. "Organization, Rationality and Spontaneity in the Civil Rights Movement." *American Sociological Review* 49(6):770–83.

Klitsch, Michael. 1988. "Court Sinks New Title X Regulations." *Family Planning Perspectives* 20(2):96–98.

Kornhauser, Anne. 1989a. "Abortion Case Has Been Boon to Both Sides." *Legal Times,* July 3, pp. 1, 11.

———. 1989b. "Kate Michelman's Permanent Campaign." *Legal Times,* November 13, pp. 1, 14–16.

———. 1990a. "ABA's Judicial Selection Role Draws New Fire." *Legal Times,* February 26, pp. 6–7.

———. 1990b. "Abortion Groups' Pleasant Problem: Extra Money." *Legal Times,* January 8, p. 2.

Ladd, Everett Carll. 1989. "Trouble for Both Parties." *Public Opinion* 12(1):3–8.

Lader, Lawrence. 1966. *Abortion.* Boston: Beacon Press.

———. 1973. *Abortion II: Making the Revolution.* Boston: Beacon Press.

Lee, Philip R. and Lauren B. LeRoy. 1985. "Abortion Politics and Public Policy." Pp. 44–58 in *Perspectives on Abortion,* ed. P. Sachdev. Metuchen, NJ: Scarecrow Press.

Leites, Nathan and Charles Wolf, Jr. 1970. *Rebellion and Authority.* Chicago: Markham.

Levine, Judith. 1985. "Blinding Us with Science." *Village Voice,* July 16, pp. 21–24.

Lo, Clarence Y. H. 1984. "Mobilizing the Tax Revolt: The Emergent Alliance Between Homeowners and Local Elites." *Research in Social Movements, Conflicts and Change* 6:293–328.

Low, Charlotte. 1987. "The Pro-Life Movement in Disarray." *American Spectator* 20(10):23–26.

Lowi, Theodore J. 1971. *The Politics of Disorder.* New York: Basic Books.

Luker, Kristin. 1984. *Abortion and the Politics of Motherhood.* Berkeley: University of California Press.

Matlack, Carol. 1989. "Mobilizing for the Abortion War." *National Journal,* July 15, pp. 1814–15.

McAdam, Doug. 1982. *Political Process and the Development of Black Insurgency.* Chicago: University of Chicago Press.

———. 1983. "Tactical Innovation and the Pace of Insurgency." *American Sociological Review* 48(6):735–54.

———. 1988. *Freedom Summer.* New York: Oxford University Press.

McCarthy, John D. 1987. "Pro-Life and Pro-Choice Mobilization: Infrastructure Deficits and New Technologies." Pp. 49–66 in *Social Movements in an Organizational Society,* ed. Mayer N. Zald and John D. McCarthy. New Brunswick, NJ: Transaction Books.

McCarthy, John D. and Mayer N. Zald. 1973. *The Trend of Social Movements in America: Professionalization and Resource Mobilization.* Morristown, NJ: General Learning Press.

———. 1977. "Resource Mobilization and Social Movements: A Partial Theory." *American Journal of Sociology* 82(6):1212–41.

Messing, Suzanne. 1989. "Pro-Choice Forces Fight Back." *New Directions for Women* 18(2):1.

Mitchell, Robert C. 1979. "National Environmental Lobbies and the Apparent Illogic of Collective Action." Pp. 87–121 in *Collective Decision Making: Applications from Public Choice Theory,* ed. Clifford S. Russell. Baltimore: Johns Hopkins University Press.

Mohr, James C. 1978. *Abortion in America: The Origins and Evolution of National Policy.* New York: Oxford University Press.

———. 1989. "Iowa's Abortion Battles of the Late 1960s and Early 1970s: Long-Term Perspectives and Short-Term Analyses." *Annals of Iowa* 50(1):63–89.

Montgomery, Kathryn C. 1989. *Target: Prime Time.* New York: Oxford University Press.

Moore, W. John. 1989. "Lobbying the Court." *National Journal,* April 15, pp. 908–13.

Morris, Aldon D. 1981. "Black Southern Student Sit-in Movement: An Analysis of Internal Organization." *American Sociological Review* 46(4):744–67.

———. 1984. *The Origins of the Civil Rights Movement: Black Communities Organizing for Change.* New York: Free Press.

Mottl, Tahi L. 1980. "The Analysis of Countermovements." *Social Problems* 27(5):620–35.

Mueller, Carol McClurg. 1987. "Collective Consciousness, Identity Transformation, and the Rise of Women in Public Office in the United States." Pp. 89–108 in *The Women's Movements in the United States and Western Europe: Consciousness, Political Opportunity and Public Policy,* ed. Mary Fainsod Katzenstein and Carol McClurg Mueller. Philadelphia: Temple University Press.

Nathanson, Bernard. 1979. *Aborting America.* Garden City, NY: Doubleday.

National Journal. 1989. "The Abortion Ruling," July 8, p. 1773.

New York Times. 1981. "Abortion Becoming a Top Priority Issue in Congress," March 13.

———. 1983. "Abortion Foes End Meeting Optimistic Despite Setbacks," July 10.

———. 1985. "Coalition Seeks High Court Support on Abortions," September 1.

———. 1987. "An Anti-Abortion PAC Falls on Difficult Times," August 9.

———. 1989. "Supreme Court to Hear Argument on Law Limiting Abortion Access," January 10.

———. 1989. "Lawyers Protest Abortion Policy at Justice Dept," March 26.

———. 1989. "Right to Abortion Draws Thousands to Capital Rally," April 10.

———. 1989. "What Is Right and Wrong with *Roe* v. *Wade*? The View From Friends of the Court," April 23.

———. 1989. "Abortion Rights Backers Adopt Tactics of Politics," July 21.

———. 1989. "The Abortion-Rights Movement Has Its Day," October 15.

———. 1989. "Abortion Rights Rallies: Capital to Coast," November 13.

———. 1989. "Pennsylvania Abortion Limits Become Law," November 19.

———. 1989. "Illinois Abortion Case Is Settled; Was Seen As Supreme Court Test," November 23.

———. 1990. "Anti-Abortion Group to Close Headquarters," February 1.

———. 1990. "Judge Fines 10 for Protests over Abortions," February 28.

———. 1990. "States Testing the Limits on Abortion," April 2.

———. 1990. "Catholic Bishops Hire Firms to Market Abortion Attack," April 6.

———. 1990. "Study Sees Little Distress After Abortion," April 6.

———. 1990. "At NOW Convention, Goal Is Putting More Women into Office," July 1.

Newsweek. 1985. "America's Abortion Dilemma," January 14, pp. 20–29.

———. 1986. "Clinics of Deception," September 1, p. 20.

———. 1989. "Abortion and the Court," May 1, pp. 28–38.

———. 1989. "Dodging on Abortion," October 2, p. 4.

———. 1990. "The Bishops Under Fire," April 23, p. 24.

Oberschall, Anthony. 1973. *Social Conflict and Social Movements*. Englewood Cliffs, NJ: Prentice-Hall.

O'Connor, Karen. 1980. *Women's Organizations' Use of the Courts*. Lexington, MA: Lexington Books.

Olasky, Marvin. 1988–89. "Engineering Social Change: Triumphs of Abortion Public Relations from the Thirties Through the Sixties." *Public Relations Quarterly* 33(4):17–21.

Oliver, Pamela and Mark Furman. 1989. "Contradictions Between National and Local Organizational Strength: The Case of the John Birch Society." *International Social Movement Research* 2:155–77.

Paige, Connie. 1983. *The Right to Lifers: Who They Are, How They Operate, Where They Get Their Money*. New York: Summit Books.

Petchesky, Rosalind Pollack. 1984. *Abortion and Woman's Choice: The State, Sexuality, and Reproductive Freedom*. Boston: Northeastern University Press.

———. 1987. "Fetal Images: The Power of Visual Culture in the Politics of Reproduction." *Feminist Studies* 13(2):263–92.

———. 1989. "Pro-Choice Challenge: Change Strategies, Change Vision." *New Directions for Women* 18(5):1, 10.

Phelan, Lana Clarke and Patricia T. Maginnis. 1969. *The Abortion Handbook for Responsible Women*. North Hollywood, CA: Contact Books.

Piven, Frances Fox and Richard A. Cloward. 1977. *Poor People's Movements: Why They Succeed, How They Fail*. New York: Vintage Books.

Potts, Malcolm, Peter Diggory, and John Peel. 1977. *Abortion*. Cambridge: Cambridge University Press.

Ridgeway, James. 1985. "The Prolife Juggernaut." *Village Voice*, July 16, pp. 28–29.

Rochon, Thomas R. 1988. *Mobilizing for Peace: The Anti-Nuclear Movements in Western Europe*. Princeton, NJ: Princeton University Press.

Rossi, Alice and Bhavani Sitaraman. 1988. "Abortion in Context: Historical Trends and Future Changes." *Family Planning Perspectives* 20(6):273–81, 301.

Rothman, Lorraine and Laura Punnett. 1978. "Menstrual Extraction." *Quest* 4(3):44–60.

Rothstein, Vivian and Naomi Weisstein. 1972. "Chicago Women's Liberation Union." *Women: A Journal of Liberation* 2(4):2–9.

Rubin, Eva R. 1987. *Abortion, Politics, and the Courts: Roe v. Wade, and Its Aftermath, Revised*. Westport, CT: Greenwood Press.

Rule, James B. 1988. *Theories of Civil Violence*. Berkeley: University of California Press.

Rupp, Leila J. and Verta Taylor. 1987. *Survival in the Doldrums: The American Women's Rights Movement, 1945 to the 1960s*. New York: Oxford University Press.

Ruzek, Sheryl. 1978. *The Women's Health Movement: Feminist Alternatives to Medical Care*. New York: Praeger.

———. 1986. "Feminist Visions of Health: An International Perspective." Pp. 184–207 in *What Is Feminism: A Re-examination*, ed. J. Mitchell and A. Oakley. New York: Pantheon.

Sackett, Victoria A. 1985. "Between Pro-Life and Pro-Choice." *Public Opinion* 8(2):53–55.

Sanford, Wendy Coppedge. 1979. "Working Together, Growing Together: A Brief History of the Boston Women's Health Book Collective." *Heresies* 2(3):83–92.

Sarat, Austin. 1982. "Abortion and the Courts: Uncertain Boundaries of Law and Politics." Pp. 113–53 in *American Politics and Public Policy*, ed. Allan P. Sindler. Washington, DC: Congressional Quarterly Press.

Schlesinger, Melinda Bart and Pauline B. Bart. 1982. "Collective Work and Self-Identity:

Working in a Feminist Illegal Abortion Collective." Pp. 139–153 in *Workplace Democracy and Social Change,* ed. Frank Lindenfeld and Joyce Rothschild-Whitt. Boston: Porter Sargent.

Schmitt, Rüdiger. 1989. "Organizational Interlocks Between New Social Movements and Traditional Elites: The Case of the West German Peace Movement." *European Journal of Political Research* 17(5):583–98.

Schneider, William. 1989a. "Trouble for the GOP." *Public Opinion* 12(1):2, 59–60.

———. 1989b. "Wrong Way for Women's Movement." *National Journal,* August 5, p. 2018.

Shapiro, Thomas M. 1985. *Population Control Politics: Women, Sterilization, and Reproductive Choice.* Philadelphia: Temple University Press.

Simpson, Peggy. 1989a. "Reconcilable Differences." *Ms.,* October, p. 70.

———. 1989b. "Video Rebuts 'Silent Scream'." *Ms.,* July–August, p. 79.

Snyder, David and William R. Kelly. 1979. "Strategies for Investigating Violence and Social Change: Illustrations from Analyses of Racial Disorders and Implications for Mobilization Research." Pp. 212–37 in *The Dynamics of Social Movements: Resource Mobilization, Social Control, and Tactics,* ed. M. N. Zald and J. D. McCarthy. Cambridge, MA: Winthrop.

The Spokeswoman. 1975. "Special Report: NOW and the Women's Movement." Vol. 6(6):1–5.

Staggenborg, Suzanne. 1986. "Coalition Work in the Pro-Choice Movement: Organizational and Environmental Opportunities and Obstacles." *Social Problems* 33(5):374–90.

———. 1988. "The Consequences of Professionalization and Formalization in the Pro-Choice Movement." *American Sociological Review* 53(4):585–605.

———. 1989a. "Organizational and Environmental Influences on the Development of the Pro-Choice Movement." *Social Forces* 68(1):204–40.

———. 1989b. "Stability and Innovation in the Women's Movement: A Comparison of Two Movement Organizations." *Social Problems* 36(1):75–92.

Steinhoff, Patricia and Milton Diamond. 1977. *Abortion Politics: The Hawaii Experience.* Honolulu: University Press of Hawaii.

Tarrow, Sidney. 1983. *Struggling to Reform: Social Movements and Policy Change During Cycles of Protest.* Ithaca, NY: Center for International Studies, Cornell University.

———. 1988. "National Politics and Collective Action: Recent Theory and Research in Western Europe and the United States." *Annual Review of Sociology* 14:421–40.

———. 1989. *Democracy and Disorder: Protest and Politics in Italy 1965–1975.* Oxford: Oxford University Press.

Tatalovich, Raymond. 1988. "Abortion: Prochoice Versus Prolife." Pp. 177–248 in *Social Regulatory Policies: Moral Controversies in American Policies,* ed. Raymond Tatalovich and Byron W. Daynes. Boulder, CO: Westview Press.

Tatalovich, Raymond and Byron W. Daynes. 1981. *The Politics of Abortion: A Study of Community Conflict in Public Policy Making.* New York: Praeger.

Taylor, Verta. 1989a. "The Future of Feminism: A Social Movement Analysis." Pp. 473–90 in *Feminist Frontiers II,* ed. Laurel Richardson and Verta Taylor. New York: Random House.

———. 1989b. "Social Movement Continuity: The Women's Movement in Abeyance." *American Sociological Review* 54(5):761–75.

Thompson, E. P. 1989. "A Third CND." *New Statesman and Society* 2(46):29–33.

Tilly, Charles. 1978. *From Mobilization to Revolution.* Reading, MA: Addison-Wesley.

Time. 1989. "The Battle over Abortion," July 17, p. 62.

Traugott, Michael and Maris A. Vinovskis. 1980. "Abortion and the 1978 Congressional Elections." *Family Planning Perspectives* 12(5):238–46.

Trinkl, John. 1988. "Struggles for Disarmament in the USA." Pp. 51–62 in *Reshaping the US Left: Popular Struggles in the 1980's,* ed. Mike Davis and Michael Sprinker. New York: Verso.

Turner, Ralph. 1981. "Collective Behavior and Resource Mobilization As Approaches to Social Movements: Issues and Continuities." *Social Movements, Conflicts and Change* 4:1–24.

Useem, Bert and Mayer N. Zald. 1982. "From Pressure Group to Social Movement: Organizational Dilemmas of the Effort to Promote Nuclear Power." *Social Problems* 30(2):144–56.

Van Kleef, Deborah. 1982. "Protesting Is Swell, but They'd Rather Be Ironing." *In These Times,* March 10–16, pp. 4–5.

Vinovskis, Maris A. 1980. "Abortion and the Presidential Election of 1976: A Multivariate Analysis of Voting Behavior." Pp. 184–205 in *The Law and Politics of Abortion,* ed. C. E. Schneider and M. A. Vinovskis. Lexington, MA: Health.

Vita, David. 1989. "Pro-abortionists Lobby Pizza Parlour." *Times Higher Education Supplement,* November 24, p. 10.

Walker, Samuel. 1990. *In Defense of American Liberties: A History of the ACLU.* New York: Oxford University Press.

Walsh, Edward J. 1988. *Democracy in the Shadows: Citizen Mobilization in the Wake of the Accident at Three Mile Island.* Westport, CT: Greenwood Press.

Washington Post. 1989. "Abortion, Once upon a Time in America," April 26.

Wharton, Ann. 1986. "Has the Pro-Life Movement Lost Its Zeal?" *Liberty Report,* May, pp. 16–19.

Wilcox, Clyde. 1989. "Political Action Committees and Abortion: A Longitudinal Analysis." *Women and Politics* 9(1):1–19.

Wills, Garry. 1989. "Operation Rescue: A Case Study in Galvanizing the Antiabortion Movement." *Time,* May 1, pp. 26–28.

Witwer, M. 1989. "Many Americans Oppose Government Intervention in Abortion Rights, but Endorse Some Restrictions." *Family Planning Perspectives* 21(5):229–30.

Zald, Mayer N. 1980. "Issues in the Theory of Social Movements." *Current Perspectives in Social Theory* 1:61–72.

———. 1988. "The Trajectory of Social Movements in America." *Research in Social Movements, Conflicts and Change* 10:19–41.

Zald, Mayer N. and Roberta Ash. 1966. "Social Movement Organizations: Growth, Decay, and Change." *Social Forces* 44(3):327–41.

Zald, Mayer N. and Michael A. Berger. 1978. "Social Movements in Organizations: Coup d'Etat, Insurgency and Mass Movements." *American Journal of Sociology* 83(4):823–61.

Zald, Mayer N. and Bert Useem. 1987. "Movement and Countermovement Interaction: Mobilization, Tactics, and State Involvement." Pp. 247–72 in *Social Movements in an Organizational Society,* ed. Mayer N. Zald and John D. McCarthy. New Brunswick, NJ: Transaction Books.

Court Cases Cited

Beal v. *Doe,* 432 U.S. 438 (1977).

Brown v. *Board of Education,* 347 U.S. 483 (1954).

City of Akron v. *Akron Center for Reproductive Health, Inc.,* 462 U.S. 416 (1983).

Doe v. *Bolton*, 410 U.S. 179 (1973).

Doe v. *Scott*, 321 F. Supp. 1385 (1971).

Griswold v. *Connecticut*, 381 U.S. 471 (1965).

Harris v. *McRae*, 100 S. Ct. 2671 (1980).

Hodgson v. *Minnesota* and *Minnesota* v. *Hodgson*, 88–1225, 88–1309.

Maher v. *Roe*, 432 U.S. 464 (1977).

Ohio v. *Akron Center for Reproductive Health*, 88–805.

People v. *Belous*, 71 Cal. 2d 954, 458 P. 2d 194 (1969).

Planned Parenthood of Central Missouri v. *Danforth*, 428 U.S. 52 (1976).

Planned Parenthood, Kansas City, Missouri v. *Ashcroft*, 462 U.S. 476 (1983).

Poelker v. *Doe*, 432 U.S. 519 (1977).

Roe v. *Wade*, 410 U.S. 113 (1973).

Simopoulos v. *Virginia*, 462 U.S. 506 (1983).

Thornburgh v. *American College of Obstetricians and Gynecologists*, 106 S. Ct. 2169 (1986).

Turnock v. *Ragsdale*, 88–790.

United States v. *Vuitch*, 402 U.S. 62 (1971).

Webster v. *Reproductive Health Services*, 109 S. Ct. 3040 (1989).

Index